P9-DEQ-205

09/21

More Praise for *CenterStage*

"*CenterStage* is another example of why Michael Kay is one of the truly gifted interviewers in the history of our industry. His ability to make all of these sports and entertainment giants feel so comfortable is extraordinary. I bet some felt afterward that maybe they became *too* comfortable. It's just one captivating interview after another. A mesmerizing book."

> —Mike Breen, play-by-play commentator
> for *NBA on ABC* and lead announcer for
> New York Knicks games on MSG Network

"A fabulous new collection . . . Kay's greatest gift is an infectious personality that shows his guests at their best, encourages them to reveal their innermost thoughts, and even, at times, uncovers secret gems about their lives. On display in *CenterStage* is a Who's Who of pop culture—from John McEnroe to Jon Bon Jovi, from Sir Charles to Sly Stallone, and including dozens more—and by the time you finish you'll really feel you personally know them."

> —Jon Heyman, insider for MLB Network
> and former writer for *Sports Illustrated*

"Even as a cub reporter Michael Kay had a unique ability to turn an interview into a conversation between friends. People trusted Michael then. They still do today, more than ever. *CenterStage* doesn't just allow readers to glimpse the souls of the rich and famous, it's a how-to for any aspiring journalist learning the craft of the Q and A."

> —Bob Klapisch, coauthor, with Paul Solotaroff,
> of *Inside the Empire*

"Michael Kay is a gifted conversationalist. He has the innate ability to make his interview subjects feel comfortable and get them to share fascinating details about their personal journeys. It's never cookie-cutter with Michael and always insightful and moving with the perfect balance of humor."

> —Ian Eagle, broadcaster for CBS Sports
> and YES Network

CENTERSTAGE

My Most Fascinating Interviews—
from A-Rod to Jay-Z

Michael Kay

SCRIBNER

New York   London   Toronto   Sydney   New Delhi

Scribner
An Imprint of Simon & Schuster, Inc.
1230 Avenue of the Americas
New York, NY 10020

Copyright © 2021 by Michael Kay

All rights reserved, including the right to reproduce this book or portions thereof
in any form whatsoever. For information, address Scribner Subsidiary Rights Department,
1230 Avenue of the Americas, New York, NY 10020.

First Scribner hardcover edition June 2021

SCRIBNER and design are registered trademarks of The Gale Group, Inc.,
used under license by Simon & Schuster, Inc., the publisher of this work.

For information about special discounts for bulk purchases,
please contact Simon & Schuster Special Sales at 1-866-506-1949
or business@simonandschuster.com.

The Simon & Schuster Speakers Bureau can bring authors to your live event.
For more information or to book an event, contact the Simon & Schuster Speakers Bureau
at 1-866-248-3049 or visit our website at www.simonspeakers.com.

Manufactured in the United States of America

1   3   5   7   9   10   8   6   4   2

Library of Congress Cataloging-in-Publication Data has been applied for.

ISBN 978-1-9821-5203-1
ISBN 978-1-9821-5205-5 (ebook)

For Jodi, Caledonia, and Charles,
who always take center stage in everything I do.

And for my sister, Debbie, her husband, Peter,
and their children—Ashley, Chelsea, and Dylan—
who long ago had to deal with my barrages of questions
before it became my job.

Contents

PART THREE

THEY MADE US LAUGH

PART FOUR

THEY PUSHED THE BOUNDARIES

Foreword

If you have watched and listened to Michael Kay on telecasts of Yankee games, a few things should be apparent. He knows baseball. He is steeped in Yankee history, the last thirty-four years of which he has experienced firsthand. He is adept at engaging with his various (and varied) broadcast partners. And here's something else: Michael sees not just pitches and plays, but story lines. He provides an ongoing narrative—of a game, a season, a career.

That last quality, missing in more announcers than you might realize, was shaped by Michael's background as a newspaper writer. The deft, unscripted turns of phrase he often delivers in big moments are a testament to a writer's regard for the beauty and importance of words well chosen. Still, a writer who is also a reporter has objectives and skills beyond the writing itself. The reporter is naturally curious. Asking good questions is how he makes his living—and his reputation. If he is to do his job honestly and well, his powers of observation and eye for telling detail are essential. He is interested not in the superficial or rote response but in the truthful and relevant answer, the pertinent observation, the honest point of view.

Which brings us to *CenterStage*. There are many types of interviews, and they require different approaches. *CenterStage* is not *60 Minutes*, *Nightline*, or *Meet the Press*. It is a conversation, not an interrogation. Seldom is there a specific issue to confront. Rather, the idea is to provide at least a slice of the guest's personal biography—to get to some of the texture and shadings of a life and career. Ideally, the conversation should be both entertaining and, in some sense, revealing. At the end of the hour, the viewer should not only have learned a bit about the events, accomplishments, and perhaps controversies for which the guest is best known. The viewer should also have a better understanding and appreciation of the *person* behind all that.

When Michael asked me to write the foreword for this compilation of his *CenterStage* shows, I was flattered to learn that my NBC interview program, *Later*, was among his influences. While there are differences, there are also substantial similarities. We both recognize the importance of thorough preparation, but also are aware that you must be nimble and spontaneous enough to put the preparation aside and react in the moment when the conversation takes you in a different direction. You must be a good listener. That allows you to follow up, to clarify, to encourage the guest to tell more.

Like *Later*, *CenterStage* is not about sound bites or mindless celebrity trivialities. The guest has a body of work. A story to tell. And the long-form format allows it to unfold. There is plenty of room for laughter. But also thoughtful (though not somber) conversation.

Over years of conducting these conversations, Michael has arrived at some of the same conclusions I did. If you have put in the time and effort to be well versed on your subject's life and career, and if it is also clear that you had some knowledge of, and interest in, that person to begin with, the person senses that, even *before* you get to all the particulars. And that sense almost always leads them to become more engaged and forthcoming.

Here's something else I have discovered and I'm sure Michael has as well: the atmosphere matters. Often, the best and most memorable responses come in reaction to specific questions. But not always. Sometimes, if the overall tone is right, if the guests trust the interviewer, if they have some regard for the reputation of the program and its host, that comfort factor leads them to share interesting thoughts and stories *on their own*. Or so it seems. Some of the best moments do seem to just happen. It *seems* as if the guest just decided to go there without any prodding. And in those instances, the host has done nothing obvious. Certainly nothing spectacular. What has happened is more subtle than that. An atmosphere has been created. An atmosphere that leads to good television.

Over the years, Michael Kay has delivered plenty of good television, much of it on *CenterStage*. The proof of that is on the pages that follow.

—Bob Costas
March 2020

A Note to the Reader

Owing to space limitations, the *CenterStage* interviews featured in this book have been reduced from their original length, with care taken to be faithful to the speaker's intended meaning while preserving the best exchanges.

Introduction

I've always been curious. I want to know how someone got rich. How someone became poor. How someone handles fame. When I was a kid and my family was driving somewhere, I'd stare up from the back seat at some of the windows of the homes that zoomed past and wonder what was going on in those apartments. What was their big issue and what was their struggle?

Ever since I've been a broadcaster, I've toyed with the idea of pitching a show with the working title *What's Your Story?* In the show, I'd take a camera and kneel down next to someone homeless in Penn Station and ask how exactly the person got to that point. Or maybe I'd just knock on a door in an apartment building and ask what was going on in the person's life.

Fame and fortune have always fascinated me. Growing up in a lower-income section of the Bronx, I dreamed of never having to worry about paying a bill or to wonder how I was going to pay for Christmas gifts. When I'd see the smiling faces on a television screen, or even on a theater stage, I'd want to know how the people had made it and what they had to overcome during their journeys.

So, I felt fortunate to be offered a job hosting the YES Network show *CenterStage*. My journey to that dream job was circuitous, but driven by the aforementioned curiosity and drive.

Since I was nine years old, I'd always dreamed of being the Yankees' announcer. Some might ask, "Why not dream of being a Yankee *player?*" My answer is that, even at a young age, I was rational and figured that my fear of getting hit by a pitch probably ruled out the major leagues. I was supported by a loving family, but even they were skeptical that I'd hit that million-to-one lottery ticket. Always wanting to encourage me, Mom and Dad let me dream, but always added to the back of it "just in case . . ."

The backup was writing. When I graduated from Fordham University in 1982, I sounded like that character John Travolta played in *Welcome Back, Kotter*, Vinnie Barbarino. There were a lot of *dems* and *doses*. Not quite ready yet for the New York airwaves, I got a job as a clerk at the *New York Post*, filing pictures, doing horse-racing agate, stats, and getting people lunch. I was also allowed to write on my own time, and if the story was good enough, it would get published. In a few years I got promoted to writer. I was always one of the first ones at an assignment and usually the last one to leave. I had to ask one more question, drive to get the answer no one else got, nail down the exclusive. By 1987 I'd been promoted to Yankees beat writer, and by 1989, I'd moved over to the *New York Daily News* to do the same job. During my five years on the Yankees beat, I was always the guy they went to on the radio to fill time during rain delays. I also became the clubhouse reporter for the MSG Network when they were the rights holder for the Yankees.

In 1992, the Yankees radio broadcast was looking for a partner to work with John Sterling, and incredibly, I got the job. I worked with John for ten years, calling five American League pennants and four World Championships. This was my dream. If I stayed in this job for the rest of my life, it would have been "mission accomplished" for a nine-year-old who called his shot.

But at the end of the 2000 season the Yankees started to tinker with the idea of starting their own television network. By July of the 2001 season, they decided to begin the YES Network, a regional cable network that would carry Yankees and NBA Nets games as well as "shoulder programming" throughout the day. This massive undertaking would change the landscape of sports. But when nascent, this humongous gamble had a good chance of not working out.

On September 10, 2001, John Filippelli—who'd been in the broadcasting business for over twenty-five years with NBC, ABC, and Fox and was a multiple Emmy winner, having worked every major sporting event in the world, including World Series, Super Bowls, Olympics, *Monday Night Football*, Wimbledon, British Opens, and *Wide World of Sports*—was hired by Yankees owner George Steinbrenner to be the executive producer in charge of production. Essentially, his job was to start the network, hire the announcers, and set the course of how the games would look on the air. Within two weeks of being hired,

Filippelli was told by Yankee president Randy Levine, "You're also doing programming." Filippelli, who is called Flip by everyone, was incredulous at his newfound responsibilities and said to Levine, "Programming. I don't know how to program a VCR." Levine, one of the visionaries of the YES Network, said, "We have faith in you, you'll figure it out." Suddenly, Filippelli was YES Network's president and executive producer in charge of production and programming. Although Flip had worked with some of the biggest names in the industry, such as Scully, Costas, McKay, and Gumbel, he knew YES was going to be a challenge like nothing he had ever done.

That quickly turned prescient.

When Filippelli took the job, he thought he'd have a year and four months to start the network. He was quickly told it was four months only, and he said, "I don't know if we can do it in four months," to which Steinbrenner replied, "You can and you will. You'd better."

With the new assignment, Flip had to come up with the other programs to surround the games, in addition to hiring all the announcers for the games. I had no idea I was even being considered until I got a call after the World Series that they wanted me to do about ninety games of play-by-play on TV. That turned out to be a hard sell for Flip since the Yankees owner really liked the pairing of Sterling and Kay on the radio and didn't want to break us up. Flip convinced Steinbrenner that TV would end up being much more important than radio in the grand scheme and said that I was the guy to lead the coverage. George said, "Fine. Do it. If it doesn't work, it's your ass."

With that, I thought my responsibilities at YES had taken full form. But, little did I know, Flip was coming up with show ideas behind the scenes, and I'd eventually fall into another dream job.

Armed with his new responsibilities, Flip sat down in his home office one day and began scribbling ideas on a napkin. One of the thoughts he wrote down was "*Inside the Actors Studio* about sports."

In talking about the process, Flip said, "I knew I wanted a long-form TV narrative about someone's life. I'd liked the show *Queen for a Day* when I was growing up, and I liked the show *Biography*, which eventually led to *Yankeeography*. I really enjoyed the *Inside the Actors Studio* show with James Lipton, but I wanted one with a sports connection."

Filippelli's first choice for host was Jack Ford, the talented ABC broadcaster, but ABC wouldn't let him out of his contract. Flip then moved on to the Hall of Fame broadcaster Lesley Visser, who considered the gig, but decided she had too much on her plate and had to decline.

Flip remembered my interviews on MSG's postgame shows and liked the style, but he initially wanted to avoid me as an option so I could focus on the Yankee games. After Ford and Visser were off the table though, he told his staff, "I bet Kay can do this show."

And that's how it began.

The first show, which is included in this book, was an interview with Steve Young, a devout Mormon, who entered a studio we had booked that was used nightly for a little show called *The Vagina Monologues.* He blushed, took a deep breath, and walked in, and we were off. Over the years we've already done close to 250 shows, interviewing the best in sports, journalism, and entertainment. It has let the curiosity of the younger me come out and ask the most famous people about the most intimate things.

The one line that runs through every story arc is dogged determination to become one of the greatest. That drive someone has, whether it's to escape poverty or chase fame, is a consistent element in the biographies of all we've talked to through the years. Some of our guests have handled their fortune well, while others have agonizingly squandered it all, providing a cautionary tale.

The idea of this book emerged in the summer of 2019, prompted by Howard Stern's book *Howard Stern Comes Again.* In that bestseller, Stern compiles the best interviews he has conducted in his career on the radio and puts them between covers. I started to think how the *CenterStage* interviews might, in a similar way, actually be more compelling on paper, because when images flicker across the TV screen there's much to be distracted by, but when you put the same words in print, they can more fully be digested and better appreciated.

The only problem was that I could in absolutely no way include all the *CenterStage* interviews in a single book because the resulting length would rival that of a set of encyclopedias. So I had to knock down the number of interviews to about thirty-five and shorten them somewhat.

I've always laughed when I've asked musicians what their favorite song is and they say, "That's like picking your favorite child." I gained a better understanding of that when, essentially, I had to make the heart-wrenching decision to throw about two hundred of my "kids" out of the book.

And each interview through the years has had a great story behind it. Leaving out the interview with actor Terry Crews was difficult. Opening up his emotional veins for all to see, he broke down and cried when he recounted his tale of sexual abuse in Hollywood, while the audience sat in stunned silence. Many such moments didn't make the cut.

Some of the stories behind the interviews that *didn't* get into the book are worth a quick visit:

- The rapper and actor LL Cool J wouldn't go onstage until our crew purchased a steamer so he could steam his T-shirt beforehand. Again, it was just a T-shirt. But he did look good.
- The actor Charlie Sheen appeared on the show right after his public meltdown following the end of his run on *Two and a Half Men*. The man with Tiger Blood was pleasant, funny, and engaging, but when we stood up to take a picture at the end of the show, I put my hand on his back and his body was vibrating like a shivering Chihuahua. It was sad.
- Of all the interviews we've ever done, my least favorite was Dennis Quaid's. He was promoting the movie *The Rookie*, and he simply didn't want to be there. He was having personal issues with his then wife, Meg Ryan, and he didn't want to sit for an hour answering questions. For the first two segments of the show he answered everything with yes or no. During a break I leaned in to him and said, "Hey, listen, the show is an hour no matter how many questions you answer with one word. I've got a thousand questions to ask, so you're the one who is going to look bad if this goes on." He was startled that I'd spoken to him like that, but was better the rest of the way.
- Academy Award–winning actor Kevin Costner was on the show, and after we were done, he leaned over to me and said, "You'd be a fun guy to hang out with." This was a big deal for a shy kid out of the Bronx.
- In the history of *CenterStage* I didn't host only two shows. One was with Lawrence Frank, then Nets coach, and the other

with Michael Imperioli of *Sopranos* fame. We were scheduled to tape both shows in one day, and my mom passed away the night before. I was in no condition to work, so my colleague Bob Lorenz filled in. To my shock, Imperioli, whom I'd never met, sent a floral bouquet to the funeral home the next day, forever entering my personal Hall of Fame for good guys.

- The legendary chef Emeril Lagassé learned from my coworkers that I'm a picky eater and made me a roast beef panini to eat during the show. I've never willingly eaten a condiment in my life, but I took a bite and thought the panini was good but a bit wet. Lagassé burst out in laughter and pointed out that I'd just eaten aioli mayonnaise. It was okay, but I never had it again.

- Steve Van Zandt, the guitarist from Bruce Springsteen's E Street Band, was in horrible back pain but insisted on doing the show anyway. His one modification to the format was that, instead of sitting in the comfy chair we have for guests, he sat backward in a small school chair leaning forward the entire hour to take stress off his back. His stories and good humor were particularly gratifying when you consider the pain he was in.

- Wrestler John Cena was engaging and funny in his hour-long interview, but particularly striking was what he'd do during commercial breaks. He'd stand up and take a picture and shake hands with every kid in the audience. Usually, we don't allow children under eighteen into the shows, but with Cena we made an exception because of his dedication to children's causes and because he'd granted the most wishes in the history of the Make-A-Wish Foundation.

Again, these are just some of the interviews that *didn't* make it. We've chosen the best of the best, and take my word that every cut was agonizing—except for Dennis Quaid. I hope you enjoy meeting in depth these thirty-five men and women who have been a major part of our popular culture.

PART ONE

THEY DID IT THEIR WAY

A-Rod

Alex Rodriguez was a member of the Texas Rangers when we interviewed him in August of 2003. Always savvy, Alex was well aware of the power of the YES Network, and I think he already had thoughts of being in the media postcareer. He quickly agreed to do the show when asked. To intimate that he foresaw eventually ending up with the Yankees the very next year would be false. How could he have known that Aaron Boone, then the Yankees' third baseman, would tear up his knee in January of 2004 and clear a road from Texas to the Bronx that might have previously seemed impossible? After Boone's injury, it was certainly convenient that the Rangers decided to get out from under Rodriguez's record-breaking contract, which the player had signed three years prior, and that the Yankees were interested in bringing him over and asking him to shift his position from shortstop, where he was a Gold Glove winner, to third, just to the right of Derek Jeter. But that's how it came down.

This interview is fascinating when you consider all that has taken place in the years since. No one knew that A-Rod would be embroiled in scandal after scandal, eventually serving a shocking full-season suspension for using performance-enhancing drugs. Try to read between the lines of this interview with the young A-Rod for clues of what was to come. When you read his answers, can you picture a man who had it all, lost it, and then ultimately grabbed a shot at redemption and engineered one of the great resurrections in sports history? Many years later I made A-Rod laugh when I dubbed him "Lazarod" for how insanely he'd risen from all of his missteps.

But at the time of this interview, he was the golden boy, putting together his third straight amazing season with the Rangers and making more money than any other pro athlete had ever earned. He had it all. Prodigious talent, matinee-idol good looks, and a glittery future that seemed certain to take him to the Hall of Fame.

But a funny thing happened on the way to Cooperstown: A-Rod's incredibly bad judgment almost brought him down to a place from which it seemed impossible to get up.

Incredibly, the only bad judgment on Alex's part back then was what he'd chosen to wear to the show. Although he knew of *CenterStage*, he likely didn't realize that most every guest wore a suit and tie. Alex showed up in jeans and a T-shirt. All these years later he laughs at his sartorial choice.

Here is the conversation we had with A-Rod, an hour of mostly sunny optimism that preceded the nightmare his life eventually became. His answers from that day are illuminating when read through the prism of what was to come.

The Interview

MICHAEL KAY: Alex Rodriguez came from humble beginnings to sit atop the world of baseball. With the rare combination of size, speed, and power, the man they call A-Rod may be the greatest player who ever played the shortstop position. Alex achieved success early with the Seattle Mariners, playing in the shadow of Ken Griffey Jr. and Randy Johnson. But Alex persevered and emerged as a true star. As one of the youngest and most accomplished free agents in baseball, A-Rod signed the largest contract in sports history with the Texas Rangers, and that's where he currently plies his trade. Talented, charitable—and well-dressed [*laughter*]—we welcome superstar shortstop Alex Rodriguez to *CenterStage*. [*Applause*]

ALEX RODRIGUEZ: Thank you.

MICHAEL KAY: I always feel a little awkward saying this, but Alex Rodriguez playing in Arlington, Texas, is like hanging the *Mona Lisa* in a garage. And that's not knocking Texas. I like Texas. [*Laughs*] But it's not New York, it's not LA.

ALEX RODRIGUEZ: [*Laughs*] Well, Dallas is a big town, it's a great town, I'm comfortable there. I love the heat. I love where I am. I love our neighborhood. And the only thing missing in Texas is winning.

And I think that's gonna come shortly. We have an incredible core of young players, as good as anyone, and I think we'll win. We still have room for growth.

MICHAEL KAY: We'll get back to that in a moment. Now, you were born in New York, and then you moved to the Dominican Republic. Is that where you learned how to play baseball?

ALEX RODRIGUEZ: I think I started here in New York early on. Ever since I was two or three years old I can remember my father having the Yankees games on and even the Mets. And my father had a baseball background. But when I was four, we moved down there, and I started playing with kids that were about two or three years older, so as a young man I was always overmatched.

MICHAEL KAY: At what age did you think, "I'm pretty good at this, I can make a living at this"?

ALEX RODRIGUEZ: It's funny, because between the ages of twelve and fourteen [after his family moved to Miami] I quit baseball completely. I was a big NBA fan, I wanted to be the next Larry Bird or Michael Jordan. But then my mom bought an NBA roster, and she said, "Okay, pick out how many Dominican or Latino players you have in the roster." So I looked for about twenty minutes and I found none. [*Laughs*] So then she pulled out a Major League Baseball roster and she says, "Now do the same." And of course about thirty or thirty-five percent were Latinos, and she said, "Well, there's your answer. You need to start playing baseball again."

MICHAEL KAY: So she actually thought that you could be a professional baseball player?

ALEX RODRIGUEZ: Well, she thought because my father almost made it to the big leagues [when he played baseball in the Dominican Republic], she felt my talents were in baseball.

MICHAEL KAY: Now, when you were nine, your father left you. But your mom was the rock.

ALEX RODRIGUEZ: [*Pauses, clears throat*] She was a great role model. I remember her leaving for work at six in the morning and coming back at midnight, working hard to support me and my [half] brother and [half] sister. She was a secretary during the day and then she was a waitress at night. It was very tough. I would go right from school to the Boys and Girls Club and stay there until midnight until my mom could pick me up. It was tough, but the Boys and Girls Club was an incredible avenue for me, and that's why I'm the spokesman for the Boys and Girls Club today.

MICHAEL KAY: Now, from what I hear, you were like a rail. Really skinny. But before you were a junior in high school, you started to lift weights, and eventually you could bench-press three hundred pounds.

ALEX RODRIGUEZ: Yeah, which benefited my baseball game. Because I got stronger. I got more confident. I started hitting the ball out of the park.

MICHAEL KAY: [With you as the star shortstop, your high school, Westminster Christian School, in Palmetto Bay, a suburb of Miami, wins the high school national championship, you bat .505 as a senior, you're voted USA Baseball Junior Player of the Year, among other honors.] You're the object of every scout's desire, people are calling you the next Cal Ripken Jr. You're in high school, and you're signing autographs. How does a sixteen- and seventeen-year-old kid process all that?

ALEX RODRIGUEZ: Obviously it was an exciting time in my life. It was crazy. We had fifteen scouts just kind of hanging around, not in the locker room but the hallways. I just felt that was bizarre. But the most exciting time I've ever had in high school was when one of my teachers called me out of class and said, "Hey, Cal Ripken is on the phone in the coach's office, he wants to talk to you." And he was my all-time favorite player. So I said, "Yeah, Cal Ripken, right," and the teacher said, "No, it's for real. And if you don't hurry up, he might hang up." So I had to run about two hundred yards to my coach's office, and I almost pulled a hamstring. [*Laughter*] And I got on the phone, and sure enough, it was Cal, and we spoke for about five or ten minutes.

MICHAEL KAY: Why did he call you?

ALEX RODRIGUEZ: Well, he knew he was my favorite player, and he was just kind of calling me to give me some words of encouragement. Kind of like LeBron James was called by a few NBA guys. It was very nice of him, something that I'll never forget.

MICHAEL KAY: Now, you were going to go to the University of Miami [on a baseball scholarship], but you were the first pick in the 1993 draft by the Mariners, and you end up not going to the university. But it was a close call, right?

ALEX RODRIGUEZ: Well, I wanted to go pro. I felt like with the Mariners, here's my chance to be in the major leagues, and obviously being the number one pick, you can't go any higher than that. But my mother was really into me going to the University of Miami—and you know, she's my mother. So I bought all my textbooks, and I'm walking toward my first class—

MICHAEL KAY: And once you go in the class you can't be signed for at least three years.

ALEX RODRIGUEZ: Right. So it was a very slow walk for me. [*Laughs*] And then one of the Mariners' scouts, one of the guys who had scouted me locally, caught up to me and said, "Alex, the Mariners brass is here and they want to meet with you one last time." So I called my mom and we go to a nearby hotel, and [finally she came around and] we signed a [three-year] deal for $1.3 million.

MICHAEL KAY: Did you ever regret not going to school?

ALEX RODRIGUEZ: Not at all. I figured that $1.3 million would be enough for me to go back to school someday. And I promised my mother I would go back and get my college degree.

MICHAEL KAY: How much pressure was it to be the number one draft pick? That's a lot of heat.

ALEX RODRIGUEZ: I was always under a lot of pressure, even in high school. And I always felt like that was great motivation to not let people down.

MICHAEL KAY: [So you played briefly for the Appleton Foxes of the Class A Midwest League and then the Jacksonville Suns of the Class AA Southern League] and then you were sent up to the Mariners as a starting shortstop [and the youngest position player in team history]. Did it happen quicker for you than you thought?

ALEX RODRIGUEZ: [Mariners manager] Lou Piniella, who I love like a father, gave me an opportunity very early on, at age eighteen. I was just a few months removed from high school and I wasn't ready—emotionally and physically and mentally I wasn't ready. [So I struggled a little bit.] But it was a great experience and it got me ready. The next year I won the batting title, so it was a good preparation.

MICHAEL KAY: Was it tough being on a team with two not-just-stars-but-megastars in Ken Griffey Jr. and Randy Johnson? Was that a benefit or a detriment?

ALEX RODRIGUEZ: It was an incredible benefit for me. Because I had an opportunity to see how major superstars handle their business, on the field, off the field, behind the cameras, on the cameras. And I had an opportunity to learn from both of them. As a young man, to learn from these guys was great.

MICHAEL KAY: Now, Seattle is a great city, with a great ballpark, but a lot of people felt that it was a waste for Alex Rodriguez to be playing in the Pacific Northwest three hours after everybody [on the East Coast] has gone to sleep. Did you feel that way?

ALEX RODRIGUEZ: [*Laughs*] I love Seattle, but let's just say I felt that seven, eight years was a long time for me in Seattle. I was born in New York, I live in Miami, I'm an East Coast person, and in my heart of hearts I knew that I wanted to come closer to home.

MICHAEL KAY: Okay, you're in Seattle, and you become a free agent. [After a lot of back-and-forth with various teams] you sign with the Texas Rangers for $252 million for ten years [at the time the most lucrative contract in sports history]. What's that like?

ALEX RODRIGUEZ: So once I got it, I was like, "Thank God that's over, now let's continue to play good baseball and go on to the next stage of my career." I mean, when I signed for $1.3 million in 1993 I felt like, "My God, I won the lottery." And that was probably a more joyous moment for me than even when I got two fifty-two. The thing the money gives you is a great opportunity to help out a lot of people. I'm able to help with the Boys and Girls Club and the Alexander Rodriguez scholarship fund and other things. But let me just say this: there's not a day that goes by that I don't realize that I'm the luckiest man in Major League Baseball, and maybe in the whole world.

MICHAEL KAY: April 2003. You hit your three hundredth home run. You're the youngest player ever to get to that point. Is that something you were keenly aware of and is it important to you?

ALEX RODRIGUEZ: It is important because it's a testament to all my hard work and my dedication and my love for the game of baseball. It was a special day, but it's also something that motivates me to keep getting better every year.

MICHAEL KAY: Do you think of Hank Aaron's [career record of 755 home runs] because you got there sooner than anybody else?

ALEX RODRIGUEZ: I kind of see that as a long ways away still. I mean, when I'm thirty-three, thirty-four, I want to sit down and see where I am and hopefully, uh, I might make a good run at some of those things.

MICHAEL KAY: In 2001 *People* magazine named you one of the fifty most beautiful people in the world. How did that go over in the clubhouse?

ALEX RODRIGUEZ: Not good. [*Laughter*] Considering I'm not really one of them. I get teased all the time about stuff like that.

MICHAEL KAY: Did you go look in the mirror and go, "Yeah!"

ALEX RODRIGUEZ: No, I looked in the mirror and said, "No, they got that wrong." [*Laughter*]

MICHAEL KAY: Can you go out in public? Do you get besieged by fans?

ALEX RODRIGUEZ: Sometimes, but usually in a nice way, though. People are very friendly. They come up, they always have nice things to say. And I've been very lucky my whole career as far as that goes.

QUESTION FROM AUDIENCE: Hi. Guys like you, Piazza, Jeter, you're constantly under the media microscope. How on earth do you tune it out, how do you stay focused?

ALEX RODRIGUEZ: Well, that's a good question. It's tough at times. But I think the number one thing is the love of the game of baseball. I mean, that's the thing I think about when I wake up and when I go to bed at night. I understand fully that that's what I do for a living. And that's what I want to continue to do, to hone my craft every day. Everything else is kind of like a bonus. Like being here today with Mike is a bonus.

MICHAEL KAY: Some bonus. [*Laughter*]

ALEX RODRIGUEZ: Everything else kind of surrounds my game. Baseball comes first, and I try to do my best at it.

MICHAEL KAY: Who was the first one to ever call you A-Rod?

ALEX RODRIGUEZ: I think it was [Mariners play-by-play announcer] Dave Niehaus.

MICHAEL KAY: Cool nickname.

ALEX RODRIGUEZ: Yeah, and it stuck. Especially in the Northwest, the kids absolutely loved it. I went two years and no one knew who Alex Rodriguez was. But they all knew A-Rod. That was cool.

QUESTION FROM AUDIENCE: Who is the toughest pitcher you've ever faced?

ALEX RODRIGUEZ: You know, that's a funny question. When you're struggling, they're all tough. And when you're locked in, they all look like they're throwing beach balls. The toughest pitcher that I've ever seen for one game was Roger Clemens in the postseason in 2000. I mean, it was unbelievable. I went into the game thinking I was locked in. I felt like everybody was throwing beach balls that postseason. And then when Roger pitched, it looked like a golf ball! [*Laughter*] It was unbelievable.

QUESTION FROM AUDIENCE: I want to ask about your life after baseball. Do you see yourself staying involved with baseball like your idol Cal Ripken?

ALEX RODRIGUEZ: I don't know. I don't see myself coaching or managing after baseball. But if I can take some of the things I've learned in baseball and put my philosophies to work, whether it's being a president of an organization, or perhaps owning a small portion of a team, that's something I might consider at some point. More than anything I'd like to get into the business world a little bit. And like I said, I promised my mother I would finish school, so that's something I want to do at some point.

MICHAEL KAY: I heard you can get a scholarship at the University of Miami. [*Laughter*] How about being an announcer? I don't know if you realize this, but I have a similar contract to yours, so there's good money in this. [*Laughter*] And you have all the tools.

ALEX RODRIGUEZ: [*Laughs*] I would consider that, probably years after I retire. I enjoy the game. I love analyzing the game, I really do enjoy breaking down the game. A lot of athletes nowadays, they don't like watching the games, they just like playing. But it's just fun for me.

MICHAEL KAY: Final thing. Is your life as perfect as it seems?

ALEX RODRIGUEZ: No, I don't think so. I mean, we're all human beings and we go through ups and downs. You go through struggles, and I think that's what in general makes life good. You go through peaks and valleys. And I always say the mark of any true man, any true person, is, how do you react when the bad times are here? But I am very thankful to be in the position I'm in right now, and every day I count my blessings.

MICHAEL KAY: Alex, it's been a pleasure.

ALEX RODRIGUEZ: Thank you.

Bill Parcells

When Bill Parcells appeared on *CenterStage* he was three years removed from his job with the New York Jets. He'd settled into retirement, was doing some broadcasting and dabbling in the ponies. His wanderlust of going from one job to the next seemed to have been satisfied. No way would he ever go back to calling plays on the sidelines.

Parcells, a tough-talking, wisecracking product of New Jersey, showed up at the show tanned and seemingly comfortable in his skin. He had two Super Bowl rings with the Giants, brought the historically lousy New England Patriots to the big game, and even managed to get the New York Jets to within thirty minutes of the Super Bowl. There wasn't anything else to accomplish—or, at least, that's what he led us to believe.

When Parcells sat down in the comfortable brown leather chair, you immediately got a sense of why he was so successful. He commanded a room with his personality, while trying to steer the conversation to a place he felt more comfortable. In a fun game of interview chess, after a while he settled in and we had an illuminating conversation that illustrated all that made him successful.

In the week leading up to the taping we also got a glimpse of the power that Parcells liked to wield. In all our interviews of people prior to his and in the countless ones that followed, only Parcells asked our producer for the questions. He liked to be in control, leaving little to chance, and he didn't want to be surprised at anything he might be asked. We refused to give him the questions and explained that the show was essentially about the arc of his life. Although uncomfortable, Parcells agreed to do the show despite not knowing what was coming, but perhaps secure in the knowledge that he'd never been overwhelmed by anything life had thrown his way, so an hour interview show wouldn't sink him.

Maybe this interview whet his appetite for more intellectual combat, as he took his final coaching gig a year later, signing to coach the Dallas Cowboys. If so, Jerry Jones has yet to thank me.

The Interview

MICHAEL KAY: Welcome, everybody. My guest has almost single-handedly turned around three separate football franchises. He won two Super Bowls with the New York Giants, he got to one with the Patriots, and he brought the Jets within one win of the big game. He's won countless coaching awards, and there are a lot of people who believe he should have been named to the football Hall of Fame in 2002. Today we've reeled in "the Big Tuna"—Bill Parcells. [*Applause*]

BILL PARCELLS: Thank you.

MICHAEL KAY: Coach, you've coached three professional teams, the Giants, the Patriots, and the Jets. Right here and now, which one are you?

BILL PARCELLS: Well, the Giants gave me a chance, so I'll be forever grateful. But my allegiance would be more to the coaches who coached for me and the players who played for me [more than for any particular team].

MICHAEL KAY: So on a Sunday when you watch a game, you're not rooting for the Giants deep down?

BILL PARCELLS: I would like for all of the teams that I worked for to be successful.

MICHAEL KAY: So why don't we just start at the beginning? You grew up on the same street as the Lombardis, you played football with the Lombardi kids. How much did Vince Lombardi mean to your coaching philosophy?

BILL PARCELLS: Well, when I first got interested in professional football, I was eleven or twelve years old, and Vince Jr. just happened to be a playmate. His dad was an assistant coach with the Giants, and so occasionally I'd go to the games. And I can remember my first game, 1954, the Giants played the Steelers, and that was kind of my first experience with pro football.

MICHAEL KAY: Did you read up on his philosophies? Did you employ some of them?

BILL PARCELLS: I was aspiring as a young coach to be a head coach in college, and so it was the Bud Wilkinsons and the Bear Bryants and the Woody Hayeses and the guys that were at the top of the profession in the collegiate level that I was really watching. But as I grew older and kind of changed my direction toward pro football, I followed the Lombardis and the Landrys and the Chuck Nolls and the guys that preceded me.

MICHAEL KAY: How do you motivate a team? Do you motivate by fear? Because you have a very tough aura about you, and the things that we've read about you that you don't take anything from anybody. Is it fear that motivates?

BILL PARCELLS: Well, first of all, I think that motivation is overrated. If a player doesn't really want to be successful, then there's nothing I can do. But if we operate on the premise that it's in the player's best interest that he succeed, and it's in my best interest that he succeed, and I can provide the proper direction to enhance that possibility, then I think we start off on level ground. And that's the way I basically try to approach new players and players that maybe had had difficulty somewhere. Because we both want the same thing.

MICHAEL KAY: Let me read a quote to you from [former New York Giants quarterback] Phil Simms. He said, "When we were playing real well as a team, Bill Parcells was miserable because he needs friction. He lives on that friction, he needs adversity, and he's got to have a spat going with a player. If there's no adversity, he'll create it." True or false?

BILL PARCELLS: True.

MICHAEL KAY: Really?

BILL PARCELLS: I don't like complacency. I like people coming to work alert, not just cruising along. We're trying to get better all the time. Even though it's going well, that doesn't mean we can't go a little further down the line.

MICHAEL KAY: Were you ever happy coaching, though?

BILL PARCELLS: Sure. But it can be a killer. The schedule that National Football League coaches are on nowadays is quite a bit different than what it was when I first started. With the free agency and the year-round effort necessary to coach on a professional level, we've made it a twelve-month job, and it used to be a ten-month job. And those eight weeks were pretty valuable as a time to recharge. It's difficult now.

MICHAEL KAY: Coach, you left the Patriots [after disagreements with owner Robert Kraft over personnel decisions], and you famously said, "If I'm going to cook the dinner, I wanna buy the groceries." Now, you bought the groceries with the Jets. Was it a tough job doing both [coaching and handling player acquisitions]?

BILL PARCELLS: Oh, sure, but I think it can be done if you're qualified to do it, and I think I had enough experience over my time in professional football. You have to have a good support staff, and you have to have someone there who's astute in the workings of professional football, and a guy that you can kind of bounce things off and who knows what he's doing. And when I was with the Jets, I had that in a guy named Dick Haley, who was our personnel guy. I could always go to him and say, "Hey, am I off base here?" And he'd tell me yes or no.

MICHAEL KAY: You had a lot of what you wanted with the Jets. [In 1998 the Jets went to the playoffs with a 12-4 record, but then they went 8-8 in 1999 and didn't make the playoffs.] Obviously when [Jets owner Leon] Hess died, that took a big proponent away from you. But the fans wanted you back, the players wanted you back, the media seemed like they wanted you back, and still you left. Why did you leave?

BILL PARCELLS: Well, when I came down, Mr. Hess said, "I want you to coach at least two years. After that, you just do what you want, but give me two years to kind of get this thing together as best you can." I just kind of felt like I'd had my time.

MICHAEL KAY: Is it just that you can only coach one team for so long?

BILL PARCELLS: No, it's not the coaching any particular team, it's just coaching itself. I was head coach in the NFL fifteen years, and you know, the last five are like dog years, you know? One year feels like seven. And I had had some physical problems, and I just didn't wanna be one of those guys that coached and coached and coached. It's a young man's game. I don't wanna be coaching when I'm seventy.

MICHAEL KAY: Okay, you left the Jets, and that was it. You said, "I'm not coming back." Do you still love coaching, though? Do you miss the actual being on the sidelines?

BILL PARCELLS: Of course, it was my whole life. It was my life, it's what I did, and I'd do it all again. So it was heart-wrenching sometimes.

MICHAEL KAY: The world would be changed if you had signed with the Phillies as a catcher [when you were a college freshman]. Were you a really good baseball player?

BILL PARCELLS: I don't know that, I was too young to judge it, but I had the opportunity. But in those days it was hard to get to the big leagues, there were only eight clubs in each league, and my dad told me, "Look, you can play baseball if you want to, but you're going to wait until you're out of college." There wasn't any discussion. [*Laughs*] It was "This is what you're doing."

MICHAEL KAY: You almost became a football player as well. You played in college, and after that you were in the Lions training camp. What happened there?

BILL PARCELLS: I wasn't good enough. And in those days [players weren't paid very much], so the economics of the business wasn't that enticing. I had an opportunity to go coach, which is what I really wanted to do, and I'm glad I did it.

MICHAEL KAY: All right, you end up coaching at Army and later as a head coach at the Air Force Academy. Did the military background affect the way you coached?

BILL PARCELLS: Well, I think you're a product of your environment. At West Point I was in my formative years as a young coach. The emphasis on the kicking game was very, very strong there, and that influenced me a great deal.

MICHAEL KAY: I guess one of the offshoots of coaching is sometimes health problems, and with you it manifested itself in heart problems. Was that because of the coaching?

BILL PARCELLS: No. It was because of dumb decisions on my part. Smoking, eating wrong foods. But smoking was the thing that put me down.

MICHAEL KAY: Now, in '91 it was very serious, right? You had heart bypass surgery. Were you scared of dying?

BILL PARCELLS: They didn't want to operate, but there was no choice. I was resigned to the fact I was doing it, and I had the attitude, well, if it happens [if I die in surgery], I'm not going to know it. But I didn't really think it was going to happen. So I would say, yes, maybe I was a little bit scared, but I wasn't anticipating that. So I had a little bit better outlook. Funny thing, this was in Philadelphia, and there was this young football player, a junior linebacker from Temple who worked part-time in the hospital. And he was wheeling me on the gurney, I had already been kind of sedated, and we were wheeling down to the operating room, and he says, "Coach, I just got to ask you for a favor. Could you sign a couple autographs before you . . . ?" So I signed them, and then I said, "So if this doesn't work, you've got my last autograph, right? That should be worth a couple of hundred bucks." [*Laughter*] And he said—he was a nice kid—"No, I'm going to be here when you come out." And the next day, he was. And now my heart's healthy.

MICHAEL KAY: You coached a lot of players over a lot of years on three teams. So I'm going to put you on the spot. Who's your favorite?

BILL PARCELLS: Favorite? I wish you'd have asked me *best* instead of *favorite*. Lawrence Taylor was the best. And it's not too close for second. He was the best.

MICHAEL KAY: Isn't it true that in a lot of sports you have to treat your stars a little bit differently? They have to have some different rules? Did you have different rules for Lawrence Taylor than you would for another player?

BILL PARCELLS: That was publicized, and he had some situations that were different than some other players. But I was trying to be right with the treatment of each guy that I dealt with. But by and large, they all had to be on time and they all had to pay attention and they all had to try to play hard, or they were getting fined or cut or whatever it was.

MICHAEL KAY: All right, who was your favorite player? Where does Phil Simms fit in?

BILL PARCELLS: Phil was right up there, you know. We needed each other.

MICHAEL KAY: Was that love/hate?

BILL PARCELLS: No, it was love. It was love with similar personalities.

More like brothers, you know? We'd fight, but don't you say anything bad about my quarterback, because I like him.

MICHAEL KAY: Now, you went with another quarterback before Phil Simms the first year that you coached.

BILL PARCELLS: Yeah, it was a mistake. Don't coaches do dumb things?

MICHAEL KAY: Was there ever animosity? Did Phil hold that against you?

BILL PARCELLS: Well, Phil got mad at the time, but, no, he never held it against me. He was mad, and I said, "Just be quiet and sit down and relax, it's going to work out." That didn't satisfy him at the time, but like I said, we needed each other. And he turned into a championship quarterback, and I think I helped him, in some ways. I'm not taking credit for it, but if it wasn't for him, I wouldn't be where I was.

MICHAEL KAY: All right, Gatorade baths. I think you were the first one that ever got one. What was that like? Did it annoy you? Did you like it?

BILL PARCELLS: It was a surprise. It always surprised me. You know, you're so attentive to what's going on, they can sneak up on you and you don't know it's coming. But I didn't mind it. You know, I busted them pretty good, and it was their way of getting back at me. If you're going to give it, you got to take a little back. So every once in a while I took it.

QUESTION FROM AUDIENCE: Hey, Coach. Which of the three teams that you've coached did you feel the most pressure from fans and management to win the championship?

BILL PARCELLS: The Jets. Because Mr. Hess was elderly at the time and I felt like I was trying as hard as I could to get him there as quick as I could. He was the best. He was a tremendous individual. I'm really glad that I had the opportunity to get to know him and to deal with him on a one-to-one basis.

MICHAEL KAY: Was that disappointing not getting to the Super Bowl?

BILL PARCELLS: It was the worst. We just made some really stupid mistakes.

MICHAEL KAY: Growing up as a Giants fan, I always identify you with the Giants. How weird was it to coach at Giants Stadium wearing Jet colors? I mean, did that ever come into play with you?

BILL PARCELLS: No, I coached there with the Patriots, too, and played against the Giants. No, your allegiance is to what you're doing, and the players that are with you on that sideline, whatever jersey they have. They're the ones that paid the price in summer camp. They're the ones that deserve your best at that time.

MICHAEL KAY: But don't you realize that Giant fans still adore you? I mean, you gave them the championship they could never have.

BILL PARCELLS: I'm very grateful to have had the opportunity. I love the organization. It's the flagship franchise of the NFL. So obviously I'm indebted and will always be forever grateful for that opportunity.

QUESTION FROM AUDIENCE: Hi, Coach. With your great success of taking losing teams and transforming them into winning teams, like our Jets and Giants and those New England Patriots, can you tell us which you consider to be your greatest accomplishment?

BILL PARCELLS: The biggest mess was the Patriots, because the ownership was in turmoil, the economics of the situation was prohibitive, and they only had five or six young and good players out of the fifty-three on the team. So it was the biggest undertaking because there was not much money, there was no quarterback, there was nothing there. And I just had to kind of start completely from scratch. That's not really the way it was at the Jets. The Jets, there was more on hand when I first got there.

QUESTION FROM AUDIENCE: As coach of many players with egos the size of Manhattan, how do you rein in the players to take direction from the coaching staff?

BILL PARCELLS: Again, the basic premise I operate on is that the player wants to do well. Now, if a player doesn't want to do well, then I'm going to try to do everything I can to get rid of him. My job is to try to give them direction and maybe a little kick if they need it, to get them headed where they tell me they want to go.

MICHAEL KAY: Tell me something that would surprise people about Bill Parcells.

BILL PARCELLS: I'm a futuristic-looking person. I'm not sentimental and I don't look back very often. I'm a guy that looks ahead.

MICHAEL KAY: So you don't enjoy successes in the past? You don't fixate on them?

BILL PARCELLS: Not at all. I'm more like, "What are we doing today? Who are we playing today? I'm ready. Let's go."

MICHAEL KAY: And what do you see in the future for yourself, since you're a futuristic guy?

BILL PARCELLS: Well, I'm going to be doing a radio show this fall, and I'm probably going to be doing some television work, so I'll be keeping close to football in a small way.

MICHAEL KAY: You're never coaching again?

BILL PARCELLS: No.

MICHAEL KAY: Really?

BILL PARCELLS: No, never coaching again.

MICHAEL KAY: You sure of that?

BILL PARCELLS: I'm sure.

MICHAEL KAY: You're the best, thanks. It was such a pleasure.

BILL PARCELLS: Thank you, Mike, I enjoyed it very much. Thank you.

Sly Stallone

When Sylvester Stallone joined us in July of 2003, his career had hit a bit of a dry patch. He was there to promote *Spy Kids 3: Game Over*, and some movie fans at the time were wondering if it might already be game over for this genius behind the *Rocky* franchise. The movie *Rocky* took the world by storm in 1976, and Stallone became a box-office warrior, racking up hit after moneymaking hit. But in the late nineties things began to get stale, and here he was in New York City hawking what was essentially a kids' movie.

But there was no sadness about Stallone. He came to the studio, was gracious with everyone, and looked great. His energy was contagious, and he told the story of his life in crisp, vivid detail. He certainly wasn't the slow-witted Rocky Balboa, but rather, razor-sharp, funny, and totally engaging. The audience loved him.

In the first ten years of *CenterStage*, audience members could step up to a microphone and ask the guests a question. We'd set up the microphone at the end of one segment and ready it for the middle of the next segment as five audience members lined up for their chance to fire away.

As this was happening during a break, I saw Stallone lose all color in his face. On the line behind the microphone was Chuck Wepner. Wepner was a former heavyweight fighter from Bayonne, New Jersey, who'd once taken Muhammad Ali to the limit in a heavyweight title bout. Stallone had frequently said that Wepner's unlikely showing against Ali was the inspiration for his character Rocky taking Apollo Creed to the fifteenth round. Well, Wepner had long thought he deserved some of the massive profits that Stallone had earned through all the *Rocky* movies. The two men reached an out-of-court settlement for an undisclosed sum three years after this taping, but at this time, it was all pretty raw.

A shaken Stallone leaned over to me and said, "Did you guys set me up by bringing that guy here?" I told him we had nothing to do with it, and that anyone could be a member of the audience by going online and getting a ticket. I assured Stallone we had no knowledge that Wepner would be here. Stallone then whispered, "This guy could charge the stage, so I want to know if you got my back." I looked at him with incredulity and said, "Got your back?!? You're Rocky." We got counted down to the next segment. Wepner ended up asking a harmless question about boxing, but he seemed to take some joy in having obviously emotionally staggered Stallone.

But Stallone never stays down for the count. Three years after this interview, he rocketed back to box-office gold with *Rocky Balboa*, another *Rambo* movie, the start of the *Expendables* franchise, as well as two *Creed* movies.

All without me having his back.

The Interview

MICHAEL KAY: Sylvester Stallone took the age-old story of an underdog fighting against the odds and turned *Rocky* into a timeless classic. He made his name tackling physical roles in films like *Rambo*, *Cliffhanger*, and *Driven*. He's also taken on more serious roles like the one of a small-town sheriff in *Cop Land*. And audiences have seen the lighter side of Sly with starring roles in *Antz* and *Spy Kids 3*. And off-screen, no matter how busy Stallone is in Hollywood, he still finds time to be a big sports fan. So let's welcome to *CenterStage* actor, writer, director, and producer Sylvester Stallone. [*Applause*]

MICHAEL KAY: Welcome to the show.

SYLVESTER STALLONE: Thank you very much.

MICHAEL KAY: A good place to start would be your childhood. I heard you really liked comic books. Is it true that you tried to fly like Commando Cody?

SYLVESTER STALLONE: Doesn't everyone? [*Laughter*] Don't tell me that children are not influenced by the media. Yes, I did that, or I tried to, and I landed in a half-finished barbecue pit and broke my collarbone.

MICHAEL KAY: You were teased as a kid because you were a little bit different. And you went to a lot of different schools. What was that about?

SYLVESTER STALLONE: Well, I had a bit of a speech impediment, and I was very, very thin. I had kind of an attention deficit disorder, and at the time that meant that you were just a bad kid, you were a rebellious kid. So I was moved around schools a lot.

MICHAEL KAY: Now, at one of these schools you learned how to play football, right?

SYLVESTER STALLONE: Actually I learned at a place called Devereux [High School in Pennsylvania]. And then I played a little bit at Lincoln [High School in Philadelphia]. But I was a very late starter in athletics. I just didn't have a lot of interaction with sports early on. As a matter of fact, in the third grade I lost the first baseball game I ever played in. I was playing catcher and someone hit a pop-up, and I just covered my head, like this. [*Hides head with hands*] To this day that haunts me. [*Laughter*]

MICHAEL KAY: You ended up going to Switzerland to go to school, too. And you're the only guy there who didn't ski.

SYLVESTER STALLONE: Exactly right. I thought, "What do I want to do—get a broken neck?" I had an inability to stand up in snow. [*Laughter*]

MICHAEL KAY: So you had some tough times [as a struggling actor] in New York. What else did you do?

SYLVESTER STALLONE: See, the trouble with acting is you need to do a lot of other things to do it. If you just stand on the corner acting, you're gone. So I took a lot of jobs that no one else wanted. I would deliver fish. I would clean lion cages at the zoo—which is horrific. I mean, there's a smell that comes out of that. And one thing after another. And then finally I got a job, after four years of college, as a movie-theater usher. Which I thought was great, except you had to use the same tux as the guy before you, and he's been sweating for six hours and everyone thinks it's your BO. [*Laughter*] But it gave me a chance. Doing that job actually is when I started to focus on writing. Because you start watching a film six times and you can start to break it down. So good things came out of it.

MICHAEL KAY: And then you end up moving to Hollywood and

you're writing a screenplay. While you're writing it, you actually go to a closed-circuit showing of the Muhammad Ali and Chuck Wepner fight [which Ali won, but in which the long-shot Wepner scored a knockdown]. And that gave you *Rocky*?

SYLVESTER STALLONE: Well, it gave me the idea that here's an interesting character who everyone underrated. I needed a story about redemption and how you can rise above the odds and so on and so forth. But it wasn't based on anything that actually happened in reality.

MICHAEL KAY: At the time you wrote the script you were dead broke. Then some producers wanted to buy the script [for $350,000], but they wanted somebody else to play the lead. But you didn't take all the money because you wanted to play the Rocky character.

SYLVESTER STALLONE: Well, I wrote [the part] for myself, and I knew it was the right thing. In life you can do a thousand things wrong. But if you just do one thing right, sometimes it makes up for the other nine hundred and ninety-nine mistakes.

MICHAEL KAY: Now, how real were the fight scenes and how much did you have to get into shape in those movies?

SYLVESTER STALLONE: A lot. A real fight is incredibly grueling, and you know you face life and death [but it doesn't last long]. But a movie fight will go on for months. You have to be able to do fight scenes over and over and over and over again, so you'll be in the ring for maybe sixty, seventy hours altogether, and then you piece it down to fifteen minutes or eight minutes.

MICHAEL KAY: Did you get hurt at all?

SYLVESTER STALLONE: Oh, man! Dolph Lundgren put me in the hospital for nine days [when filming *Rocky IV*]. Nine days! But it was an accident. I told Dolph, "I want you to get up there and just try to clock me, knock me out. For the first minute of the fight it's gonna be a free-for-all." So he comes out there, and I'm, like, five-ten, and he's, like, six-twelve. [*Laughter*] And he was also the world champion kickboxer so he knows how to fight. Boom! I get it in the chest. And then that night I started feeling palpitations, and they said, "Oh my God," they put me on a low-altitude flight [from location in Canada] back to Saint John's Hospital in California. I knew I was in trouble when I showed up at the hospital and the nuns greeted me. [*Laughter*] I was in the ICU for nine days.

MICHAEL KAY: You were so convincing as Rocky. At the height of your training, do you think you could have beaten a professional fighter?

SYLVESTER STALLONE: [*Laughs*] Probably not. Actually I had a few reality checks. In *Rocky I* I was just so awkward. But in *Rocky III* we brought Joe Frazier in, and he was in the ring for maybe eleven seconds and I had to get four stitches.

MICHAEL KAY: Get out!

SYLVESTER STALLONE: I swear to God, four stitches. Then I brought in Earnie Shavers. He never hit me in the jaw, he just started to move around, so I figured I'll outrun him, no problem. They've always said Earnie was kind of slow. The bell rings, he starts moving at halfback speed, and the next thing I know I'm in the corner, he starts to unload, and he's hitting me in the arms. It was like being hit by a Buick, and I started to squeal this new kind of sound—it was like my feminine side coming out. [*Laughter*] And then I did one with Roberto Durán, and he was extraordinary. And I thought, "I really shouldn't be in the ring with this guy."

MICHAEL KAY: Your dog [a bullmastiff named Butkus] appeared in *Rocky*. Why *Butkus*?

SYLVESTER STALLONE: Well, I named him after [Chicago Bears linebacker] Dick Butkus. It was a facial thing, because [Dick Butkus] had a very large head, like the dog. But he wasn't very pleased. I ran into Dick Butkus and [NFL fullback] Larry Csonka one night, and Dick Butkus says, "So why do you call your dog Butkus?" And I said it's an *homage*, and he had no idea what that was. He thought I said it was an omelet. [*Laughter*] Then Larry Csonka goes, "Yeah, he doesn't like that." So now two of the biggest heads in the world were coming at me in stereo. And of course I did what every brave guy would do, I completely backed off. I said, "That dog is a proud, powerful animal. If you were gonna take a dog and make him a linebacker, it would be that dog."

MICHAEL KAY: Let's go to another action-driven movie that you did. *Driven*.

SYLVESTER STALLONE: Well, *Driven* kind of like missed, but it was about the extraordinary world of motor racing. Two things that people do are, they fight against the odds and they race against time. Fighting, racing, fighting, racing. And that's why we race everything, from jets to cars to turtles to hamsters to Jack Russell terriers. And I thought there's an extraordinary story in here somewhere. It didn't quite all come together, but that is an amazing sport.

MICHAEL KAY: Did you ever go two hundred miles an hour [during the filming]?

SYLVESTER STALLONE: Yeah, I went about two oh five, two oh eight.

MICHAEL KAY: Why do you do these things?

SYLVESTER STALLONE: Because I'm stupid. [*Laughter*] I mean, I could try to give you a dramatic answer, like "Well, I decided I wanted to push the limits of myself." But it was because I'm a moron.

MICHAEL KAY: You're a star. You can't be doing that stuff. You did some of your own stunts in *Cliffhanger*?

SYLVESTER STALLONE: Oh my God, yes. I think mountain climbing is insane. Truly. Because not only do you risk your life getting up to the top, now you gotta go back down. [*Laughter*] The first day there [for filming in the Italian Alps], I swear to you, I got on my hands and knees and I crawled to the edge [of a cliff], and I'm probably about twenty-five hundred feet up. There's a [safety] wire, but it's a little thin thing, like this. And then, after about three weeks, I'm standing there with my back to the edge, eating lunch.

MICHAEL KAY: You know what I always thought about when you do all these movies? I mean, *Cliffhanger*, *Driven*, and all that. How do you get insurance? Do the producers in Hollywood go, "Oh no, he's doing this again."

SYLVESTER STALLONE: There's a lot of insurance involved. [*Laughs*]

MICHAEL KAY: Now, I heard that when you were watching Miami Heat games at the American Airlines Arena, they actually played the *Rocky* song and they showed you on the screen. And you were a really good sport about it. Does it ever bother you, like, "Oh, stop, man, I'm trying to watch the game"?

SYLVESTER STALLONE: Not with *Rocky*. If they were showing *Stop! Or My Mom Will Shoot*, I would get upset. [*Laughs*] Or *Rhinestone*. Then I'd be really upset, yeah. But *Rocky*, it's okay, it's nice.

MICHAEL KAY: So you're really cool about that. You're okay with being Rocky?

SYLVESTER STALLONE: Totally. Are you kidding? I mean, I wish I was Rocky. Because he's not a bad guy, he's okay, you know? He's such an ethical guy and he maintains his childlike enthusiasm and he basically puts other people first. But that's not me at all.

MICHAEL KAY: I loved the *Rocky* movies, all of them. But *Rocky V* [in which Rocky retires after losing all his money] got me because I did not want to see Rocky go out a bum again. It broke my heart. It killed me.

SYLVESTER STALLONE: Killed you? You didn't get the reviews. I got buried alive. [*Laughter*] But, yeah, that was a big mistake on my part. Nobody wants to see the overweight Elvis. Nobody wants to see Frank Sinatra inebriated or the Judy Garland character taking pills. Fighters do have curves in their lives, it's up and down, peaks and valleys. But when they've gone up for ten years, you don't want to see the valley. It was shortsighted on my part. I thought, "Okay, this is dramatic," and it was dramatically right, but it was philosophically wrong to the audience. That's why there's a nagging part of me that wants to end it on another beat.

MICHAEL KAY: Good. Now, you're in such great shape. I wondered about that *Cop Land* role [in which you play an out-of-shape small-town sheriff].

SYLVESTER STALLONE: I loved that film. But, yeah, I put on about forty pounds. Pizza, pancakes, fries, cheesecake, you eat before you go to bed and you sleep with French toast [*laughter*], then you wake up and eat some more. You just pound food. Then the movie opens up with a shot of my stomach, and the audience went, "Whoa!" It was, like, a shock. I think with certain actors there's an expectation from the audience. The audience expects a certain kind of behavior. If John Wayne wants to do the *Nutcracker Suite*, even if he has the ability to do it, we're not watching it, okay? You don't want to see people vacillate. If a guy's a great pitcher, I don't want to see him play catcher. But maybe the guy wants to play catcher, he wants to prove he can do it.

MICHAEL KAY: You were great in that movie, but were you trying to separate yourself from *Rocky* and *Rambo*?

SYLVESTER STALLONE: I was, and I think it was self-defeating because even though that character was physically the antithesis of

Rocky, he's still Rocky-esque. I think heroes come in all sizes and shapes. It's not about muscles or whatever. A real hero knows that he can't possibly survive but he'll still do it anyway. That's a hero.

QUESTION FROM AUDIENCE: After the movie, how hard was it for you to lose all the weight that you gained and get back to great physical condition?

SYLVESTER STALLONE: So afterwards I thought it would be easy to take it off, but it wasn't. It was not that easy. The body chemistry has to go through a whole process. So I started going on a very, very heavy-protein diet, but then again that can also make you a little tired. It took about two months. But it's an ego thing, you know, flabs to abs. [*Laughter*]

MICHAEL KAY: You'll always be remembered for Rocky and Rambo. But take that part out, what would you like your legacy to be?

SYLVESTER STALLONE: You know, someone sent me a pillow once, and on it they had embroidered this message. It said, "You fought many wars, you lost a few battles, but you never quit." So that's basically it. I just want to be a guy who is a raging optimist and wants to hang in until the final bell.

MICHAEL KAY: You seem pretty happy with yourself and your life and comfortable in your skin. Are you that way?

SYLVESTER STALLONE: Yeah, but it took a while to get there. I went through that whole period of being pensive and petulant and, you know, bitter about some things. Like, "How come somebody else gets something and I don't?" I try to drill it into my children early on, get rid of envy, it will only kill you. Get rid of envy and then everything starts to come to you. It's like what they say with the Lakers: don't keep chasing the game. It'll come around, don't chase it. You know, I just turned fifty-seven, and I realize that it's blink, blink, and suddenly your life is over. But I'm still here—and I'm incredibly grateful.

MICHAEL KAY: It was really nice to meet you.

SYLVESTER STALLONE: Yeah, thank you.

Joe Namath

Joe Namath would be on the list of top-five favorite hangs for every sports fan old enough to have witnessed his heroics with the New York Jets. Who *wouldn't* want to spend a significant amount of time with Broadway Joe, finding out how the man became the legend? And when we got the chance to talk with Namath, he didn't disappoint. He's an incredible storyteller and has been one of the more famous people on the planet since stepping onto the campus of the University of Alabama to play quarterback for Bear Bryant.

Both men and women find Namath fascinating, and it remains for each person to tell specifically what about this kid from Beaver Falls, Pennsylvania, draws them in. But he certainly has that something.

He's a Hall of Fame quarterback, the MVP of arguably the most significant Super Bowl win when he quarterbacked the Jets to a historic upset of the Baltimore Colts—and he has appeared in commercials, plays, shows, and movies, while also broadcasting the game he is best known for.

Namath has had some of the world's most beautiful women on his arm, but he's always behaved like a gentleman, declining to tell tales. Instead, with a twinkle in his eye he casually brushes aside requests for details.

The ravages of the vicious sport he played have taken some of the spring from his step, and the lines in his face testify to the years and experiences he has accumulated along the way, but Namath lights up in the spotlight, and when he walks into a room, people stop. They stare. *That's Joe Namath!* All these years since his greatest moment in 1969 in Super Bowl III, Namath still commands the spotlight on *CenterStage*. His stories amaze and entertain. He has lived one of the coolest American lives, and on the show he allowed us to reexperience the ride with him.

The Interview

MICHAEL KAY: Today's guest is a New York icon whose brash, bold style defined the Big Apple's persona decades ago. But he remains an icon of cool. A natural athlete in all sports when he was growing up in a small Pennsylvania steel town, he chose football to make his mark and will forever be remembered for guaranteeing a New York Jets win in Super Bowl III over the highly favored Colts. Oh, yes, many of us remember the long hair and Fu Manchu mustache, the fur coats, photos of him with the world's most beautiful women, tales of all-night carousing. The ladies swooned, and other men envied his good looks, natural charm, and winning style. Not only do I promise that this will be a great show—I got that from Joe—I guarantee it. [*Laughter*] Please welcome the greatest quarterback ever to wear the Jets green, Broadway Joe Namath. [*Applause*]

JOE NAMATH: Thank you, guys. Beautiful.

MICHAEL KAY: A good place to start would be when you left Alabama, and you got the $427,000 contract to sign with the Jets. Were you shocked at that money?

JOE NAMATH: I was shocked all right. My dad was still working in a mill, he was making fifty-one hundred dollars a year, and my mother was still working. The original negotiation was with the St. Louis Cardinals. These two guys representing the Cardinals showed up unannounced at my dorm room, I was alone, and they asked me what I wanted. Coach Bryant had already talked to me about it. He said, "Do you know what you are gonna ask those people for whenever they talk contract?" And I said, "Well, sir, last year Don Trull signed for one hundred thousand dollars." Coach Bryant said, "You go ahead and ask 'em for two hundred thousand dollars. That's a better place to start." So I told these guys from the Cardinals, "I want two hundred thousand dollars—and I also want a Lincoln Continental convertible." And they both acted like they had heart attacks. [*Laughter*] But they pulled out some papers for me to sign right there.

MICHAEL KAY: What stopped you?

JOE NAMATH: I hadn't talked to anybody else. And we still had a bowl game to play; I couldn't sign anyway.

MICHAEL KAY: The Jets get involved, because of the AFL against the NFL. And the number gets to $427,000.

JOE NAMATH: Well, it worked out. The most important thing Coach Bryant told me was "First of all, before the money, get to know the people you are gonna work for. Get to know your owners. Get to know your coach." I had a chance to play for [Jets coach] Weeb Ewbank, a guy who coached Johnny Unitas to a world championship, and what quarterback wouldn't want to do that? And the Jets ownership was just spectacular. I was supposed to be a Jet, that's all there was to it.

MICHAEL KAY: Did you think you would fit into New York City as seamlessly as you did? Were you scared of the big city? [*Laughter*]

JOE NAMATH: I wasn't scared of the big city. I had been here once, to the World's Fair. [*Laughter*]

MICHAEL KAY: Now, it worked out obviously for the Jets and for you. In '68 you beat the Oakland Raiders in the AFL Championship Game, and then you go up against the Colts. And you guaranteed the win. Why were you so confident when Vegas had you as a big underdog?

JOE NAMATH: It was a combination of effort and belief in the team. I was a confident ballplayer, but don't get cocky mixed up with confident. Coach Bryant didn't have cocky guys, he had confident guys.

MICHAEL KAY: It wasn't just trying to get your team to believe. You really believed you could beat the Colts?

JOE NAMATH: I don't know any other way to go out on a football field. You have to believe you are gonna win, and you are going into the game thinking you are gonna win.

MICHAEL KAY: What was it like growing up in the steel town of Beaver Falls, Pennsylvania? Was it tough?

JOE NAMATH: We thought it was tough. When you're a kid, the grass is always greener somewhere else. But in reflecting on it, it was absolutely wonderful for kids. The town is in a valley, with the river on one side, and railroad tracks on the other side. We had baseball, basketball, football, the river, the railroad tracks, the factories and the foundries—and school. It was wonderful.

MICHAEL KAY: Now, you also played basketball and baseball in high school. You were a great baseball player—so much so that the Cubs offered you fifty thousand dollars to play for them.

JOE NAMATH: *Great* is a word that's overused. I was a prospect. I could play. I could run, I could throw, I could catch, I could hit.

MICHAEL KAY: You mentioned what your dad made earlier. Was it tough to turn down fifty thousand dollars?

JOE NAMATH: It was a no-contest for me. My mother wanted me to go to school. She just said, "I want Joey to go to college." And that was that.

MICHAEL KAY: So the kid from Beaver Falls goes down to University of Alabama to play for Paul "Bear" Bryant. Was it a culture shock?

JOE NAMATH: The first day it was. I went to the Greyhound bus station, and that's where I first encountered the COLORED and WHITE water fountains, and the segregated bathrooms, and I realized what a different society it was.

MICHAEL KAY: How shocking was that for you? Beaver Falls was ethnically diverse, and you didn't see color when you were growing up.

JOE NAMATH: It sounds like an excuse, but I was so naive and ignorant. All I ever did was play baseball, basketball, football, and work. I didn't know what went on around the rest of the country, or around the rest of the world. I never did accept it [racial segregation], but it took a while to communicate my feelings. In '64 [black students] Vivian Malone [and James Hood] entered the university [after Governor George Wallace tried to block the doorway], and that was a major step forward, of course. But it was a slow process. And it wasn't just the Deep South. People carry hatred with them all over the world, for a variety of reasons.

MICHAEL KAY: Bear Bryant is such a huge figure, Joe. He had a way of getting people's attention, and he got your attention in the one special way. . . .

JOE NAMATH: [*Laughs*] Yes, he did. As a freshman, running an option play around right end, and I pitched a ball and it was a bad pitch. And Coach Bryant was yelling something to me—"Namath!"—but I didn't hear the rest. And as I was walking back, I had my head down, and the next thing I knew my face mask was yanked up, and he looked at me and said, "Boy, when I talk to you, you look me in the eye and say, 'Sir.'" And I said, "Yes, sir, yes, sir, yes, sir." [*Laughter*] And for the next four years, if he was three football fields away and said, "Namath," I would yell out, "Yes, sir!" [*Laughter*]

MICHAEL KAY: So he was scary.

JOE NAMATH: Yes! It was old-style coaching, but the old style isn't always bad. I certainly don't believe in physical abuse, but you gotta find a way to get through to some players. And certain coaches have that ability.

MICHAEL KAY: You always had your shoes taped, but there was one game against North Carolina State that you didn't. And that's when you suffered your first knee injury.

JOE NAMATH: It was the fourth game of the season, and things were wrong. I put my thigh pads on backwards, I didn't tape my shoes. I was discombobulated for some reason. I was running around right end with a run/pass option and my knee just gave out, and I tore some things. And from that time on, it was a matter of taking care of the knee, playing and hurting it again, and then playing again, until I got it fixed reasonably well when I came to the Jets.

MICHAEL KAY: How tough was it for you to reconcile being hurt like that?

JOE NAMATH: I learned to adjust my style of play. You don't plant [your foot] this way, you don't run that way, you don't put pressure on it and expect it to stand. You play the hand you're dealt.

MICHAEL KAY: You were twenty-nine and four with Alabama and ended up winning the national championship. And then you join the Jets, and the Manhattan jet set. Was there jealousy on your teammates' part?

JOE NAMATH: That's always sensitive turf, the walk-on for a rookie coming in to play with veterans in professional sports. And when the rookie is coming in, he might be making more money than some veterans who had earned their way through several years. There were some attitudes, of course.

MICHAEL KAY: You end up becoming "Broadway Joe," but you were more or less Upper East Side Joe, or Second Avenue Joe. [*Laughter*] But how did *Broadway* come about, and who gave you that name?

JOE NAMATH: Our offensive left tackle, Sherman Plunkett. He was a leader on our team, a real veteran. No one ever knew how much Sherman weighed because the scales only went up to three hundred at that time. [*Laughter*] We had come in from practice one day at Shea, and on our stools in front of our lockers was the *Sports Illus-*

trated magazine with me standing on Broadway in a football uniform. Veterans have a way of letting you know that you are a rookie, and some of the comments were tough. But then Sherman is looking at the magazine cover and a big ol' smile breaks out on his face, and he said, "Look at Broadway Joe." [*Laughter*] That's the first time I heard it. And it's been dear to me ever since because it was Sherman.

MICHAEL KAY: Well, you were doing great on the football field, and from the stories that are always told, you were doing great off the football field as well. [*Laughter*] Now, I don't want to put you on the spot or embarrass you, but did every woman in New York want Joe Namath at that time?

JOE NAMATH: Oh, I hope so. [*Laughter*] But everything came after football. Going out at night was only after watching films of the guys we were getting ready to play. But it was different in the off-season. [*Laughter*]

MICHAEL KAY: We all know about Super Bowl III. But with the Jets, there was a lot of losing as well. And you had only known winning with Alabama. How tough was it to take the losing?

JOE NAMATH: When I was a freshman at Alabama, we had our first meeting with Coach Bryant, and he had talked to us about the peaks and valleys we would experience. There were some tough valleys. It's not fun to make mistakes, to lose football games, to have that feeling that you and your team have failed and let everyone down. It stinks to lose.

MICHAEL KAY: You were the first quarterback ever to throw for four thousand yards in a season, and you did it in fourteen games. You liked to throw the ball, and you had a lot of interceptions in your career. Was it because you had bad teams, or you just wanted to air it out all the time?

JOE NAMATH: The interceptions? Oh, no, they were all great defensive plays. [*Laughter*] I even tried to con myself by thinking, "Oh, it's an interception. Just think how happy his family is." [*Laughter*]

MICHAEL KAY: So you win the Super Bowl, and you are twenty-five years old. What was it like to be Joe Namath, after that win, after the guarantee?

JOE NAMATH: I was consumed with the elation of winning the championship. I lived on that feeling for quite a while. It was a huge accomplishment for the AFL and for our team. Remember, we were more than just a team then. We were representing the AFL, and the fans, and it's a feeling that I still enjoy today. I've been asked, if we had lost the game, what would I have done? And I know what I would have done. If you lose, you shut up, go back to work, and do it the next time.

MICHAEL KAY: Your life went into hyper-overdrive after that. All the beautiful women that were surrounding you. Was it tough to stay single? Were people trying to marry you all the time? [*Laughter*]

JOE NAMATH: I never lived with a lady until I was forty years old. I was raised a Catholic, and my mother would visit me, and there was no way I could justify to my mother that I was living with a lady before being married. Or at least I used that as an excuse. [*Laughter*]

MICHAEL KAY: You also did a lot of commercials, and you broke new ground. One of the commercials you did, the one that's always remembered, was the pantyhose one. [*Laughter*] How did that come about?

JOE NAMATH: It was the ad agency's idea. I remember seeing the storyboard. And I laughed, I thought it was funny. But a lady in our office said, "I don't think my dad would like that." And that postponed things about a week, figuring out how people would feel about a ballplayer wearing pantyhose. And after that, I said, "Timeout. This was funny when we first looked at it. We do it, so what?" When I went back to Alabama one time, I was in a restaurant and a man in his eighties said to me, "Son, I don't mind you wearing them there pantyhose, but, boy, did you shave your legs?" [*Laughter*] And I said, "Well, sir, when you play football and tape your ankles and tape your knees, you'd better shave your legs." [*Laughter*]

MICHAEL KAY: The years 1970 through '73, you played only twenty-eight of fifty-eight games.

JOE NAMATH: You're kidding.

MICHAEL KAY: [*Laughter*] How much pain were you in, Joe?

JOE NAMATH: [*Laughs*] I don't remember. But I learned that the body is a wonderful piece of work. We can rehab and heal it, with the right guidance. And things could always be worse. I hated missing playing time. And the first five years I played, I didn't miss a game. I was feeling pretty good, five years without missing a game. But then Lady Luck took a little different turn.

MICHAEL KAY: You have talked about the injuries and how much pain you were in. And it led you to self-medicate because of the pain, and that's why you started drinking.

JOE NAMATH: Well, as a high schooler, we might have had wine sometimes, but we really didn't drink. We were athletes. Then when I was a rookie, I picked up a safety blitz with my left hip at Boston, and it hurt so bad I couldn't even sit on the plane. I got back to my apartment on Eighty-Sixth Street, and I was hurting. I found the funkiest-smelling stuff—it was my roommate's Scotch—and I started drinking. I never considered it a problem—but it became a problem.

MICHAEL KAY: Now, there was what everybody knows as the "Suzy Kolber incident" [in which you said during a live TV interview in 2003 that you wanted to kiss the ESPN reporter]. What happened, Joe?

JOE NAMATH: I had too much to drink and I made a fool of myself. I disappointed my family and my friends and the Jet fans, and I acted like a jerk. The next day I felt awful, and I realized I needed to get some help. When I first got married [in 1984] and started a family, my wife had told me if I didn't quit drinking, we were gonna have a problem. And I did quit drinking. I was what you would call a "dry drunk" for thirteen years. I didn't touch a drop, and it was great. It was so good, I used to wonder why I ever drank. Then I went through some changes [a divorce], and I found some excuses to start drinking again. That lasted for about three years, until the Suzy night. I apologized to her, and I went to rehab, got some information, got an education, [and I haven't had a drink since]. And things are good. It took me a long time to figure out that life is so much better without it.

MICHAEL KAY: When we started this show, the ovation for you was thunderous. You could feel the love. What's it like, that kind of adoration?

JOE NAMATH: Well, I know how I feel about people and life. I respect my relationship with people. It makes me feel awful good to have the relationship I do with the sports fans, with the people that I meet. It's a blessing just being able to see somebody and have 'em smile. I just like where I am right now.

MICHAEL KAY: Thank you so much.

JOE NAMATH: Hey, thank you. [*Applause*]

Red Auerbach

In 2004 we interviewed Celtic legend Red Auerbach. He was promoting a book he'd written with John Feinstein, and he came on *CenterStage* to tell the story of his legendary life. A particular memory stands out about that day. The taping began with Red sitting down in the comfy dark brown chair (the color of the chairs has changed over the years) and holding his trademark cigar. People figured he'd just hold the cigar during the interview—and he did until the final twenty minutes. Then, during a break between segments, he began lighting his stogie. One of the producers ran onstage and nervously said, "Mr. Auerbach, there's a New York City ordinance against smoking indoors." Red looked up at him, let out a deep, almost dismissive chortle, and in his raspy, New York–tinged, Boston-influenced accent, said, "Yeah, right. An ordinance." He lit the cigar, knowing no one was going to stop him. The producer looked on in exasperation, sighed, put his head down, and walked away.

Red was incredibly proud of his 938 coaching wins and nine NBA championships in ten seasons. He'd also been GM and president of the Celtics and, in those roles, had won seven more titles, giving him sixteen in his twenty-nine years in Boston.

And his influence was far-reaching, since he played a large role in the ascension of the league from distant afterthought to major player in entertainment. While doing so, he helped break down color barriers and drafted the first black player, Chuck Cooper. He also sent onto the court the first all-black starting five in 1964. The only color Red saw was Celtic green. If you could help him win, he wanted you on his team.

And win he did. He became somewhat infamous for lighting up his cigar when he thought victory was about to be nailed down. The day of my interview with him, in the city of his birth, our discussion ranged over a lifetime of remarkable triumphs. That day, no one was telling this eighty-eight-year-old icon that he couldn't celebrate another win. He would die a year later.

The Interview

MICHAEL KAY: *Red Auerbach* is synonymous with championships. With talent, determination, and savvy trades, Auerbach coached the Boston Celtics to nine world titles, with eight of them in a row, from 1959 to 1966. He coached eleven Hall of Famers, including Bill Russell, Bob Cousy, and John Havlicek. And after he removed himself from the bench, Red continued to work magic in the Celtics' front office, orchestrating the arrivals of Larry Bird, Kevin McHale, Robert Parish, Bill Walton, and many others. Coach Auerbach has won countless awards, including being named the greatest coach in the history of the NBA by the Professional Basketball Writers Association. He literally changed the game of pro basketball. In his fifty-five seasons as a member of the Boston Celtics family, he has plenty of tales to tell. And many of them are in his latest book, *Let Me Tell You a Story*, cowritten with John Feinstein. Today we are so honored to let him tell us some stories. Please welcome the legendary coach Red Auerbach. [*Applause*] Coach, welcome.

RED AUERBACH: Thank you.

MICHAEL KAY: You know, the words *legend* and *genius* get thrown around a lot these days. But they really do apply to you. Does it make you uncomfortable when people say "legendary" and "genius"?

RED AUERBACH: I don't pay attention to it. I've been through the wars, and when you are through [with your career], people think you are better than you were when you starred. [For example] I was picked in the top fifty ballplayers at George Washington University, but I wasn't that good. [*Laughter*] I really wasn't. Maybe the top seventy, but not the top fifty. But it was what I did other than actually playing at GW that got me that vote.

MICHAEL KAY: But when you think of all you've accomplished, it must give you a sense of satisfaction.

RED AUERBACH: I was pretty fortunate. But you gotta be realistic. You've got to be a little lucky. Talent is fine, but you gotta be a little lucky. For example, one year we're in the seventh game [of the finals], in overtime, and someone—it was either Frank Ramsey or Don Nelson—takes a shot, the ball hits the rim, it hits the backboard, it hits the rim again, rolls around, and then it goes in. I guess that made me a helluva coach. [*Laughter*] And like with [Holy Cross College star and future Hall of Famer Bob] Cousy. [When I started with the Celtics in 1950,] everybody in Boston wanted to draft Cousy. I said, "All I'm interested in is winning, I'm not interested in the local yokels." Then when Chicago folded, there were three players available, and Cousy was one of 'em, 'cause they had drafted him. And he was my last pick of the three, I wanted him last, 'cause I thought he was just this fancy kid. As it turned out, we had to draw names out of a hat, and I wound up with Cousy. [*Laughter*] Luck. That's what I am telling you. You gotta be lucky.

MICHAEL KAY: Well, let's start where this all began, and that was in Brooklyn. People identify you so closely with Boston, but you were born and raised in Brooklyn and you played basketball at Eastern District High School, in the Williamsburg section.

RED AUERBACH: One of the great thrills of my life, I still remember to this day. You remember the old [*New York*] *Herald Tribune*? They had a weekly list, the five "Players of the Week," and one week I was picked. This was a big honor. Also I made all-Brooklyn second team. So I used to tell some of my ballplayers, "I made all-Brooklyn second team," and they got hysterical. "What the hell is all-Brooklyn second team?" You know? [*Laughter*] I would tell 'em we had more teams and better teams in Brooklyn than you had in the whole state of Indiana or Iowa or anywhere like that. But I couldn't convince 'em.

MICHAEL KAY: Well, you end up going from Brooklyn to George Washington University [in Washington, DC]. Forget about the top fifty, and things like that. What kind of ballplayer were you at George Washington?

RED AUERBACH: Well, I was what they call a point guard, which means you're supposed to be a smart-ass, you know? We had a good ball club, and we had one of the toughest schedules in the country.

If they had ratings in those days, we would have been in the top five or six. We had a helluva ball club.

MICHAEL KAY: Now, when you get out of George Washington, you end up going into high school coaching. And then [in World War II] you end up in the navy coaching a navy basketball team. Then your first pro coaching job was with the Washington Capitols.

RED AUERBACH: Yeah, when they got a franchise with the NBA—it was called the BAA [Basketball Association of America] in those days—somehow or other I was able to sell myself to be the coach. I had my old coaching job waiting for me at the high school I had worked at in Washington, but I took a chance. That's the way life is. You gotta take a chance.

MICHAEL KAY: So you're with the Capitols for a couple of years, then the Tri-Cities Blackhawks, and then you start with the Celtics in 1950–51, making ten thousand dollars a year. You mentioned Cousy and the local yokels. When did he win you over? When did you say, "Hey, this guy isn't just flashy, he can really play"?

RED AUERBACH: Well, the first day. He was a very bright guy. And I explained to him, I said, "Bob, with all that behind-the-back dribbling and behind-the-back passing and over-your-head stuff, I don't give a damn how you pass the ball. I don't care if you kick it—but somebody better catch it." [*Laughter*] That was that. As soon as we understood each other, we were all right.

MICHAEL KAY: Let's fast-forward about five years. You get the rights to Bill Russell, and he became an unbelievable asset for you, one of the best players ever. But you two also had a very unique relationship. Why did you guys form that special bond, more than coach and player?

RED AUERBACH: Well, he was a very sensitive guy. See, I don't handle players. I never "handled" players. You handle animals. You "deal" with players. And Russell was so intelligent, you could talk to him. A lot of people thought that I had a double set of standards, you know, one for the other guys and one for Russell. But that's not so. It never was so.

MICHAEL KAY: One thing that makes you stand out was, in 1950 you were the first [NBA] coach to draft a black player [Chuck Cooper]. And obviously, you had a great relationship with Russell. Were you truly color-blind when it came to people?

RED AUERBACH: Hey, I was brought up in New York. [*Laughter*] I didn't care if a guy was green. What the hell difference does it make? If he could play ball, he was gonna play.

MICHAEL KAY: Let's talk about how you got Larry Bird. It turned out to be one of the greatest moves in NBA history.

RED AUERBACH: Well, I didn't know he was gonna be that good. [*Laughter*] I thought he would be damn good. But I didn't know Larry Bird was that bright, I didn't know Larry Bird would play when he was hurt, I didn't know Larry Bird was such a great passer. He had a lot of basketball smarts. But when people talked about Larry Bird, he was the "country bumpkin from French Lick," you know what I mean?

MICHAEL KAY: He had a lot of leverage, though. Was that a tough negotiation with him?

RED AUERBACH: His agent, a guy by the name of Bob Woolf, came in with Larry Bird to talk to me about the contract. So I said, "Look, he's a great player, he should be a great pro. But we don't know, he hasn't played a game yet. So I'm gonna give you one hundred thousand dollars." He looks at me, and he says, "I thought we would get a million." And we would fight and [then] argue in the newspapers. And eventually we would settle for about five hundred thousand dollars. I said, "That's the highest amount of money ever paid a rookie. What the hell more do you want?" So finally he said, "Well, give me fifty thousand dollars more." And that was probably his cut, you know? For fifty thousand dollars, I don't want to kill the deal, so I said, "Okay. You got it." And then he reaches into his pocket, and he pulls out a typewritten page. And he says, "Oh, of course, we would like to have these." He had a list of perks he wanted. I looked at them, and I started to laugh. "If Larry Bird decides to go back to college to finish the last year, the Celtics would pay his tuition. If Larry Bird's mother would like to come to the games, the Celtics would pay for her tickets." That kind of stuff. And I said, "You're talking a couple hundred dollars. He's getting $550,000, plus a deal from Converse. He's making over a million dollars, and you're bugging me with, you know, a couple hundred dollars? What's wrong with you?" I said, "Look, all I want to know is how much do I have to give you to play basketball? I'm not into all that other stuff." So finally he said, "Okay, okay, we got a deal." And I took that list and I ripped it up and I threw it at him. [*Laughter*]

MICHAEL KAY: We have talked a lot about your Celtic players. And one guy we haven't hit yet is John Havlicek, [who was known for his ability to steal the ball.] Whenever Havlicek stole the ball, what went through your mind?

RED AUERBACH: Oh, I could have kissed him. [*Laughter*] John Havlicek was one of the greatest athletes I ever coached. He was a coach's dream. No problems. Came to work, worked hard, team oriented. Just name it, and he had it. He was the ideal athlete.

MICHAEL KAY: Red, you are smoking that cigar right now. You always lit up a cigar when you had a game well in hand. It became famous. When did that start?

RED AUERBACH: Well, you see these coaches now, their team is twenty-five, thirty points ahead, three minutes to go. And the coach is pacing up and down, yelling and screaming. And I'm thinking, "The damn game is over, for crying out loud. Sit down!" [*Laughter*] Now, see, in the days when I coached, a lot of ballplayers smoked. They used to smoke on the bench. [*Laughter*]

MICHAEL KAY: Really?

RED AUERBACH: Sure. Anyway, say there was four minutes to go, and we are twenty-some-odd points ahead, I would sit down. So one day I sat down, and I was bored, so I pulled out a cigar and I lit it. And just like that, whoom! Everybody made a big deal of it, see? So they played it up in such a way that the other teams got mad. But honestly I never did it to antagonize or gloat over the other team. I did it 'cause I was just relaxing. So one day, we go into Cincinnati, and they give out five thousand cigars, figuring that if they beat us, everybody in the joint would light up a cigar and blow smoke in my face. But then we knocked the hell out of them. [*Laughter*]

MICHAEL KAY: Did you ever light up a cigar and then you guys ended up losing?

RED AUERBACH: Almost. One time we were ahead, and I lit the cigar, then one of my guys made a boo-boo, and I'll be damned if the other team didn't tie it up. But we won in overtime, so I forgave him. [*Laughter*]

MICHAEL KAY: Now, you weren't just a coach. You actually set up some of the promotional situations at games. Did anything ever go wrong?

RED AUERBACH: Yeah. One time we gave out three thousand bats at a game. Imagine what coulda happened? [*Laughter*] After I did it, I realized what a jerk I was. Another time I gave out [drinking] glasses with everybody's signatures on them. Then I thought, "Gosh, what happens if we have a couple of bad calls and they throw a glass at the referee or something?" We gave out everything from caps to gym bags, but I never spent more than a dollar and twenty-five cents each for any giveaway.

MICHAEL KAY: Did you feel good about the bronze statue they erected of you at Faneuil Hall in Boston [showing you sitting down and holding a cigar]?

RED AUERBACH: Oh, yeah. Wow.

MICHAEL KAY: Does it look like you?

RED AUERBACH: Well, I posed for it. [*Laughter*] I'll tell you something funny. This friend of mine comes out, he wants to see the statue, so I take him into town, and there is no statue. It's gone! [*Laughter*] Finally I get a guy who works there and I said, "What the hell happened to the statue?" And he says, "Well, you know, the birds do things on it, so they had to clean it." [*Laughter*] They had to bring in a derrick, it weighs a couple of tons, and they had taken it out of there for about four months, and nobody told me. [*Laughter*] That was a scary thing, you know?

QUESTION FROM AUDIENCE: Mr. Auerbach, as the game of basketball has continued to evolve, are today's players as well-coached in the fundamentals as when you coached?

RED AUERBACH: No. They are not coached as well fundamentally because they got too many [assistant] coaches. Most teams have five, six assistants—for one lousy game, with five guys out there on the court. [*Laughter*] They get in each other's way. In my opinion, even today the most you need is two assistants. They worry too much about the X's and O's and all the details and stuff like that. They have three-hour practices, and so forth and so on. What the hell could be more boring than if you are with the same coach for seven, eight years, and you go to practice and you're thinking, "I'm gonna be here three hours, going through the same damn drills I done for eight years"? It's gotta wear on you, see? And that's why a lot of guys, when they are free agents, they don't really want to move, but they move anyway, for two reasons. One, to get a new coach. And the other is for money.

MICHAEL KAY: Who is the best coach now?

RED AUERBACH: Well, I can't say that, because the other thirty will get mad at me. I got enough troubles. [*Laughter*]

QUESTION FROM AUDIENCE: What is your opinion of players who jump from high school to the NBA?

RED AUERBACH: Well, number one, the kids who come from high school to the NBA are not gonna be brain surgeons. [*Laughter*] So what are they gonna do in college except mature and get better as players—and mature as people? However, there are certain exceptions to that. Because some kids at eighteen years of age are men. They are developed more than the average guy of twenty-one or twenty-two. Like LeBron James. He has a man's body and a man's head. And there's another thing. If a high school kid is projected into the first round, he has got to go to the pros. Because what happens if he goes to college and he gets hurt, he breaks a leg or gets an eye injury? What happens? Who takes care of him? Nobody. But if he goes to the pros, he gets a guaranteed contract for at least three years. He gets a few million dollars, he could put it in the bank, he could live on it.

MICHAEL KAY: Coach, let me ask you. If there is a kid that wants to become a basketball player, what advice would you give him?

RED AUERBACH: Just play. Play a lot, as much as you can. If you can't play with other guys, one-on-one, two-on-two, play by yourself. Just get the feel.

MICHAEL KAY: You once said that the Boston Celtics are not just a basketball team, they are a way of life. They have been your way of life for over fifty-five years. Do you ever wonder, if you didn't become a Celtic, what you would have done with your life?

RED AUERBACH: Yeah, I think I would have been a teacher. I love to teach.

MICHAEL KAY: And that's really the way you coach, right? It wasn't just sitting there diagramming plays. You were teaching.

RED AUERBACH: Yeah. They don't teach much today.

MICHAEL KAY: But would you have been satisfied teaching kids, and not having become the legend that you are?

RED AUERBACH: Well, I don't know about that. [*Laughter*]

MICHAEL KAY: What's your greatest accomplishment in your entire career?

RED AUERBACH: I don't know. I really don't. I've just been very fortunate.

MICHAEL KAY: You have had a remarkable life.

RED AUERBACH: Yeah, it's been interesting. It has been interesting. [*Laughter*]

MICHAEL KAY: Red, I'll tell you what. It's been an honor to have you. And we thank you so much.

RED AUERBACH: Well, my pleasure. Thank you. [*Applause*]

Jerry Jones

Jerry Jones is an American original. This billionaire businessman hocked his entire life savings to put together the money to purchase the Cowboys in 1989 for the then unheard-of sum of $140 million. Businesspeople and sports owners snickered at the enormous price Jones paid to join the NFL fraternity. All these years later, Jones is the one laughing as the Cowboys continually jockey with the Yankees for the title of most valuable franchise in the world, hovering around the $5 billion mark.

And the Cowboys didn't become the gold standard because of inertia, but rather, through Jones's talent for moving and shaking. Following Jones's purchase of the team, the new owner shockingly fired iconic Tom Landry, the only coach the franchise had ever known. And that was just the start. In the years since, Jones has continually battled the NFL's staid authority figures, making each of the league's other owners billions more than they would have if he hadn't arrived on the scene. When he appeared on *CenterStage* in 2008, he and the Yankees had just partnered in Legends Hospitality, which has since become one of the most valuable brands in the catering sector.

Since that show, Jones has built the jewel of all stadiums in Arlington, Texas, a breathtaking home to the Cowboys and their brand. He doesn't seem to be slowing down, either; rather, he's always looking for new ways to monetize the NFL shield and, most important, his beloved Cowboys.

Jones is easy with a story and quick with a quip, and all of that was on display when we sat together for a fascinating hour to explore what makes Jerry run.

The Interview

MICHAEL KAY: Thank you, everybody, and welcome to *CenterStage*. Today's guest was raised in Little Rock, Arkansas, where he was a high school football star at running back. He went on to the University of Arkansas and helped them to an undefeated season and a national championship. After a short stint at his father's insurance company, he became the owner of the hugely successful Jones Oil and Land Lease Company. He bought the Dallas Cowboys in 1989 and immediately incurred the wrath of their fans by firing their legendary coach Tom Landry and then trading their star running back. But all was forgiven four seasons later when the Cowboys would win the first of three Super Bowls over a four-year period. He is perhaps the most hands-on owner in the NFL and as general manager makes the player personnel decisions. He has also put his mark on the entire league through unique and innovative broadcasting, merchandising, and marketing deals. Please welcome the owner of the Dallas Cowboys, one of sports' most distinguished, proud, and successful franchises, Mr. Jerry Jones. [*Applause, standing ovation*]

MICHAEL KAY: Jerry, I gotta tell you, we have done about one hundred and thirty shows, and that's the first standing ovation any guest has gotten.

JERRY JONES: Well, I think they've been drinking all afternoon. [*Laughs*] No. I have always appreciated—no matter where we go— the interest in the Cowboys, the interest in sports. It's about emotion, and it's about getting involved with your team. And we certainly have had some of the greatest rivalries in the East, and that helps make the Cowboys the most visible team in television. So it's fun.

MICHAEL KAY: All right. Let's start off right with that, because according to *Forbes*, the Dallas Cowboys are the most valuable franchise in all of sports. They are America's Team. Why the interest in what is really the fourth-largest market? It's not the first, it's the fourth. But you guys are America's Team. Why?

JERRY JONES: Well, first of all, I never got involved in the Cowboys with the idea that the team would be "valuable" or "not valuable." I had really been very fortunate—better than I deserved—and had some money. And I gave that money up to get to be a part of the future of the Dallas Cowboys. But I really don't think I "own" the Dallas Cowboys. I know what it's like to "own" something—to own a car or a house or a business. But you can't own the University of Notre Dame, and you can't own the Dallas Cowboys. *Fans* own the Dallas Cowboys. I just get to husband 'em for a little while. [*Laughter*] I get to use whatever skills I have to run with the ball and make the Cowboys franchise all it can be.

MICHAEL KAY: Now, when you bought the team, there was a famous quote that you were "not gonna be about jocks and socks." You are not just the owner who is signing the checks; you are making the decisions. Now, most of the owners in the NFL don't do that. Why did you decide "Hey, I want to make the player personnel decisions" or "I want to do everything"?

JERRY JONES: From an ownership standpoint, sports is one of the few areas that I know of where you really can get a lot of criticism for being too much hands-on. You get criticized for talking to the team; some people say that it "undermines the coach." I don't look at it that way. If I'm on the sideline, I'm interested in seeing the guys and seeing where the intensity is and where it isn't. Are their eyes glossed over, or do they have their minds on how to make the next play and win it? If they look like they're in shock, I don't go up and tell 'em to snap out of it. But the next time their contract comes up, I'm gonna remember that look in their eyes one way or the other. [*Laughter*]

MICHAEL KAY: When you bought the team, Jerry, I remember people saying, "Oh my God, he spent so much money for this team, the stadium's broken down, the team's no good." But now, all these years later, it's worth ten times what you bought it for.

JERRY JONES: Twenty years ago the Cowboys were losing one million dollars a month in cash. And I paid the most that had ever been paid for anything in sports in the *world*. And that's not an exaggeration—in the *world*. The capital costs of what I paid for them—even back then—were seventy-five thousand dollars a day, on top of losing that much a month.

MICHAEL KAY: Wow. Now you are building—like the Yankees—a new stadium that's gonna be worth over a billion dollars. What makes your facility so special?

JERRY JONES: Well, they should pass legislation not to allow someone as passionate and as tunnel-visioned as I am to have enough credit to build a stadium like this. It's nuts. [*Laughs*] We could have had a wonderful stadium for three-quarters of what I'm spending to build this stadium. But this is *the Dallas Cowboys*. This is the most visible team in television, and we lead the NFL, so we just had to do it. We had to put the wow factor in it.

MICHAEL KAY: What's the old line, "You put the hole in the roof because God has to watch the Cowboys"?

JERRY JONES: [*Laughs*] Yes, no doubt.

MICHAEL KAY: Now, Jerry, it started in North Little Rock, Arkansas. What was life like there for the Jones family?

JERRY JONES: I was so fortunate. I had a mom and a daddy who had a small business, with all the ups and downs of that. We had a grocery store, and we lived above the store. So I got to see that in my very formative years. When I was nine years old, Dad had me with a little bow tie on, greeting our customers when they came through the door at the grocery store. So I was very sensitive to customers—or fans—very early on. Mom and Dad wanted me to participate in sports, but I always had to do my two hours a night in the store, stocking the shelves or whatever. No matter what time I finished ball practice, I had to go back down there and do two hours in that store. But I have never got mad about working; for me, working was like breathing.

MICHAEL KAY: Did you ever think of going anywhere other than the University of Arkansas?

JERRY JONES: I didn't know there was anything other than the University of Arkansas. [*Laughs*]

MICHAEL KAY: We mentioned at the start that you were a running back in high school, and you moved to the offensive line at Arkansas. In 1964, you won the national championship after an undefeated season. I can't think of another owner of a professional team that has won at the level that you have won as a player. Did you want to go to the next level playing-wise? Were you good enough?

JERRY JONES: I wanted to be as successful as I could, financially, so as far as playing, I passed on that. But from the get-go I had hope that somehow I might be involved in the management of sports.

MICHAEL KAY: You graduated from the University of Arkansas in 1965 with a business degree, and you started selling insurance. Why did you go that route?

JERRY JONES: Selling is the best way to reflect your energy, your ambition, your will to succeed. And the better you could do financially, the better you could do the things that you wanted to accomplish. So from very early on it was just instinctive for me to do business. But to show you how wise I am, when I was a senior in college, I had the opportunity to get the franchising [rights] for a large portion of the state of Missouri for McDonald's or for Kentucky Fried Chicken—both of which were pretty new in the area—or for a pizza parlor chain. Well, my logic was that everybody knows how to cook fried chicken at home, and every restaurant in the world knows a hamburger when they see it, so the thing I wanted to do was get in the pizza parlor business [and that didn't work out]. [*Laughter*] I could share with you several legal pads of all the mess-ups and miscues I have done. But hopefully at the end of the day you can cut your bad decisions short and let your good ones run long, and you'll end up ahead.

MICHAEL KAY: All right. Let's talk about one of the good ones—a real good one—Jones Oil and Land Lease. How did that come about?

JERRY JONES: As a young person I was trying to hire other people to sell insurance in Oklahoma. And when I would be visiting with people, I would hear about all these families that had done well in the oil-and-gas business. I didn't bother to do more homework and find out that most of that "doing well" had happened twenty years earlier. [*Laughter*] Then I ran into someone who was a better salesman than me, and he got me involved, and we initially made some good wells. I didn't tell my family about it, and I didn't tell my banker about it, because at that time the oil-and-gas business was like going to Las Vegas. I had some good fortune—and that's how it started.

MICHAEL KAY: Well, you got enough good fortune, but I am sure that in the back of your mind football was still there. And the Dallas Cowboys became available. Take me through the process of how you purchased that team, because you were young, very successful, and you probably had the money for it. So how did that come about?

JERRY JONES: Well, I was actually in Mexico with one of my sons, on a fishing trip, and one night I had too much tequila. [*Laughter*]

So he went fishing, and I stayed in that morning. And I was thumbing through this newspaper, and I saw a little note there that Mr. Bum Bright in Dallas was gonna sell the Dallas Cowboys. And I called him and I said, "Look, I feel like I am dying, but if I live"—[*laughter*]—"I'm gonna come back and buy the Dallas Cowboys." That's how we got involved.

MICHAEL KAY: Did price matter to you? Because I heard that somebody tried to step in and give Bum Bright ten million dollars more than you offered. . . .

JERRY JONES: Yeah. But Mr. Bright was very honorable. After we shook hands [we didn't have a formal contract yet], he called me the next morning and said, "I have a guy that will pay ten million more than you. But the team is still yours if you want it."

MICHAEL KAY: Wow. Now, one of the first things that you do when you buy the team is that you fire Tom Landry. Tom Landry kind of *is* the Cowboys. He was the only coach they ever had. How tough was that? I mean, was that something that you dreaded, or did you realize, "I have got to do this"?

JERRY JONES: Of course the criticism was that it was not handled with respect. But I had such respect for him. He had transcended the Dallas Cowboys, frankly, as far as an institution is concerned. And I was in uncharted water for me and my decision making. Certainly, if I had that to do over again, I might have done that a lot differently. But exactly the same time we announced that we had bought the team, we announced that we had made that change. And that's not smart. That's not the way you do those things. And I paid a high price for that.

MICHAEL KAY: If you could have done it differently, would you have kept him just a year and have a transitional period before you brought in Jimmy Johnson? Is that what you mean when you say, "I could have done it differently"?

JERRY JONES: Yeah, that certainly was a consideration. But I wanted to get there in a hurry—probably too big a hurry. I wanted to get on with it.

MICHAEL KAY: Why Jimmy Johnson [as coach]? The first year you guys are together, you win one game. I know you were a teammate of his at Arkansas, but why were you convinced that he was the one?

JERRY JONES: Well, Jimmy is one of the smartest people that I have ever been around. Jimmy could have been successful in anything he tried. Anything he wanted to do, he would have been successful. The bottom line is I believed in him, and it worked, and we had a wonderful thing happen to us in the five years that he was coach of the Dallas Cowboys.

MICHAEL KAY: If you look at the linchpins of what turned around the Cowboys, in '89 you draft Troy Aikman, and that's obviously huge. But then you engineer one of the biggest trades in NFL history, and this is probably what turned the Cowboys around. You trade Herschel Walker for a boatload of picks from the Minnesota Vikings. Obviously the Landry thing had gotten people upset. And Herschel Walker was big in Dallas, and he was your best player. Was it a tough one to pull the trigger on?

JERRY JONES: Not really. We knew that we had a building job to do. The bottom line is that we got not only our picks for three consecutive picks—and our picks were high picks 'cause we weren't playing well, that's the way it works in the NFL—but we got all of Minnesota's picks for three years. When you load up like that, then you can do some great drafting. That's what the Herschel trade did for us.

MICHAEL KAY: The second season you go seven and nine. And the next season, in '91, you go eleven and five, and you are back in the playoffs for the first time in six years. The Triplets—Michael Irvin, Troy Aikman, Emmitt Smith—they really were what you built your team around. And then you come to 1992, with the Triplets and all the talent that you have around them. In that first championship year, you go thirteen and three, you play the Bills in the Super Bowl and wax 'em. You win the Super Bowl. Are you thinking to yourself, "I'm vindicated. Everybody who has criticized me with the Landry stuff, bringing in Johnson, well, this vindicates me. I am on the top of the mountain."

JERRY JONES: Yeah, I did. [*Laughter*] It was nice, real nice.

MICHAEL KAY: Now, when you won the Super Bowl the next year, that's two in a row, are you thinking, "This is easy, I have conquered this"?

JERRY JONES: Well, I got accustomed to it, let's put it like that. [*Laugh-*

ter] I have been going through withdrawals not getting to go to the Super Bowl [since 1996]. . . .

MICHAEL KAY: Now, Jerry, do you believe that [singer/actress] Jessica [Simpson] is a distraction to Tony Romo? [*Laughter*]

JERRY JONES: No, no.

MICHAEL KAY: Because she is a distraction to me. [*Laughter*]

JERRY JONES: No, I don't. Gosh, I wish everyone could see the intensity and the way that Tony addresses his business and his football. And [that relationship] is as pure as mother's milk. That's innocent stuff. I could show you some off-the-field stuff that's serious—and I've been dealing with it for twenty years. [*Laughs*]

MICHAEL KAY: What's the best piece of advice anyone ever gave you?

JERRY JONES: Sam Walton, the founder of Walmart, once told me, "If you are not undermanned, you are overstaffed, and you'll never get a chance to see who your heroes are."

MICHAEL KAY: Wow. Sam Walton knows what he is talking about. Final thing. When you look at the whole body of work—your whole life—do you get up in the morning and pinch yourself and go, "This is pretty cool."

JERRY JONES: Well, there hasn't been time to sit around and say, "Boy, this has been a heckuva deal." But I'll say this: the big-time plusses wouldn't have been anything like they were if I hadn't had my fanny kicked and been down. It's made it that much better.

MICHAEL KAY: This has been great. Thank you so much.

George Foreman

George Foreman has had quite a life. Two-time heavyweight champion, Olympic gold medalist, master salesman, minister, and incredibly successful businessman. And it all started with a tough upbringing in Houston's Fifth Ward. There's so much to the Foreman story that a filmmaker could likely turn it into two or three movies and still not cover it fully.

The transformation of the man is most shocking. In his first iteration as heavyweight champ, he was sullen, nasty, and wanted no part of the give-and-take of fame. He was downright scary. But that was his first act.

The second act occurred after he'd left boxing for ten years and came back as a somewhat beefy fighter at the age of thirty-eight. He was a completely different man, having undergone a spiritual awakening that changed his outlook and personality. He was now a gregarious, lovable type who was easy to root for. He was your fun uncle, who happened to be able to knock you out. And when, at age forty-five, he KO'd Michael Moorer, Foreman gained fame and fortune unlike anything he could have imagined.

But incredibly, his fighting prowess eventually took a back seat to his business acumen. He was world renowned as much for his George Foreman Grill as for his boxing skills.

It's an amazing life, and Foreman tells the story in an easy, albeit dramatic way. He knows his is a cautionary tale and, if shared, can help others avoid some of the traps into which he fell. From the moment he walked onstage with his big smile and easy way, Foreman owned the audience. He's a master showman with an incredible story to tell, and he told it masterfully.

The Interview

MICHAEL KAY: Welcome, everybody. George Foreman overcame a childhood filled with rebellion, crime, and poverty to become one of the best fighters of all time. An intimidating bully, he knocked out Joe Frazier for his first heavyweight championship in '73 and was later on the losing end of one of the greatest upsets of all time, when Muhammad Ali rope-a-doped his way back to the title. In '77, Foreman abruptly retired from the sport and became an ordained minister, in the process shedding his surly demeanor that had frightened his opponents as well as boxing fans. He reentered the ring ten years later as a new man, a fan favorite, and ultimately knocked out a much younger Michael Moorer to become the oldest boxer to ever win the heavyweight championship. Foreman is also a hugely successful product spokesman, best known for the George Foreman Grill, Meineke mufflers, and Casual Male Big and Tall Shops. Hall of Fame boxer, Olympic gold medalist, minister, author, and former heavyweight champion of the world, George Foreman. [*Applause*]

MICHAEL KAY: Tough childhood. You grew up poor in Houston. What was it like?

GEORGE FOREMAN: I never had anything. I remember I hated school because they had lunch, but I couldn't get any [because I couldn't pay]. You don't like school, that means you're not going to school, and you're going to get into a lot of trouble. I dropped out of school at fifteen, and it was one piece of trouble after another.

MICHAEL KAY: A lot of people say—you said it yourself—you were a bully?

GEORGE FOREMAN: That's all I knew. I wanted attention. You have to find a way to attract attention. I found out early, I was a lot bigger than most guys and I could take what I want. So I was the bully.

MICHAEL KAY: Were you disliked in the neighborhood?

GEORGE FOREMAN: I had a lot of friends 'cause no one wanted to be my enemy. [*Laughs*]

MICHAEL KAY: You said you got into a lot of trouble. What kind of trouble?

GEORGE FOREMAN: By the time I was a teenager I was really a masterful mugger. My friends and I would go out and actually rob people. Take their money and run. I was so ignorant, it was years before I realized it was a crime to steal. But everyone was doing it, so I just started doing it. You can imagine some young people in prison right now, eighteen, nineteen years old, they don't even know what they've done until the judge hits the hammer and says, you got ten, twenty years. They're just so ignorant they have no idea they were committing a crime.

MICHAEL KAY: Did you ever get caught by the police?

GEORGE FOREMAN: One time the police got behind me, they were chasing me, I had to crawl under a house to hide. And I started thinking, "They're gonna send the dogs out, they're gonna sniff me out and find me." I remembered from the TV, whenever the criminals were being pursued, they'd go into the water and the dogs couldn't sniff them. And I looked around under the house, and there was a sewer pipe that had burst, and I said, "Well, it's water. . . ." And I started to dig myself into this sewer water and covered myself. There I was under that house, a thief running from the police, covered in sewer water, and I said, "I'm not this, this isn't me." I never stole a thing again. When I crawled from under that house, I changed my life.

MICHAEL KAY: So that was like an epiphany to you.

GEORGE FOREMAN: Yeah, I had to change. Then on TV I heard Jim Brown, the great football player, do a commercial for the Job Corps program. They said if you're looking for a second chance in life, you can get an education and a vocational skill. I joined the Job Corps, and that's where I got my real start. I went to Grants Pass, Oregon, and for the first time I was treated like a human being. People suggested that I read, so I started reading books. Life changed for me. I stopped being a bully from that point on.

MICHAEL KAY: Somebody in the Job Corps turned you into a fighter, right?

GEORGE FOREMAN: In '65 I was listening to Cassius Clay fighting Floyd Patterson on the radio. All the kids in the dayroom looked at me and said, "If you think you're so tough, why don't you become a boxer?" I said, "Yeah, I'll show you, I'll be a boxer." I got transferred to [the Job Corps center at] Pleasanton, California, and I met [Charles]

"Doc" Broadus, the boxing coach. I said, "I want to be a boxer," and he said, "Well, you're big enough and you're ugly enough. Come on down to the gym." [*Laughter*] I was seventeen, I was a big guy, and I thought I could just go down there and beat everybody up. And I saw the first guy I was gonna box. He was skinny, you could see his ribs. But I couldn't even lay a hand on the guy. He did something called jabbing, and he kept moving out of the way. [*Laughter*] So I tried to wrestle him and I picked him up, and everybody screamed, "No, you can't pick him up, you gotta put him down." But Doc Broadus stayed on me. He said, "If you stay out of fighting in the streets and dedicate yourself, you can be an [Olympic] gold medalist." So he put me in a tournament, and I won, and then some Golden Gloves, and I won, and then in 1968 I was a gold medalist [at the Mexico City Olympics]. They put the gold medal on your neck, and you hear the national anthem in the background. People had always told me, "You will never be anything," but I was what you call a demonstration of a compassionate society that never gives up on its underprivileged. That was an important day of my life. I will never forget it if I live to be a hundred.

MICHAEL KAY: [In 1973, in the "Sunshine Showdown" in Jamaica, Foreman is 37-0 as a pro, with 34 knockouts, and now it's a title fight against heavyweight champion Joe Frazier.] It was one of the more amazing boxing matches that we'll ever see, and it brought into the vernacular "Down goes Frazier, down goes Frazier," six knockdowns. Explain what happened that night. And how shocked were you?

GEORGE FOREMAN: The first time I got into the ring with him, I was real scared of Joe Frazier. Your trainers and managers tell you, "This guy's weak, you'll knock him out, he doesn't have a punch"—they'd always tell you this to psych you up. But I'm going to the dressing room before the Joe Frazier fight and I'm thinking, "Don't even go in there." So I get in the ring and I knock him down the first time, and he gets up, then I knock him down again, I'm thinking, "If I don't hurry up and get out of here, he's gonna get me."

MICHAEL KAY: [*Laughs*] After you won [in a TKO], what's going through your mind? All that work, being poor growing up, and now you're the heavyweight champion of the world. What was that like?

GEORGE FOREMAN: All that was going through my mind was that

I was glad Joe Frazier didn't kill me. [*Laughter*] But then I started to believe what they said about me, that I really was the hardest puncher alive.

MICHAEL KAY: Everybody thought that when you fought Ali in the "Rumble in the Jungle" [in Zaire in 1974], there was no way he was gonna beat you, but it didn't turn out that way. [For the first time you suffered a knockdown, and you lost the fight.] What was that like being on the ground?

GEORGE FOREMAN: Yeah, I get knocked down and my whole life changed. One day everybody was patting me on the back and everybody was afraid of me, and then the next day they're patting me on the back and saying, "It's gonna be okay." From praise to pity—I've never been so devastated in my life. I was undefeated as a pro, no one had ever stood up to my punching power, and how Ali did it, I'll never know. I didn't want to accept the fact that I lost. So I made excuses from out of the sky. "Uh, the ring ropes were loosened" [to help Ali's "rope-a-dope strategy"] or "They put poison in my food."

MICHAEL KAY: So you were grasping at anything?

GEORGE FOREMAN: Anything just to save my pride. I hate that, because here I was fighting one of the greatest athletes of all time, and I go out and tarnish his name [by alleging] the ropes were loose and they put something in my food. That's one thing I'm sorry for. I wish I had never done that. He beat me fair and square.

MICHAEL KAY: You and he are best friends now, but at the time you hated him.

GEORGE FOREMAN: I hated Ali, and I was jealous of him. Everybody loved him, he always had something to say, he put on this show. There were a lot of us boxers and athletes who were jealous of Muhammad Ali. But I love him now.

MICHAEL KAY: [In 1977 you had what you described as a near-death experience in the dressing room after you lost a twelve-round decision to Jimmy Young.] You become a born-again Christian, and then you become an ordained minister and you're away from the ring for ten years. Did you miss boxing at all?

GEORGE FOREMAN: No. I didn't even make a fist in all that time.

MICHAEL KAY: How did you support yourself those ten years—the money had to run out, right?

GEORGE FOREMAN: I had some money. But I also had some people with sticky fingers trying to get that money, too. [*Laughter*]

MICHAEL KAY: Is that why you came back to the ring in '87?

GEORGE FOREMAN: I looked up one day, and I had ten kids, and I had a youth center, and parents would drop these kids off and I was supporting them. And I didn't have enough money. I remember I was in a church in Georgia, this preacher asked me to come spend three days and run a revival, and he would give me some money for my youth center. I stood there in the pulpit next to him, and he said, "Let's give money and help George and his kids," and the people [some of them poor people] gave some money. I was so embarrassed, I said I would never do this again. I said, "I know how to get money. I'm gonna be heavyweight champion of the world again."

MICHAEL KAY: [So you come back at age thirty-eight] and you won a lot of fights.

GEORGE FOREMAN: Yeah, because I dedicated myself. I got the youth center working, and I took care of my family. And I was different. As I taught the kids in the youth center, you don't need a killer instinct, you don't need to kill anybody, get the chip off your shoulder. I taught them how to box without anger, and in return I learned that myself.

MICHAEL KAY: You knocked out Michael Moorer in '94 [in Las Vegas], and at age forty-five you become world champion again—the oldest man ever to do so. What was that like?

GEORGE FOREMAN: Oh, that was an important moment. I was so happy because I had a chance to really go back and be an athlete at forty-five years old, when everybody said I was gonna be killed. I fell to my knees and thanked God for that great opportunity.

MICHAEL KAY: First time, as we said earlier, you were mean. This time you were this lovable guy that everybody loved.

GEORGE FOREMAN: I met a lot of good people [when I was making my comeback]. That's what made me change. People are the best invention ever.

MICHAEL KAY: Now you want to come back again.

GEORGE FOREMAN: Oh, yeah, I want to box again. I'm fifty-five. I want to show the world that fifty-five, sixty-five, seventy-five, is just a number. You can dream, and you can keep dreaming if you want to. They are probing for life on Mars right now, but they should be probing some of us older guys. You'll see more life here than you'll ever find on Mars. [*Laughter*]

MICHAEL KAY: But aren't you afraid at your age?

GEORGE FOREMAN: I think that everybody should be afraid at fifty-five, sixty-five, and seventy-five. Why retire and be comfortable and lose all fear? You think I'm gonna spend the rest of my life watching the Dow Jones go up and down, buy a condominium and a Rolls-Royce? That's no way to live. I need an adventure. Everybody needs an adventure.

MICHAEL KAY: George, how different is it training when you're fifty-five than when you were twenty-five?

GEORGE FOREMAN: It never was nice. It's worse then and it's worse now.

MICHAEL KAY: [*Laughs*] Is there a lot of pain when you're training at fifty-five?

GEORGE FOREMAN: It's not about pain, it's about the commitment. Do I really want to get up in the morning? That's when the commitment starts.

MICHAEL KAY: So then it becomes George Foreman, punch man turned pitchman. Now you're a fashion designer with Casual Male Big and Tall Shops.

GEORGE FOREMAN: I couldn't find clothes that fit me. I had this small waist, big arms, big shoulders, big thighs. I had to find a big-and-tall store to fit a person like me. This is a chance to spread the message: "George Foreman Comfort Zone, fine clothes so everybody can look good—as good as George Foreman when I dress up."

MICHAEL KAY: [*Laughs*] Have you ever thought about growing your hair back?

GEORGE FOREMAN: No. I always say, I used to have an Afro, but now I have a zero. [*Laughter*] The zero is here to stay.

MICHAEL KAY: The product that's now become synonymous with you is the George Foreman Lean Mean Grilling Machine.

GEORGE FOREMAN: "It knocks the fat right out of your diet." [*Laughter*]

MICHAEL KAY: Everybody in this audience owns one. Did you think it could ever be this big?

GEORGE FOREMAN: When some people asked me to [be a spokesman for the grill], I said, "How much are you gonna pay me?" They said, "Nothing, but you can have the grill, put your name on it, we'll just be your partner." I said, "Yeah, right." So they sent one home for me to try, and after my wife had been using it for a few weeks, she finally asked me to use it. Lo and behold, it was slanted, all the grease went away, and the food was still tasty. It was easy to clean and put away. I started using it. Finally we did an infomercial, and people would walk up to me and say, "George, the doctor told me the grill could help, and look at how much weight I've lost." It was something to smile about, it made me happy. The last thing that came to my mind was making money with that grill. It was a service.

MICHAEL KAY: George Foreman, a two-time heavyweight champion, is almost more identified with the grill than with being the champ. Does that bother you at all?

GEORGE FOREMAN: Not at all. One time I was in Memphis, walking down the street, and there were some teachers with some Head Start kids. And one of the teachers says, "Look, that's George Foreman," and she started explaining that I was an Olympic gold medalist and heavyweight champion two times. And this little kid looked at me and said, "Naw, that's the cookin' man." [*Laughter*] So the grill has taken over.

MICHAEL KAY: [*Laughs*] Obviously you must have a lot of grills in the house because you have ten kids, [including] five boys all named George [George Jr., George III, George IV, George V, and George VI]. When you're sitting around the dinner table and you say, "Pass the potatoes, George," who does it?

GEORGE FOREMAN: Whatever George it is knows who I'm talking about.

MICHAEL KAY: [*Laughs*] And one of your daughters is Georgetta. How come the other girls didn't have a Georgetta?

GEORGE FOREMAN: My wife told me to stop it. [*Laughter*]

MICHAEL KAY: Your wife's name is Mary, but you call her [by her middle name,] Joan. At least it's not George.

GEORGE FOREMAN: I've asked her to change her name to George [but she wouldn't do it]. [*Laughter*]

QUESTION FROM AUDIENCE: What was the hardest shot you ever took and who delivered it?

GEORGE FOREMAN: Ron Lyle in 1976. He hit me so hard it didn't even hurt. I felt like a piece of rag. I got up and he knocked me down again, and I got up and he kept knocking me down and I kept getting up. He beat me so bad. But finally he fainted—he was tired of beating me. [*Laughter*] And I won the boxing match.

QUESTION FROM AUDIENCE: George, did you ever have any personal regrets after knowing you've hurt an opponent?

GEORGE FOREMAN: I'm happy because I've seen many of the fighters I had fought early on, and they were all in good shape and healthy. I was so happy I never hurt anyone.

QUESTION FROM AUDIENCE: Who would you like to have fought but never did?

GEORGE FOREMAN: I didn't really like boxing, it was just something I had to do. I would have liked to have seen Joe Louis fight, along with Archie Moore. But to get in the ring with them? No, no.

MICHAEL KAY: About boxing. There are so many problems with it. You mentioned before, some boxers get robbed. What do you think about a national boxing commission?

GEORGE FOREMAN: Anything that would help us, keep us a little safer, and enable boxers to hold on to some money. It's a short career. And there are so many guys that end up without money.

MICHAEL KAY: Do you shake your head when you see some of these young boxers make these millions of dollars, and they have these posses around them, taking all their money?

GEORGE FOREMAN: What I see coming is another George Foreman. I remember I had that the first time around, too, and you think it's gonna go on forever. Then you look up one day and you are as broke as a goat. You have nothing. I'm looking into ways of being able to help these guys and explain to them about saving their money.

MICHAEL KAY: Here's a hard one. Say you could go back in time and beat Muhammad Ali in Africa, but if that happened, no one would have ever heard of the Lean Mean Grilling Machine. Would you take that trade?

GEORGE FOREMAN: No. I'm so happy about the way my life has gone. I wouldn't want to change anything about it.

MICHAEL KAY: George, it's been a pleasure.

GEORGE FOREMAN: Thank you.

Andre Agassi

Andre Agassi came on *CenterStage* in November of 2009 to talk about his book, *Open: An Autobiography*. The book reached number one on the *New York Times* bestseller list, and when you read this interview, you can certainly understand why. Although blessed with incredible talent, and untold riches, Agassi didn't have the easiest path to stardom. Agassi's father groomed his son to be a tennis champion from the time he could hold a racket and in that pursuit was emotionally abusive and demanding of Andre physically.

Those rocky beginnings shaped some of the trouble that Agassi would encounter along the way. Robbed of the simple joys of youth, Agassi became a tennis corporation at an early age and had to keep up appearances throughout his young life. He was more a brand than a person. Because of that, he was forced to wear a hairpiece so he could continue to play the role of the rock-and-roll tennis star. That immense pressure eventually led to his hating the game, rather than embracing his rare gifts.

But Agassi eventually found his way out of an emotional wilderness. After dating Barbra Streisand, twenty-eight years his senior, and ending a failed marriage to Brooke Shields, he married fellow tennis great Steffi Graf and settled down to raise the family he'd always dreamed about.

As he relates so vividly in our conversation, the path to stardom was anything but perfect, but the eventual endgame made the journey seem worthwhile.

The Interview

MICHAEL KAY: Thank you, everybody, and welcome to *CenterStage*. Today's guest was born in Las Vegas and, as a toddler, was driven to be a tennis champion by his father. The child prodigy turned pro at age sixteen. With his rebel image of long hair, earrings, and colorful attire, he mirrored one of his many sponsors' taglines: image is everything. His first Grand Slam title came in 1992 at Wimbledon. At times he was romantically linked to many of Hollywood's biggest stars, but the truth was his image was not reality, as he struggled with his self-confidence and self-identity. Then out came the razor, and off came the mane of hair, and a Jordan-esque bald-headed tennis player took to the courts. He would eventually total eight Grand Slam singles titles, all the while overcoming a lost year, and almost a lost career, to a crystal meth addiction. His charismatic style, skill, and energy made him a fan favorite. He is married and has two children with tennis great Steffi Graf. He has demonstrated his humanitarian heart with his many efforts to help children, especially those at risk. His new book is the surprisingly revealing *Open: An Autobiography*. Please welcome one of only six men to win the career Grand Slam in tennis, Andre Agassi.

ANDRE AGASSI: Thank you, thank you.

MICHAEL KAY: Well, this book, it is raw, it is open, as the title says. It's one of the best autobiographies I've ever read. But I have one question to ask: Why? Why would you open yourself up to this?

ANDRE AGASSI: I've lived a very public life, and many things said about me, both good and bad, were just simply not accurate. Many things I said about myself, good or bad, just weren't true. I had the rare privilege that most people don't get of getting a second chance. And I think we all would do a lot with our lives if we had a second chance. I think this book can offer some people tools or inspiration to help them out of a life that they find themselves in, to help them with a life that maybe they didn't choose, to help someone who's in a marriage that maybe they don't want to be in, or maybe help somebody get out of the pitfalls that I was trapped in. If it can help that one person, whatever price it comes with, it's a price that is worth paying.

MICHAEL KAY: All right, let's get to some of the points in your life. It began in Las Vegas, but was it always tennis for you? Did you like any other sports as a kid?

ANDRE AGASSI: I played soccer for about five years. My father wanted me to play soccer because he thought it would be good for my footwork in tennis.

MICHAEL KAY: Now, you liked the aspect of a team sport where it wasn't you alone. That's what soccer gave you.

ANDRE AGASSI: Yeah, I didn't feel like the weight of the world was on my shoulders if I didn't score that day, or we didn't win.

MICHAEL KAY: That's why tennis players talk to themselves, right, because they're all alone?

ANDRE AGASSI: Yeah, you're on an island. It's like solitary confinement, and that always leads to self-talk. You don't only talk to yourself, you answer yourself. [*Laughs*] I'm not kidding.

MICHAEL KAY: Why was your dad so fixated on tennis? Because he was a boxer growing up [in Iran].

ANDRE AGASSI: Tennis is mortal combat without the contact. My father bonded with it for that reason. But he was a boxer because he had to fight. His mom used to make him wear hand-me-down girl's clothes to school as punishment when he got in trouble, so he had to fight as a boy. Then he put it to formal use, boxing in two Olympics, winning two Golden Gloves. He came to America when he was eighteen years old, not speaking a word of English, and he put himself through school, raised four kids, held two jobs most of his life. He was pretty hard on us—not abusive, but hard—but he was really hard on himself.

MICHAEL KAY: Give me some of his training methods. How did he make you what you are?

ANDRE AGASSI: He had this ball machine, this souped-up ball machine, I called it the Dragon, to shoot the ball at a hundred and ten miles an hour. He would push it as close to the net as possible and point it directly at me. The ball would come at me at one hundred and ten miles per hour, and then I would have to adjust and figure out a way to hit it back faster, harder, more often.

MICHAEL KAY: Now, you're doing this when you're seven years old. At what point do you say, "I hate this, I can't stand this"?

ANDRE AGASSI: Seven. [*Laughter*]

MICHAEL KAY: Now, [as a boy] you practiced with guys like Nastase, Tanner, Jimmy Connors, Bobby Riggs.

ANDRE AGASSI: Yeah. My dad was incapable of being embarrassed, so he would go up to these guys and tell them that I was going to be the next number one player in the world. That's how he used to introduce me. I had conflicting feelings about it. You know, part of me was "I'm embarrassed, I don't like this," while the other part of me was kind of proud. It's like, "My dad believes in me, he thinks I'm going to be great." So I thought, "Well, I gotta be great."

MICHAEL KAY: And were these guys fun to hit the ball with?

ANDRE AGASSI: Yeah, occasionally I relaxed and enjoyed it. You know, Connors hit with me once, and I remember him telling my dad, "Your kid's going to be pretty good if he keeps this up." And my dad says, "What do you mean 'pretty good'? He's going to be number one in the world."

MICHAEL KAY: Jimmy Connors comes off as kind of an egomaniacal jerk in the book. Is that what you got from him?

ANDRE AGASSI: I've spoken to Jimmy about seven minutes in my life, and five of those were when I was seven years old. When we got out to the US Open, I introduced myself, thinking he's going to remember me, and he just blew me off. And I get on the court to have him swearing at me on the changeover, and having him and the crowd calling me a punk. And I'm eighteen years old.

MICHAEL KAY: Who was the most famous celebrity you hustled as a kid?

ANDRE AGASSI: [NFL player] Jim Brown. I was nine years old, and my father bet him ten thousand dollars that I would beat him, which was, like, our life savings, but the manager of the club talked it down to five hundred dollars. So we went out there and I was relaxed because we were only playing for five hundred dollars and not our life savings. And I beat him bad.

MICHAEL KAY: Now, at age thirteen you go to the Nick Bollettieri Tennis Academy in Florida. You're supposed to go for three months, but you stay a lot longer. But it was not a great place, right?

ANDRE AGASSI: No. It was an environment designed to make great athletes and horrible students. You go to school four hours a day, you play tennis six hours a day. You sleep, drink, eat tennis, and how you do on the tennis court decides the pecking order, which has real relevance in your life.

MICHAEL KAY: When you first go there, it seems like you're a decent kid. But once you're there, you're known as a punk, and you're mean, and you're vulgar. Is that an accurate description? And how did you become that?

ANDRE AGASSI: The things I did were punkish, and jerkish. There's no question about that. But, you know, that's part of the evolution I've gone through, and it's part of the message I'm trying to give in [my book]—which is, don't label kids. Because they're in the process of trying to figure it out, and maybe their antics are not an attempt to stand out, but an attempt to hide who they really are, or what they're really scared of.

MICHAEL KAY: Were you rebelling against your dad putting you there?

ANDRE AGASSI: That was part of it. I used to grow a long pinkie nail and paint it, and I got an earring, and then I wore eyeliner, like punk rockers used to do back in the day.

MICHAEL KAY: And your dad was dead set against that?

ANDRE AGASSI: Oh, please—

MICHAEL KAY: Now, you end up turning professional on May first, 1986, two days after your sixteenth birthday. Was that a real tough call for you?

ANDRE AGASSI: I didn't have a choice. There was nothing else I was going to do at that point. I knew I had the potential of being one of the best in the world, and I had a responsibility to my family, to my dad. After that tournament I called my father because I won about eleven hundred dollars, and if I took the money, I would be a pro, and I asked him, "Should I do this?" And he's like, "I don't understand what you're asking me. Take the money! What else are you going to do, be a doctor? How are you going to be a doctor? You left school in ninth grade!" So I took the money and I went pro.

MICHAEL KAY: Now, by the end of '88 you've won over two million dollars in prize money. Are you surprised by the success? Are you happy with the life?

ANDRE AGASSI: Things got easier. It was neat to see how that changed the pressures that existed at home.

MICHAEL KAY: As you were playing this great tennis, you were also getting into the glam rock, the flamboyant clothes, the denim shorts and stuff like that. Was that calculated or did it just happen?

ANDRE AGASSI: There were things about it that were just rebellious. There were things about it that kept me hiding myself from the world. I mean, what better way to distract people from who you really are than by wearing a mullet, right?

MICHAEL KAY: You didn't play in the Australian Open the first eight years of your career, and Wimbledon from 1988 to 1990. These are Grand Slam events, so why not?

ANDRE AGASSI: It was not that important to me. That was part of my rebellion. I just didn't like it. I looked for any reason not to do it.

MICHAEL KAY: At Wimbledon they make you wear predominantly white, and at the time you said that that was one of the excuses [for why you didn't play there]. Was it legitimately an excuse, that you didn't want to wear white clothing?

ANDRE AGASSI: I just thought it was obnoxious to tell me what I have to wear. It's like, "Who the hell are you?" That's what I thought.

MICHAEL KAY: Now, while all this is happening, Andre, you don't have a great relationship with the press. At best, it's adversarial, and sometimes it gets nasty. What didn't you like about the press?

ANDRE AGASSI: They always talked about the subject I knew least about, which was myself. I don't mind talking about things I know. I never minded talking about tennis. And I don't mind talking about myself *now*.

MICHAEL KAY: In '95, what a year you had: seventy-two and nine, member of the US Davis Cup Team, you're ranked number one in the world, you've won Grand Slam titles. You had it all. But it wasn't perfect. What was going on there?

ANDRE AGASSI: Well, it can appear like somebody has it all, but in a lot of cases it's only a magnifying glass on what you're actually missing. You know, I never played tennis for me. When I was a child, it was for my father. And then I get sent away at age thirteen to a glorified prison camp, you know, the Nick Bollettieri Tennis Academy, which was like *Lord of the Flies* with tennis rackets. [*Laughter*] And I'm playing to get out of there, just to get away. Success to me was just getting out of that place. I turned professional and I found my teenage rebellions to be on a world stage. It was never a choice of mine. It became the only thing I knew. I didn't have an education, I didn't have options, and it wasn't until I was twenty-seven years old that I actually chose my life.

MICHAEL KAY: A prevailing theme through your life is that you hate tennis. Hate tennis, hate tennis. But tennis has given you fabulous riches, a great life, two great children, a great wife. In retrospect, do you really hate tennis? Because you wouldn't have had those things without tennis.

ANDRE AGASSI: Yeah, you make a good point. Do I have a love/hate relationship with tennis? No, I have a hate/love relationship with it.

MICHAEL KAY: Now, in 1997, you started to experiment with crystal meth for a year. How did that come about, and what would make a guy who makes his living with his body abuse his body?

ANDRE AGASSI: Well, first, it was less than a year. But I didn't care about tennis, and I damn sure didn't care about myself. Really, in hindsight, I was in depression, but I had no idea that's what it was. You're in this life where you're doing something that you hate, and then you're in a marriage that you don't want to be in—

MICHAEL KAY: That was with Brooke Shields?

ANDRE AGASSI: Yeah. Then something came along and gave me an escape. And I took it.

MICHAEL KAY: You end up testing positive for the drug, but you don't get suspended. Explain what happened. How did you not get suspended?

ANDRE AGASSI: It started with a lie. I hadn't done the drug in a period of time, and I'm in LaGuardia Airport when I get a phone call from a doctor from the ATP, who tells me I was tested positive for crystal methamphetamine. And I don't even know what that is. The truth is, my assistant would get it, he would prepare it, and I would do it.

MICHAEL KAY: What did it do for you, though?

ANDRE AGASSI: It gave me energy, a ridiculous amount of energy. But the positive test was a brutal, brutal moment because I was really afraid. Nobody in my life knew that I was doing any drugs on any level, even my friends, even my wife. So I didn't tell anybody what had happened. I asked [the ATP] what the procedure was, and they told me to write a letter declaring my innocence or admitting my guilt. And I wrote a letter that was a lie, but with a lot of truths in it. I said that my assistant had a problem, which he did. I said that he spikes his sodas with this stuff, which he used to hide his usage, and I accidentally sipped it, and that's why it was in my system. I asked for leniency, and I signed it, and I've never been so ashamed in my life.

MICHAEL KAY: So after hitting rock bottom, you go from one twenty-two in the rankings to six, you win the French Open in 1999, so obviously you did rebound. And eventually you decide to shave the mullet and go bald. What was that like, and what drove you to do that finally? Because again, the hair was a big part of the image.

ANDRE AGASSI: Yeah, it was. Brooke was a big factor in that. When a supermodel tells you you are still gonna be cute if you're bald, you go, "Okay." [*Laughter*] And when I took it off, it was immediate liberation.

MICHAEL KAY: Now, in '03, you win your final Grand Slam, at the Australian Open. Then in the '04 season, you are ranked eighth in the world. And it's a weird transformation, because now from the youngster that started at sixteen, you become the grand old man of tennis.

ANDRE AGASSI: Yeah. I mean, when you're still playing and you hear people say, "I grew up watching you," you know you're getting old. [*Laughter*]

MICHAEL KAY: In '06, you end up playing your final US Open, and at the end of your last match you get a standing ovation from the crowd—which goes on forever. Then you get a standing ovation in the players' lounge from the players, and then you get a standing ovation from the *press*—the people that used to *hate* you. So my question is, which standing ovation meant the most to you that day?

ANDRE AGASSI: Oh, from my peers. You will *never* get a more rewarding applause in your life than one you get from people you compete against in the heat of battle, saying, "Well done, we respect you." That's the ultimate compliment. And then it would be the applause from the fans. And then it would be the press.

MICHAEL KAY: The press never claps for *anybody*.

ANDRE AGASSI: [*Laughs*]

MICHAEL KAY: Do you and Steffi ever go in the backyard and play tennis?

ANDRE AGASSI: We don't have a court in the backyard.

MICHAEL KAY: Do you ever play tennis at all?

ANDRE AGASSI: Sometimes we'll do some charity events and stuff, and then we'll go out and get ready for it. And occasionally she'll want to get out and exercise. We make a deal that she just has to hit the ball [straight] back to me, because I refuse to run. And she wants me to run her left and right, so it's *perfect*, you know? She hits it back to me, and I make her run.

MICHAEL KAY: Now, when you wrote your book, were you worried that you were gonna hurt your father's feelings? And has he read the book?

ANDRE AGASSI: I believe it's an honest but loving portrait of him. It's a story of me coming to terms, about forgiveness of him, forgiveness of myself, about understanding of him, understanding of myself. I talked to him the other day and I said, "You know, Dad, I hope you are doing okay with all this. They are sensationalizing a few things." And he says, "I don't care what people say. Because if I did it all over again, I'd do the same thing." And he told me he's not going to read it. He said, "What the hell do I need to read it for? I was *there*." [*Laughter*]

MICHAEL KAY: Now, from listening to this show and reading your book, what life lesson would you want a young man or young woman to take out of this, to get to a successful and happy life?

ANDRE AGASSI: Well, I think it's never too late to turn your life around. It's never too late to make your life what you want it to be. To understand what you want and then to go out and, and *get* it. And that applies to the *relationships* that you are in, and it applies to the *work* that you are in.

MICHAEL KAY: Thanks so much for coming in. [*Applause*]

ANDRE AGASSI: You are welcome. Good luck.

Mike Tyson

We were all a little nervous about having Mike Tyson on *CenterStage*. I know I was—because I'd been told by many friends in the boxing community that you never knew what you were going to get. Mike might be in a good mood, an angry mood, or a sad mood. Everything depended on, well, his mood.

The show was set to tape at 10:00 a.m. and Tyson was late. He left us waiting for over an hour before he and a couple of friends strolled in. No harm, no foul—it would just cost YES more money to keep the crew longer. But after the world-famous fighter got there, he and his buddies disappeared into his dressing room. I was waiting down the hall and was soon knocked over by an incredibly strong odor wafting down from his room. I naively shouted, "What is that stink? Jeez, it smells like a skunk. It's brutal." One of our production assistants raced down to where I was standing and put her finger to her mouth to shush me. I said, "What's wrong?" And she whispered, "That's skunk pot. He's smoking pot in his dressing room."

Mike finally emerged, and his emotions ran the gamut. He was intense, he laughed, he cried, got angry, then laughed again. The hour turned into a riveting portrayal of this complicated man.

As you'll see when you read this interview, he found success early, becoming the youngest man to win a heavyweight title when he knocked out Trevor Berbick in 1986 at the age of twenty. From there his life became an emotional roller coaster, with dizzying highs and stomach-emptying lows. The wounds from that journey are still open, incredibly raw. It's hard for an outsider to process what happened to Mike Tyson under the glare of stardom, and it seems even more difficult for Mike Tyson to understand it.

At the end of the interview, during which Mike's wildly swinging emotions spilled all over the studio, he happily stayed backstage for about a half hour, taking pictures with the crew and some members of the audience. It seemed odd that the tension that had filled the past sixty-plus minutes—a span in which he, at times, seemed incapable of holding it together—was seemingly gone. It was as if a cloud had lifted from his being. He seemed almost joyous, finally getting a chance to be in the moment after having taken a trip into the dark corners of his past.

The Interview

MICHAEL KAY: Today's guest was born and raised in Brooklyn. As a child he ran the mean streets of Brownsville, until being sent to reform school in upstate New York. There he learned to box and eventually caught the eye of legendary trainer Cus D'Amato. Under D'Amato's tutelage Tyson quickly rose through the ranks to become the youngest heavyweight champion in the history of boxing. A frightening physical specimen, he instilled terror in his opponents even before the fights began. He was the model of a supreme gladiator, unbeaten and unbeatable, dispatching opponents in short order. He thrilled boxing fans, and his fights became must-see events and box-office gold. After monumental upset losses, his image inside and outside the ring spiraled downward due to several bizarre incidents and a prison term. In 2008 he was the subject of a profoundly honest documentary that displayed his human side. He is currently taping and starring in a new TV show that examines the world of pigeon racing. Please welcome the champ, Iron Mike Tyson. [*Applause*]

MIKE TYSON: Thank you.

MICHAEL KAY: How you doing?

MIKE TYSON: Man, I don't know, I'm just, um . . . I feel awesome. You know, normally when people ask me how I'm doing, I'm not great. What is great? But right now I'm just really feeling awesome.

MICHAEL KAY: And you get the love from the crowd. Do you sense that people love you?

MIKE TYSON: I don't know. Recently it's becoming more tangible to me. But I go through spells of a lot of self-loathing, you know?

That's just something I deal with. But I'm truly appreciative and grateful.

MICHAEL KAY: Let's try to understand your upbringing, Mike. At two years old your dad left the family; then what happened from that point?

MIKE TYSON: I remember this place, Fort Greene [in Brooklyn], and Bedford-Stuyvesant, then I remember moving to Brownsville, and that was just a totally different dynamic, you know? All these people outside, late at night, drinking, smoking, cursing, using profanity, and I think my mother, she wasn't in her element. There was no security there, you know, you were just open game.

MICHAEL KAY: I heard that when you were a young kid, you were a pretty docile person.

MIKE TYSON: I'm pretty docile now. [*Laughter*] No, certain things would trigger me when I was younger, you know what I'm saying? They would put me in a state of insecurity, and when I was insecure and frightened, I would strike out.

MICHAEL KAY: What kind of things triggered you, Mike?

MIKE TYSON: Just people picking on me, taking my money, messing with my pigeons.

MICHAEL KAY: Why did people pick on you, specifically?

MIKE TYSON: Because I had a high-pitched voice, and I was really obesely overweight. But then when I was ten years old, this bigger guy took one of my pigeons, and my friend said I should fight him, and I fought him, and I don't know, I guess I beat him up and stuff, and some of my friends watched and everybody applauded.

MICHAEL KAY: And you had never fought before?

MIKE TYSON: Never in my life.

MICHAEL KAY: Then you got in some trouble.

MIKE TYSON: Yeah, I did a robbery, and somebody had told on me, and I went to a reformatory for kids in the Bronx. And when I went there, it's just so ironic, this is probably '78, '77, Muhammad Ali came in there to visit the kids. And I saw him, and a feeling came over me like I never felt before. You know, Ali's an incredible person, and I just wanted what he had, the energy he had when he came in the room. But I was still getting in trouble, I think I stabbed somebody there, so they shipped me to another place that was really horrible.

MICHAEL KAY: Was that Tryon [School for Boys in Johnstown, New York]?

MIKE TYSON: Yeah. And it was horrible. But there was this Irish guy in there, [counselor and former boxer] Bobby Stewart, and he was teaching these guys to box. He wasn't a big guy, maybe a hundred and seventy pounds, but [the first time I got in the ring with him], I'm just whaling away, I don't know anything about fighting, but I'm strong. And then he hit me in the stomach, and everything I ate for the past two weeks seemed to come up. [*Laughter*] And I says, "Sir, can you teach me how to do that?" I never thought about no professional-fighter shit, I just wanted to knock out some people in the street so I could steal their money. And he said, "If you want to learn [to box], first you clean your room and do good in school." So I did all that stuff, I was getting grades, I mean, I didn't know how to spell *cat*, but I was getting on the little honor rolls.

MICHAEL KAY: And then Stewart took you to meet [longtime trainer] Cus D'Amato [who was running the Catskill Boxing Club]. What type of guy was he, and why did he take an interest in you?

MIKE TYSON: I have no idea. I have no idea why he wanted to even be around, I was disgusting.

MICHAEL KAY: Did you feel a connection with him?

MIKE TYSON: No, he was this arrogant, mean Italian guy and I was afraid of him. And I thought he was a weirdo. [*Laughter*]

MICHAEL KAY: But he saw something in you, though. Did you ever ask him what it was after you got close with him?

MIKE TYSON: Well, if it had nothing to do with boxing, I didn't ask him basically anything.

MICHAEL KAY: Now, he didn't just teach you boxing, Mike, he also taught you psychological aspects of things as well. He delved deep into you, right?

MIKE TYSON: Oh, absolutely, he believed that you could do anything with your mind. He thought I could be champ at fifteen years old, but he said I didn't have enough belief in myself. So he broke me down, man, so he could design whatever kind of fighter he wanted.

MICHAEL KAY: Did you love him, or were you afraid of him?

MIKE TYSON: Both.

MICHAEL KAY: How did you reconcile that, loving a man and being afraid of him?

MIKE TYSON: I was just his slave. You know, I just did what he told me. If he told me to kill you, I would kill you.

MICHAEL KAY: [You went pro at age eighteen], you had eleven fights, eight knockouts in the first round, and they're billing you as the next great heavyweight. And then Cus dies of pneumonia in November of 1985.

MIKE TYSON: He didn't believe in doctors and hospitals, that's why probably he died, he never went to the hospital. He said they kill more people than anything. You know, he was born in 1908, so that was just the mentality back then.

MICHAEL KAY: All right, now you continue to mow through contenders. Twenty months after turning pro, you're twenty-seven and oh, and then on November 22, 1986, you get your title shot against Trevor Berbick. How nervous were you?

MIKE TYSON: Hey, I was nervous, but I knew this had to happen. I saw the [1981] fight with him and [an aging and out-of-shape] Muhammad Ali, and I just thought that he unmercifully just beat the crap out of Ali. He didn't have to do that, Ali was absolutely helpless, he couldn't do nothing. Then Ali came to me before the fight and said, "Kick his ass for me." And so I said, "Oh, you got that." [Laughter]

MICHAEL KAY: You end up beating him in the second round, a TKO, and you're the heavyweight champ of the [World Boxing Council], at age twenty, the youngest champ ever. Then in 1987 you beat Tony Tucker, and now you're the undisputed heavyweight champ, and that's really the beginning of Tyson mania. I mean, the whole world is going crazy for you. Was it going too fast for you?

MIKE TYSON: Yes and no. Since I was twelve, you know, I was pretty much groomed for it. But then I get all this money, millions of dollars, and I have no restrictions, there's nobody to say, "Mike, put that away for a rainy day."

MICHAEL KAY: Were you spending it as quickly as you were making it?

MIKE TYSON: I had a lot of fun, yeah. [Laughter]

MICHAEL KAY: Now, in '88 you meet the great Larry Holmes, and that's the only time he was knocked out in his career. And when he was here on the show, he said that he tried to give young fighters advice about Don King and saving their money. Did he ever talk to you about that stuff?

MIKE TYSON: Well, I was with Don King, so anybody who don't like Don, I don't like them. If I'm with somebody, if you don't like him, then I'm going to attack you.

MICHAEL KAY: When you met Don King, did you like him right away?

MIKE TYSON: I don't know. I thought he was cool, he was pretty flashy, he talked my lingo back then. Yeah, he's a scoundrel, but it takes one to know one, you know? I'm no church choirboy, and I'm no imam. I was just as rotten as he was back then. That's why we got along so well. I got just as much as I took, and I guess he got the same. I'm not the guy you guys think I am. I'm not the poor black guy who's been abused for his money, and Don King is not a man who took advantage of that poor black guy. Whatever happened to me, I deserved it, I put it on myself. Of course, I'm not a total moron. I've read about [what happened to] Ray Robinson, I've read about Sugar, Joe Louis, and I've seen Ali's situation.

MICHAEL KAY: Now, you're the heavyweight champ in '88, and you knock out Tony Tubbs in two rounds in March in Japan, and that sets the stage for the big showdown with Michael Spinks. And a lot of boxing writers at the time said what a great match this is going to be. Then it lasted for ninety-one seconds before you knocked him out. Looking back, do you think that was the pinnacle of your boxing career?

MIKE TYSON: No, no, no, no. Because when you look at the situation, there was no way that Michael Spinks could ever beat me. You know, it wasn't fair. He was fighting for money, he wasn't fighting to win the fight. He was fighting for money. When I got his age, I understood, it's really just "Get in there, don't get hurt, and let's get some money." So he got the money.

MICHAEL KAY: In 1990 you fight Buster Douglas and you end up losing that fight. Everybody knocks you and says you weren't in shape.

MIKE TYSON: People confused it, I was in great physical condition, but the fact is I wasn't in any psychological shape. Buster did an awesome job. But I always tell people, I think that was my best fight I ever had. Because Cus used to always tell me, he said, "You can beat everybody up, but what's gonna happen when somebody starts beating you up? Can you take it?" And that fight proved that I could take it.

MICHAEL KAY: People look at that now and say it's one of the biggest upsets in the history of sports. After it happened, when you're leaving the ring, could you believe that you had lost?

MIKE TYSON: No, no, I couldn't believe that I had lost. But once I lost, the only thing I was thinking about was being champion again.

MICHAEL KAY: So after you lose to Buster Douglas, you start on the comeback trail—two really tough fights that you win against Donovan "Razor" Ruddock, and that sets up a championship fight with Evander Holyfield. But that fight didn't happen, due to your conviction on sexual assault charges in Indianapolis.

MIKE TYSON: See, that was rape, they said I raped her, it wasn't no sexual assault. Listen, when you're with me, don't try to sugarcoat anything, man. Don't do that, man.

MICHAEL KAY: Okay. Do you regret what happened in Indianapolis?

MIKE TYSON: No, no, I didn't regret. I regret those guys falsely accusing me, but the experience was awesome, because if I didn't go to prison, I would've never been champion again. Because before I was in prison, the desire wasn't there no more.

MICHAEL KAY: But you got it back, because when you got out of prison [after serving almost three years] you have a couple warm-up fights, then you win the WBC [World Boxing Council] title, and the WBA [World Boxing Association] title. Then you have the long-awaited Evander Holyfield match in '96. You lost that fight in a TKO, but in '97 you have the famous rematch with Holyfield in Las Vegas. He's headbutting you and you bite his ear. Mike, I guess the only question I have is—why would you bite him? [*Laughter*]

MIKE TYSON: I was just pissed off and I was an undisciplined soldier. I'm a spoiled brat and it wasn't going my way and I wanted to hurt him. I had always been jealous of him, and I got emotional, just a spoiled fucking kid—forgive my language—and I bit him.

MICHAEL KAY: Looking back on it now, how do you judge it?

MIKE TYSON: [*Pause*] If I'm objective about it, I look at it and say, "This man is totally undisciplined, this man should be banned from boxing." But when I look at it from a pity perspective, it's like, "Well, he headbutted me!" But, no, I was wrong, I was dead wrong

MICHAEL KAY: After you lost to Holyfield, you sued Don King for $100 million for [allegedly] stealing millions from you. Did you ever collect anything off that?

MIKE TYSON: Oh, yeah, I got a lotta money from people, but, you know, that was just all irrelevant. I mean, it wasn't like someone gave me some money and I said, "Well, I'm gonna put it away and save it for my future." I was just living my life, I was just gambling with life back then.

MICHAEL KAY: You never thought about the future, Mike?

MIKE TYSON: No, I never thought I would live to see the future.

MICHAEL KAY: All right, so you had your boxing license taken away for a while, but you come back again. Then you get another title shot against Lennox Lewis, and you guys had a fight at the press conference, where you bit his leg. [*Laughter*] What happened there?

MIKE TYSON: I don't know, I'm just a crazy man. [*Laughter*] I'm just crazy outta my motherfucking mind—I'm sorry, guys—[*laughter*]—I am sorry, God damn, man.

MICHAEL KAY: So you lose the Lennox Lewis fight. Then in 2005 you quit before the seventh round in a fight with Kevin McBride. Was that when you decided, "I've had enough of boxing, that's it, I'm done"?

MIKE TYSON: Yeah. I was boxing just for money and ego, it was just a useless thing. I didn't want to see Mike Tyson getting beat every day, fighting twenty-five fights after he should have retired.

MICHAEL KAY: You had tremendous success, but you also had trouble with bankruptcy and the law and drugs. If you were granted a do-over, Mike, what would you have done differently?

MIKE TYSON: I don't know. I left a lotta wreckage and stuff, you know, and I wasn't a good dad—and I have some awesome kids, I don't even deserve to have the kids I have. All that stuff comes back to haunt you.

MICHAEL KAY: I gotta ask you this, Mike. You've never even hinted at it, but we've heard some rumors that you and Don King have kind of made up. They'd pay you so much money, would you come back [to boxing]?

MIKE TYSON: No, I would never do that. No way. I'd be afraid to do it now, actually, physically afraid to do it. And my psyche is not there no more. I don't like that way of life no more. It's the most humiliating thing in the world to just be physically beat up and stuff, you know what I mean? The money just wouldn't matter, you could give me a billion dollars, 'cause money never was the point. It was just my ego, I wanted to be the best. I was nothing, and then I was the best in the world at something at one time. Who cares about money? I was the greatest in the world. But it doesn't match up with the life I have now.

MICHAEL KAY: So you're happy now?

MIKE TYSON: I don't know about happiness. What is happiness? Everybody has different opinions about happiness and stuff. I don't know if it's true, but some people say that to know who you are is pretty much happiness, the good and the bad, to practice some self-examination. I've tried that, but it hurts. I have a lot of pain and I don't know how to let it go. I used to be this tough guy, toughest guy on the planet, and next thing I know I cry at the slightest fucking thing. I don't know what's wrong with me. I think I'm falling to pieces sometimes.

MICHAEL KAY: Well, this has been fascinating, Mike, thank you so much.

MIKE TYSON: Thank you. [*Applause*]

Bob Costas

When I was a Yankees beat writer with the *New York Post* in 1988, I was walking with a friend on Seventh Avenue across Twenty-Third Street in New York City. After crossing the street to the southwest corner of Seventh Avenue, I found myself standing next to someone I'd long admired, Bob Costas. I was astonished when he recognized me and introduced himself. I subsequently introduced him to my friend Donna, and we chatted for a short while, then went on our ways. Now, fast-forward ten years, and Donna, who was working at the NBA, ran into Costas at Madison Square Garden. She'd never seen him since that day in 1988, and he walked up to her and said, "Hi, Donna, I'm Bob Costas. I met you once with Michael Kay."

Mind blown.

That story reflects some of the genius of Costas. His memory is astonishingly sharp. He never forgets a name or a face or a fact. Imagine how much that has meant to him in his career. His mind is a vault of information that he seamlessly spins into stories that apply perfectly to what people are watching. He's the gold standard in the broadcasting industry, superb not just at hosting but also interviewing, doing play-by-play, and composing essays. His scope is endless and his excellence is unmatched.

He hosted the Olympics for NBC for close to thirty years, worked NFL, NBA, and MLB play-by-play, and did studio hosting for the NFL, NBA, NHL, NASCAR, horse racing, and baseball. At every job that aspiring broadcasters dream of being somewhat proficient at, he has excelled.

As I mentioned at the start of this book, *CenterStage* was styled after *Inside the Actors Studio*, but I also wanted it to be somewhat like the transcendent *Later with Bob Costas*, which ran for six years late-night on NBC. That might be Bob's best work in a life of Hall of Fame work. The ease with which he got the biggest-name guests to tell their stories almost made it seem as if it weren't a difficult task. It was.

So with a résumé that makes most in the business envious, Costas was the perfect *CenterStage* guest. He was so good, he was one of just a few who ever had a second show. The first time Costas appeared was in 2002, then he came back fifteen years later. We've combined the best of the two interviews to give you a detailed look at his life and career.

Since we last talked with Costas, he's left his longtime home at NBC, in 2019, and is now with MLB Network, doing play-by-play as well as an interview show, *Studio 42 with Bob Costas*.

The Interview

MICHAEL KAY: Thank you, everybody, and welcome to *CenterStage*. Today's guest was born and raised in Queens and Long Island. While finishing college at Syracuse, he takes a job announcing games for the fledgling ABA. A few years later, he was hired by NBC, where he became one of television's most prolific sports announcers and, later, one of its most respected interviewers and cultural commentators. Combined with his encyclopedic knowledge is a devilish sense of humor. He served as a prime-time host of a record eleven Olympic Games. He's also been part of seven Super Bowl telecasts, was voted Sportscaster of the Year a record eight times, and has been awarded more than two dozen Emmys. Please welcome one of the preeminent broadcasters of this generation, Bob Costas. [*Applause*]

BOB COSTAS: Thank you.

MICHAEL KAY: Now, you covered it all. What's your favorite sport to cover?

BOB COSTAS: Baseball by far. Not even close.

MICHAEL KAY: What started that love affair? Why baseball? Because you're good at everything you do.

BOB COSTAS: If you're talking about play-by-play, for a certain kind of announcer, someone who's anecdotal, someone who likes history, who enjoys byplay, it's baseball. You do it every day and every night from April to October, and it's just a different kind of thing from calling a basketball game or a hockey game or a football game. It isn't that the sport is necessarily better, but it's better for me.

MICHAEL KAY: Like you, I love baseball. But also like you, I'm a little concerned about it. What are some of your concerns? Do you think the game's in good shape?

BOB COSTAS: I think the game is generally in good shape. Pace of play is a problem. Look, the game is supposed to have an appealing, leisurely pace, but it's not supposed to have a lethargic pace. A game that's two to one should not take three hours and twenty minutes. It's a question of pace. The constant trips to the mound by the catcher, the pitchers taking forever to throw a pitch.

MICHAEL KAY: So tell me about Commack, Long Island.

BOB COSTAS: Well, that's where I lived when I went to junior high school and high school in the 1960s. I was already a huge baseball fan, but that's where my dad and I bonded over baseball. We went to a lot of baseball games, Yankee and Mets games, and watched a lot of them on TV. At that time, most teams didn't televise the majority of their games, and the Yankees and Mets televised virtually all of them. And it was still the golden era of sportscasting. Vin Scully had decamped along with the Dodgers to the West Coast. But think of those voices: Mel Allen was still doing Yankee games in the early sixties, and Red Barber, and later Joe Garagiola, did Yankee games. Lindsey Nelson was one of the voices of the Mets, along with Bob Murphy, and Ralph Kiner, who wasn't a classic announcer, but he was a wonderful storyteller and, and baseball analyst. Marty Glickman was doing Knicks games, then succeeded by Marv Albert. You'd hear Jack Whitaker on NFL games. And to me there was something romantic and intriguing about being a broadcaster.

MICHAEL KAY: And when did that click? When did you say, "This is what I want to do for a living?"

BOB COSTAS: When I was about ten or eleven. Because I was very astute as a child [*laughter*], I knew that if I was ever gonna get into Yankee Stadium without buying a ticket, it would be to sit where Red Barber had sat, not to stand where Mickey Mantle was standing. [*Laughter*]

MICHAEL KAY: Now, your dad occasionally liked to place a bet, right?

BOB COSTAS: Occasionally, as in almost every day. [*Laughter*]

MICHAEL KAY: Did you ever gamble?

BOB COSTAS: No. Other than five bucks, ten bucks, playing golf or something. My dad's gambling created emotional highs and lows for our family, there was a traumatic imbalance there. My dad died when I was eighteen, and he was forty-two. Some people gravitate toward what their parents were like, good or bad, but I walked away from it.

MICHAEL KAY: Now, you're ten years old and you want to be a sportscaster. What was your first paid gig?

BOB COSTAS: First paid gig was when I was still a senior at Syracuse, doing games in the old Eastern Hockey League, the actual league that the Paul Newman hockey movie, *Slap Shot*, was based on. I got thirty dollars a game, five dollars a day meal money on the road. In the Eastern Hockey League, there wasn't just a fight a night. There were police actions at several games, there were riots. There were games that were forfeited between periods because the fans rioted. There was one game in Johnstown where it starts with a fight on the ice, then it spills over with fans in the penalty box, then the trainers pair off and fight, and then the coaches are going at each other, they're wearing sports coats and they're not on skates, so they're slipping and sliding around. I'm up in this rickety broadcast booth by myself, I'm the announcer, I'm the engineer, I'm the statistician, I'm the whole thing. And then I look up in the stands and I see our *bus driver* is up there fighting with fans. [*Laughter*] And I'm thinking, "How the hell are we gonna get back to Syracuse?" [*Laughter*]

MICHAEL KAY: You're a very youthful-looking person, and I'm sure that when you were younger, you were more youthful looking. Did it play against you?

BOB COSTAS: I was afraid that it would. Obviously I got jobs, but I was concerned, not so much about being on the radio, but being on TV. When I first got to NBC, I was twenty-seven, and Don Ohlmeyer was running NBC. Ohlmeyer was already a legendary figure in television, an intimidating presence, and he calls me into his office. And he says, "You know, we like your work, we think you have a future here. But how old are you?" I said twenty-seven, and he said, "Goddammit, you look like you're fourteen!" So then he says, "How much older do you think you would look if you grew a beard?" And he's serious, it's, like, his brainstorm. And I said, "I'd look at least five years older—because that's how long it would take me to grow it." [*Laughter*]

MICHAEL KAY: All right, so how does the kid from New York City and Syracuse end up at KMOX in St. Louis?

BOB COSTAS: Well, I sent a tape of a game I had done on the campus radio station at Syracuse to KMOX in St. Louis. That's when the Spirits of St. Louis came into existence, and I wanted to do play-by-play. They had been the Carolina Cougars, but they moved to St. Louis, and they were there for the last two seasons of the ABA. I was twenty-two years old, and lo and behold, I got the job.

MICHAEL KAY: Then you went from the Spirits of St. Louis to do play-by-play for the Chicago Bulls.

BOB COSTAS: Yeah. I did one season. It was pre–Michael Jordan, so they were not a contender, they didn't make the playoffs.

MICHAEL KAY: Then you end up at NBC. How did they discover you, where did they find you?

BOB COSTAS: I actually had done some regional games, both basketball and NFL games, in the mid- to late seventies for CBS, because KMOX was a CBS-owned-and-operated station. Jack Buck was their signature voice, he had done marquee football games for CBS forever. So when they needed someone to do, like, the seventh or eighth regional game, they called the general manager at KMOX, and he said, "Well, I've got this one guy here, he looks very young, but he's pretty good." So I was doing a handful of those games, and then Don Ohlmeyer and the people at NBC noticed me. And one thing just kind of led to another. When I first got to NBC, Bryant Gumbel was the preeminent host of all their sports coverage. And then when he went to the *Today* show, Michael Weisman, who was the executive producer then at NBC, he told me, "You know, we think you can take Bryant's spot on these various shows." And I explained to him that I had never seen a teleprompter, I had never really worked in the studio before, I had only done play-by-play. And for the first five years that I hosted the NFL, I ad-libbed everything. There was no teleprompter at all. Eventually we started to use a teleprompter because the production became more sophisticated, but I still, to the very end, on the Olympics or whatever, would ad-lib in and around the teleprompter. The trick was for the audience not to know when I was ad-libbing and when I was reading.

MICHAEL KAY: Now, did you ever get accused of, quote, "rhapsodizing about the infield fly rule"?

BOB COSTAS: Yes. In 1983, I took the train down from New York to Baltimore to be at the first two World Series games. I'm talking with Al Michaels, and he's doing the games with Howard Cosell and Earl Weaver, and Cosell is standing outside the broadcast booth of the old Memorial Stadium wearing that hideous yellow ABC blazer, the toupee precariously perched atop his head, and brandishing a cigar about half the size of a Louisville Slugger. [*Laughter*] I had never met Howard Cosell, so I walk up to him and I say, "Mr. Cosell, my name is Bob Costas, it's a pleasure to meet you." And he goes, "I know who you are. You're the child who rhapsodizes about the infield fly rule. I'm sure you'll have a fine career." And he flicks the cigar ash and walks back into the booth. And my first thought was "This is the biggest schmuck I've ever met." But my next thought was "This is great, I just got the full Cosell treatment." [*Laughter*] And here we are, more than thirty years later, and I'm still telling the story.

MICHAEL KAY: Did you ever have a better relationship with him?

BOB COSTAS: We never had a great relationship. Howard was a complicated character. At his best, he was brilliant and courageous. At his worst, he was a caricature of himself. And he was very resentful. I think the people he resented the most were those he knew that he could not truthfully dismiss as lightweights. He resented Al Michaels for that reason, and I think he might have resented me for that reason. The last conversation I ever had with him, I told him directly, "You ought to be to all of us what Walter Cronkite is to people in the news business. You should be the guy we turn to. You should be the gray eminence, the emeritus guy. But because you resent so many people and have alienated so many people, you can't do that." And he said, "Maybe you're right, kid, maybe you're right. We'll talk again soon." But we never did. He died shortly after that.

MICHAEL KAY: Now, in 2014 in Sochi, Russia, you get an eye infection and you have to give up your Olympics hosting duties. I have a two-year-old and a four-year-old, so I appreciate pink eye.

BOB COSTAS: Well, I would have appreciated getting it when I was two or four [*laughter*] instead of when I was sixty.

MICHAEL KAY: I know that must have been painful for you, because I know that hosting the Olympics meant something for you.

BOB COSTAS: You know, we've all gone to work not feeling well. If I'd just had the flu, if I had a broken leg, they put it in a cast, I stick it under the desk, no one knows. You just grit your teeth and you get through it. But this was literally written on my face. And of all the timing! I woke up the morning of the opening ceremony, and I go to shave and my right eye is a slit. And I'm thinking, "Well, there must be something they can do about this." And at first they said, "Well, it's some kind of bacterial infection or something, and we can give you antibiotics, it will go away in a few days." But then it jumped to the left eye, and they knew that it was viral. And the only thing you can do is wait it out. And you know, by that point, to be honest, hosting the Olympics didn't mean as much to me personally as it did in terms of relationships and responsibility. You're carrying the ball for your colleagues, who have worked their tails off, you have them running around the world to do these athlete profiles for a year or more, and you're kind of the front man for that. So that's why I tried to hang in as long as I could, but then it got to the point after five or six days where I couldn't get through a segment without my eyes tearing up, so I had to step aside for a while.

MICHAEL KAY: Some people have said that part of your success is your broad demographic appeal, especially to women. Do you think of yourself as a sex symbol?

BOB COSTAS: Uh, of course I do. [*Laughter*] Actually, if I ever was, I think I peaked sometime in the nineties. [*Laughter*] Boyish works well through your thirties and forties, but it doesn't work so well after you've turned sixty.

MICHAEL KAY: Now, the last time you were here, we talked at length about the great eulogy you gave at Mickey Mantle's funeral. In 2013, you did the same for Stan Musial, and it was magnificent. Tell me some of the highlights for that, and how close had you gotten to Stan.

BOB COSTAS: I was pretty close with Stan, having lived in St. Louis for the better part of my adult life. He was the nicest man and the least pretentious superstar you could ever come across. And the difference between Stan's and Mickey's situation was, Mickey was sixty-three, and it was a tragic death, and he had a life that had many regrets. Stan was ninety-two, lived a full life, and had no regrets as a ballplayer, and if he had any as a man, they were few. He lived a full and happy life.

MICHAEL KAY: And you used Mantle in the eulogy, right?

BOB COSTAS: Yeah, it was a true story and it connected the two of them. Mickey stayed at our house in St. Louis a couple of nights sometime in the nineties. He had agreed to do a charity event for me, and he stayed with us. So in order for him to feel a little more comfortable, we invited Stan and Lil over for dinner, so that he'd be with someone that he knew. So it was a very nice evening, and then everyone had gone off to bed, and it was just me and Mickey, up late talking. You know how sometimes someone who is not particularly eloquent, or you don't think of them as eloquent, can be eloquent in simplicity, because it just cuts to the heart of the matter? And Mickey, you know how humble he was, he never bragged. But he said, unprompted, "You know, I could have been a better ballplayer than Stan. No one had more power than me, no one could run any faster than me before I got hurt. But you know why he was a better player than me? Because he's a better man than me. And that's why he'll never live with all the regret that I live with about my career and about my life." That's what he said.

MICHAEL KAY: Wow. I mean, what do you say to him when he says that?

BOB COSTAS: Well, sometime later, just before he died, I said to him, "Do you realize how many millions of people love you? How connected you are to their childhoods or to their relationships with their dad, or their best friend, or whatever it might be?" But this humble, unassuming kid from Commerce, Oklahoma, could never quite get his arms around it. He was a naturally shy person, and for all he achieved, he always felt that he had let people down. He didn't understand the adulation. But I think before he died, he finally got it.

MICHAEL KAY: You've met so many people because of the positions that you've been in. Have you ever been kind of startled by people you don't know but who consider you somebody that they know?

BOB COSTAS: Yeah, and when you think about it, it makes sense, because in an increasingly fractionalized world of niche entertainment, one of the things that cuts through is big sports events, like the Olympics or the World Series or *Sunday Night Football,* or whatever. So this story goes back more than twenty-five years. I'm having dinner late one night in Little Italy with Norm Stewart, who then was the coach of the Missouri Tigers, and his wife and some people who had come from St. Louis. I take them to dinner in Little Italy, at this restaurant, and I look up, and who should be walking in but [mobster] John Gotti, the Dapper Don, and he was every inch that—two-thousand-dollar cashmere overcoat, perfectly coiffed. The waiter practically dropped the rigatoni in my lap as he raced off to greet him. And the maître d' removed Gotti's coat like it was a prince's cape. And I later found out that the Ravenite Social Club, where he conducted his business, was just down the block, and he was a regular at this restaurant. And so he's led to his table, and I lean over to Norm's wife, Virginia, and I go [*whispers*], "John Gotti, murderer." So she says, a little scared, "Should we leave?" And I said, "You don't understand. Unless you somehow have crossed Mr. Gotti, you're now in the safest place in all of New York. So enjoy the rigatoni." [*Laughter*] So a few more minutes go by, and the maître d' comes over and he says, "Mr. Costas, Mr. Gotti would like to buy you a drink." By this point we've all had enough to drink, but on the other hand, I put this in the category of an offer you could not refuse. [*Laughter*] So I say, "All right, we'll have a little more Chianti," and I look over at Gotti and I say, "Mr. Gotti, thank you." And he goes, "Bob, I like your work." And what am I supposed to say? "I like your work, too"? "Nice rubout at Sparks Steak House"? "That Paul Castellano really had it coming"? But instead, I say, "Thank you, have a nice evening." [*Laughter, applause*]

MICHAEL KAY: So we'll go back to the beginning, when you grew up wanting to broadcast for a team. Are you happy with the way things have turned out?

BOB COSTAS: Yes. I'm happy with the way things have turned out. If I have a small regret, and I'm not really entitled to regrets, it's that I never had a long enough run as a baseball announcer to find out how good I could have been. I was never the equivalent of a Jack Buck or an Ernie Harwell or the gold standard, Vin Scully. I might have been able to be, but if I did all they did, then I wouldn't have done the Olympics or other things I've done. But it's like sitting there having the best steak you could ever possibly have, and then saying, "You know, I wish I had ordered the swordfish, too." You can't have everything on the menu.

MICHAEL KAY: Very cool. And we will see you in another fifteen years, right?

BOB COSTAS: Yeah, and hopefully I'll have some new stories to tell.

MICHAEL KAY: Thanks so much.

PART TWO

THEY SHOWED US
WHAT IS POSSIBLE

Bill Russell

Full disclosure: Bill Russell intimidated me. When I heard we'd booked Russell for *CenterStage*, I was equal parts thrilled and terrified. Thrilled, because I'd have the opportunity to talk with one of the greatest winners in the history of sports. (The man won eleven NBA titles in his thirteen-year career with the Celtics, two NCAA championships with the University of San Francisco, and a gold medal at the 1956 Olympics.) Terrified, because he was tough with the media and didn't suffer fools, I wanted to be prepared to interview him so we could have a revealing back-and-forth that didn't derail because of tension or because of my not having my facts.

Russell was there to promote his book *Red and Me: My Coach, My Lifelong Friend*, and I think that his knowing we'd interviewed Red Auerbach years before served to somewhat soften the entrance into his guarded persona.

Russell is tough to interview even if he's agreeable because he has an incredibly odd cadence in speaking. His pauses are of such length that you think he's done talking, but as you begin talking again, he revs back up. Picture being in a car with a faulty transmission that lurches forward just as you think it's slowing down, and you'll have an idea of what a conversation with Russell feels like.

He also has a loud cackle of a laugh that is unnerving when you first experience it. The laugh comes when you're not expecting it, throwing you off even further.

But once you get over these speed bumps, and it does take a while, the conversation is riveting. Russell has lived one of the great and most influential of American lives. Despite his excellence on the court, he has committed his life to battling social injustices, and he simply never accepts a wrong without trying to right it.

This talk is essential reading for those who love the NBA, but also anyone who wants to study the life of a prominent black man in the 1950s and 1960s who made it through with his head high and his values intact.

The Interview

MICHAEL KAY: As a young man from Louisiana, today's guest struggled to master the game of basketball. Growing up in Oakland, California, he blossomed late in high school and received a scholarship to the University of San Francisco. While there, he led the Dons to two consecutive NCAA championships. He then captained the US Olympic men's basketball team to a gold medal. During his illustrious thirteen-year career as the centerpiece of the Boston Celtics dynasty, he helped them win eleven NBA championships. A five-time winner of the NBA Most Valuable Player award, he is widely considered as the best defensive player in NBA history. He was noted for his intensity, stellar basketball IQ, and sheer will to win. In 1966, as player/coach of the Celtics, he became the first African American to coach a major professional team. Please welcome the greatest winner in the history of professional sports, Mr. Bill Russell. [*Applause*]

MICHAEL KAY: I would think that, for an athlete, being called "the greatest winner in the history of sports" is probably the best compliment you could have. How do you feel about being called that?

BILL RUSSELL: It depends on who's doing the calling. [*Laughter*]

MICHAEL KAY: Was it a fear of losing, Bill, or was it the exhilaration of winning that drove you?

BILL RUSSELL: Winning. Always. I can't remember being afraid of anything. Fear of losing was not something that ever even occurred to me. I remember one of the greatest thrills I had in basketball was when my high school team won the Northern California championship. And in the tournament, I didn't play, I was the fifteenth man on the team. So I watched the whole tournament, and we won the championship, and even though I didn't play, I was so thrilled being on the championship team, I couldn't sleep for three days.

MICHAEL KAY: You were the fifteenth man on a fourteen-man team. So you were a late bloomer.

BILL RUSSELL: [*Laughs*] I was a late *grower*. I grew another inch and a half in college.

MICHAEL KAY: Talk to me about when you knew that you wanted to play basketball, even though you weren't good until you got to be a little bit older.

BILL RUSSELL: I was living in Louisiana until I was nine. I had never seen a basketball. And then I moved to California, in the projects, and they had a basketball court. So I would go out there and start playing—not very well, but I had fun. I got cut from junior varsity in the eleventh grade [because of an argument with the coach], and that night I went out and played basketball for five straight hours because it was irrelevant where I played, I just wanted to play. And then when I got to be a senior in high school and in college, I developed a gunfighter mentality. I always wanted to find somebody that I could really play against, to measure myself against them. And so far I have never seen anyone that was better. [*Laughter*]

MICHAEL KAY: You had one scholarship offer, and that was to USF. On the basketball court, things were going well. In your junior year, your team goes twenty-eight and one and they win the national championship [and you were MVP at the Final Four]. Did you say to yourself, "I'm really good at this and I'm gonna make a living at it"?

BILL RUSSELL: I said, "I am really good," but I didn't think about making a living. I just knew I was good at it.

MICHAEL KAY: Now, obviously, the Celtic years are the years a lot of people identify you with. How did you get there?

BILL RUSSELL: We had a guy at Oakland that had played for the Celtics. He was a local hero; he had played for UCLA, and he was an African American. He calls me and says, "The Celtics are a good bunch of people. That would be a good place to go." I met [Celtics owner] Walter Brown and [Celtics coach] Red Auerbach, and they seemed nice enough guys. So I signed with Boston [in 1956].

MICHAEL KAY: Let's talk about Boston, because at the time it was considered somewhat of a racist city.

BILL RUSSELL: Not "somewhat" racist. Overtly racist. Proudly racist. [*Laughs*]

MICHAEL KAY: How tough was that for you, in that town?

BILL RUSSELL: It was not difficult for me. I was born in segregated Louisiana, and the segregation there was harsh, very harsh. That was the reason my family moved to California, to get away from that. I went to public schools in Oakland, California, which were segregated, so all the kids I went to school with were black kids. The only experience I had with white folks in great numbers was at the University of San Francisco. So when I got to Boston, it was routine. The reason that everybody thought it was difficult was because my folks had taught me to never take anything from anybody without accountability. So if someone came up to me and said things that were out of order, I responded that it was out of order. In the projects where I grew up, if someone said something out of line and you walked away, they would hit you in the back of the head. So if someone would say something out of order, I was aggressive. And I threatened a few lives and things like that. [*Laughter*] If you came up to me and tried to give me a bad day, I made sure that you were the one that left there with the bad day.

MICHAEL KAY: What brought you and Red Auerbach together? Obviously the business relationship did, but what made you friends? What was that common bond? He was a Jewish kid from Brooklyn, in Irish Catholic Boston, and we just talked about the things that you encountered.

BILL RUSSELL: We came from two different tribes. What I brought to the relationship were the things that I learned from my tribe: my father, my mother, and my community. And he brought the same things from his tribe. It was two tribes meeting, and no tribe thought that their tribe was superior to the other tribe. And that's all. Over the years we each had a job and a position within the unit, but no job or position was superior to the other one. So he never told me how to play, and I never told him how to coach. The only thing that both he and I were interested in was winning. And we did that pretty well.

MICHAEL KAY: You did that eleven of thirteen years. Do you look back and consider how amazing that was?

BILL RUSSELL: To us, it was not amazing. We knew we were the best.

MICHAEL KAY: One of the things that is always said about you is that you had an incredible work ethic, and that you got that from your dad.

BILL RUSSELL: Yes. My father, who was always my hero, had a couple of things he used to tell me. First, he said, "If you take a job, and they pay you five dollars a day, you give them seven dollars' a day worth of work. Because if they are paying you five and you are giving them seven, you are more valuable to them than they are to you, and you can look any man in the eye and tell him to go straight to hell." And the other thing he said was "I don't know what you are gonna do when you grow up, but let's say that you decide to be a ditchdigger. Nobody thinks much of ditchdiggers, but if you decide to be a ditch-digger here in Monroe, Louisiana, you take ditchdigging and make it an art. I want people in Miami, New York, Chicago, San Francisco, to say, 'There's this guy down in Louisiana digging ditches, and you can't believe what he can do with a ditch. It's worth the trip to go down and see him.'" [*Laughter*] So when I started to be serious about basket-ball, I took it beyond being a journeyman and made myself an artist.

MICHAEL KAY: A couple of years into your Celtic life, Wilt Cham-berlain appears [playing for the Philadelphia Warriors, later playing for the Philadelphia 76ers and the Los Angeles Lakers], and they call it "the big collision." You said you were seeking out the best people to play against. Did you feel that playing against Chamberlain was a great litmus test for your defensive talent?

BILL RUSSELL: Not necessarily. After I played against him a few times, I made a conscious decision: I'm gonna continue to play the way I have been playing before he got here. And if either of us is gonna adjust and move toward the way the other guy plays, it will be him. But we were friends from when he was in college, and it was like when you play against your brother, you still try to beat him. He was five inches taller, about fifty pounds heavier, and a great athlete. And he was really smart. That creates a major problem. [*Laughter*] You couldn't play him the same way every night. So over the first couple of years, I developed six different ways to play him. And sometimes I would have to change it in the middle of a game because that ain't working that night.

MICHAEL KAY: We talked about the incredible run the Celtics had, the eight championships in a row. If you look at sports now, if the Yankees win three out of four years, it's a big deal. How did the Celt-ics sustain that record?

BILL RUSSELL: First of all, we had the classiest, more intelligent teammates any guy could ever hope for. And Red had a system that he could get the best out of all of 'em. And they worked just as hard as I did. That was the attitude.

MICHAEL KAY: So after Red retires and becomes [general manager], he makes you the player/coach. Did you want that job?

BILL RUSSELL: No. First he says to me, "I'm gonna retire," and I said, "Don't do that, come on, stay another year," and he says, "No, this is it." And I never brought it up again. If you and I are friends, and you ask me a question, and I say no, and you try to convince me to change my mind—well, what you are telling me is that what you want me to do is more important than what I want to do. It's not right.

MICHAEL KAY: In the '68–'69 season, your third year as a player/coach, you guys have a mediocre season for the Celtics, but you beat the 76ers, then the Knicks. And then you play the Lakers [in the NBA finals]. How important was it for you to win that series?

BILL RUSSELL: That's when we got behind two to nothing, and then we beat 'em three of the next four. Seventh game, we're playing the Lakers in Los Angeles, and before the game [Lakers owner Jack Kent Cooke] put out a postgame program, saying what was gonna happen after the game. It starts out, "After the Lakers win the championship the USC band will come out and play 'Happy Days Are Here Again.' We're going to release ten thousand balloons from the ceiling, and for the season-ticket holders there are ten cases of champagne in the Forum Club." So I take this program and I sit with my players as we're getting ready to go out. I say, "Guys, look at this program, the Lakers think they are gonna win. First of all, that's impossible. The Lakers cannot possibly win this game. If they were to play the best game any team in the history of this franchise had ever played, they would still lose."

MICHAEL KAY: And you won the game and championship. You were obviously on top of the world, but then you just walk away. Did you know before the game that that was it?

BILL RUSSELL: I knew before the season. I had decided to leave a year before. I was at the end of a marriage that wasn't working out, but I did not want my kids to grow up in a broken family, so I wanted to take a year to try to save [the marriage]. But there was another thing. We flew home Tuesday, and we were gonna have a parade on Friday. Thursday morning a reporter from one of the Boston papers walks into Red's office and said, "Are you satisfied with the coaching you had this year?" Red says, "What are you talking about? We won the championship three days ago." And the reporter says, "Yeah, but if you had a better coach, couldn't you have won more regular-season games?" One of the realities was that the Boston press—as a whole—did not want me to be the coach of the Celtics.

MICHAEL KAY: Why was that?

BILL RUSSELL: First of all, race was important. Why should their best team have a black guy running it? And an arrogant black guy at that? When a guy asks a question like that—"Are you satisfied?"—after you just won a championship, I told Red, "I'm not gonna do this anymore. I'm finished." Red says, "I gotta talk you out of it," and I said, "I've made up my mind." And we never discussed it again.

MICHAEL KAY: Now, you coached [other teams] after you had left the Celtics. But at one point you said, I want to fade away, I just don't want people to know me or even think about me. What happened there?

BILL RUSSELL: My life's ambition at that age was to go home and close the door behind me. [*Laughs*] Because my favorite place on the planet is my house. But what I've wanted to do the last couple of years is to do everything I can to help the next generation of Americans be the best generation that they can be. I spoke at a school in Texas many years ago, when the Vietnam War was winding down, and at the end of my speech I said, "We need to take the money away from war and rehabilitate our educational system, because that's the most important thing that we have on the plate. Period." So after the speech, a guy walked up to me and says, "You know, what you talk about is a lot of tax money. Why should I pay taxes to educate other people's kids?" And I said, "Sir, there are no 'other people's kids' in the United States of America. That is the next generation of Americans. And if they're not educated, we're gonna be in a world of trouble."

MICHAEL KAY: Now, Bill, the motto of your basketball journey with Red Auerbach was "Play like children without being childish." Do you feel like you accomplished that?

BILL RUSSELL: Yes. We had more fun than any team ever could have thought of. We lived a full life.

MICHAEL KAY: Bill, it's been an honor. Thank you.

Joe Montana

Joe Montana is part of forever. His exalted work as a quarterback in the NFL puts him in the conversation as one of the greatest champions in any sport.

With the San Francisco 49ers Montana won four Super Bowls and was chosen MVP of that game three times. But in a manic game, Joe never seemed rushed; instead, he exuded cool. He was the epitome of relaxation when all around him was spinning out of control. That ability to slow it down when things were going faster for mere mortals propelled Montana to greatness.

The trip from New Eagle, Pennsylvania, to Notre Dame and eventually to the West Coast was a journey that Montana was more than willing to share. His style while being interviewed was the same as his style on the field. His demeanor never lets you see him perspire, no matter how tough the question or how difficult the answer.

Montana is one of the greatest of all time, and when you get an opportunity to document his incredible life, you seize it. There's a certain buzz when someone of Montana's stature walks into a room. People want to know the man behind the fairy tale. Fans wonder how someone becomes so accomplished and seem to want to hungrily devour the secrets to his success and apply it to their existence. The room first stirs when Montana enters, then gets quiet as people lean on his every word. His whole life has been like this, so he's used to the adulation, and essentially, he gives people what they want.

Our hour with Montana is a window into his greatness and all that made him Joe Cool.

The Interview

MICHAEL KAY: Thank you, everybody, and welcome to *CenterStage*. Coming out of Notre Dame the scouts evaluated today's guest as a six point five on a nine-point-zero scale. They said, quote, "He can thread the needle, but he usually goes with his primary receiver and forces the ball to him even when he's in the crowd. He's a gutty, cocky type. Doesn't have great tools but could eventually be a starter." Well, this eventual starter went on to be selected to eight Pro Bowls and was twice the NFL's Most Valuable Player. He won four Super Bowls and was elected to the NFL's Seventy-Fifth Anniversary All-Time Team. And today he's also the standard by which all future great quarterbacks are measured. In 2002, he was diagnosed with high blood pressure and has worked since then to create public awareness on the issue and educate people on how they can live with and treat the condition. Please welcome the man they call Joe Cool, Joe Montana. [*Applause*]

MICHAEL KAY: Joe, how you doing?

JOE MONTANA: I'm doing great.

MICHAEL KAY: Now, let's go right back to the beginning. Growing up in Pennsylvania, your father checked you into a peewee league when you were eight years old and you excelled in the league. How important was your dad to your success?

JOE MONTANA: My dad was very important. Every time he'd come home from work I always had a ball. He taught me the fundamentals that he knew about, and some of the things that you don't think about.

MICHAEL KAY: Now, I heard that you had a unique passing drill. What happened with that?

JOE MONTANA: When you're a kid, it's hard to find a lot of kids willing to go run routes for you while you drop back and practice your throwing. So he would always do that, and then he got tired of running around. And my neighbor had a tire swing in the back. So my dad used to make me roll out and throw the ball while the tire was moving, trying to work on accuracy.

MICHAEL KAY: Now, it was starting to be bad times in the rust belt. How was it for kids at that time, was it a depressing time?

JOE MONTANA: Well, I think as a kid you don't really realize what you're living through and what your parents are really going through. Where I grew up, there were [closed] steel mills up and down the river, there was a [shut-down] coal mine in our town. But as a kid you don't really notice, it's just normal.

MICHAEL KAY: Let me throw some names at you, Joe—Johnny Lujack, George Blanda, Johnny Unitas, Terry Hanratty, and Joe Namath. They all come from Pennsylvania, all these great quarterbacks. What's in the water there?

JOE MONTANA: Well, I think it was the beer. [*Laughter*] No, I think it's that blue-collar work ethic. I know my family could never have afforded to send me to college. And so they saw sports as a way to get me out of what they were going through and living through, and trying to make it better for me.

MICHAEL KAY: Now, your high school coach, Jeff Petrucci, said you were born to be a quarterback. He turned an oh-and-nine team into an eight-and-one team. And you got All-American honors as well. When this was all taking place, although you're playing baseball and basketball, are you thinking, "I'm a football player, this is what I want to do"?

JOE MONTANA: I had no idea, really. At that point in time I was thinking I loved basketball. You know, I liked football a lot, but I didn't like practicing it as much as I loved the whole game of basketball.

MICHAEL KAY: Now, you were offered a basketball scholarship to North Carolina State. If you had not been offered a Notre Dame football scholarship, would you have been a basketball player?

JOE MONTANA: I probably would have been a basketball player. But at that point I had no idea what I would do if I didn't get an offer from Notre Dame. There was just something about the aura of Notre Dame. There were a lot of people from western Pennsylvania at Notre Dame at the time also, and I wanted to go there. That was my goal.

MICHAEL KAY: So you're in Notre Dame now, and you were part of Ara Parseghian's last recruiting class. Then he retires for medical reasons and it's Dan Devine you play for. Was it a disappointment never to play for Ara?

JOE MONTANA: Oh, yeah. It was a sad day when Ara had to leave. It was totally understandable, but it was a little disappointing.

MICHAEL KAY: When you first got there, you were the seventh-string quarterback?

JOE MONTANA: I was the seventh freshman string. So there were a lot more guys in front of me.

MICHAEL KAY: How did it not get you down? That's a long way to get to the top.

JOE MONTANA: When I first got there, I was very intimidated by the team that was there; it was probably the biggest team I've ever seen. I mean, you had guys like Mike Fanning, who was six-eight, Steve Niehaus, who was six-five. Even the corners were six-one, one guy was six-three, the other guy was six-two. The safeties were six-two and six-one or six-three, and the linebackers were all huge. And I was running the prep-team stuff, and these guys are in full contact mode. That wasn't fun.

MICHAEL KAY: You end up getting a separated shoulder in preseason in your sophomore year. And then by junior year you're still the third-string quarterback. What's your mind-set? Are you thinking about giving up?

JOE MONTANA: No, not really. I was playing a lot better so I really thought that at some point in time I would have an opportunity.

MICHAEL KAY: Now you get an opportunity. You're playing Purdue in your junior year, the senior quarterback gets hurt. [Finally they bring you in] and that's the first of the great comebacks. You get in late in the third quarter, Notre Dame's down twenty-four to fourteen. Then they win thirty-one to twenty-four, and I guess you never looked back. From that point on you guys roll and you win the national championship. You graduate [with a degree in business administration], and then you go on to the NFL draft. You're third round, eighty-second pick [by the San Francisco 49ers]. Were you surprised you were going that low, did you think you'd go higher?

JOE MONTANA: Well, going into the draft, I really didn't have great numbers. I didn't have the strongest arm, and I was a hundred and ninety pounds, so I wasn't the biggest guy, either. I think a lot of [teams] didn't think I'd make it physically through one season, let alone sixteen or seventeen. I was just happy to be getting an opportunity to get into the NFL.

MICHAEL KAY: [49ers coach] Bill [Walsh] started you slowly, he didn't really play you in the first year. In the second year you're still backing up [Steve] DeBerg, and you get into some games, and then you get into a game where you're down twenty-eight points at halftime, and it's the greatest comeback of all time. Did you know then you could play in the NFL after you engineered that?

JOE MONTANA: Yeah, after that comeback with New Orleans, it was one of those things that told me, "Hey, you can play at this level."

MICHAEL KAY: Now, that year you make the playoffs, you meet the Cowboys. And you were trailing twenty-seven to twenty-one with under five minutes remaining. And then it's "The Catch" to Dwight Clark, one of the most famous plays in NFL history [that eventually won the game]. You go to the Super Bowl and you beat the Bengals twenty-six to twenty-one. That's not a bad first full season for a quarterback. What was that like, winning the Super Bowl?

JOE MONTANA: Well, when I first walked out, it was such a tremendous feeling just to be there. But then once the game got going, it was, it was a real ugly game for us offensively.

MICHAEL KAY: Now, three years later you go to the Super Bowl again. You're fifteen and one in the regular season, you meet the Dolphins, and you beat them. A lot of people say that might have been the best team in NFL history.

JOE MONTANA: I think as an all-round team that was probably the best team. We had some teams that might have been more talented [individually] later on, but together that team played the best that I've seen in a long time.

MICHAEL KAY: And [the 49ers] got even more talented. The next year they get Jerry Rice, so they have Montana and Rice. Did you know right away that this guy is the real deal, that he was gonna be as great as he turned out to be?

JOE MONTANA: It was funny. Bill was telling us about this great wide receiver, he's thrown for touchdowns, he's run for touchdowns, and he's set records for catching touchdowns. Then the first day at practice, the ball was just beating him up, it was just bouncing off of him everywhere. [*Laughter*] But you know, they teach wide receivers that when they catch the ball in practice, to turn and run up the field five or ten yards, just to get used to making that move. Well, the first time Jerry catches the ball, he turns and he sprints as fast as he can go all the way to the end zone! And we sit there and go, "Oh God, look at this rookie trying to impress the coaches." But that's what he did every time he touched the ball in practice, I don't care if it was nine yards or ninety yards, he would run and score a touchdown. So is it a coincidence that he's the NFL all-time touchdown-reception leader? The answer is no, because that's how he worked every day. And the funny thing is, it became contagious to the other guys. John Taylor started doing it every time, and then Roger Craig would do it. Or you'd throw to one of them and all three of them would race to the end zone.

MICHAEL KAY: So in '86 you rupture a disk in your back. Doctors tell you it might be a good idea for you to just give it up. But you don't. You've accomplished a lot by then. Did you really ever consider saying maybe I shouldn't go back?

JOE MONTANA: I thought about it initially when I first found out the seriousness of my injury. But I had played the game so long, and I loved the game. The guy who did the surgery on my back told me, "This could end your career, but it might not. It just depends on how well it heals and what goes on from there. And a lot of it is up to you." So I thought I would at least give it one more try, try to rehabilitate as fast as I possibly could and get back as fast as I could to see whether I could make it or not.

MICHAEL KAY: Now, in '87, Steve Young arrives. You're still battling injuries, trying to come back from the back injury and everything. It's almost like a reverse Montana-DeBerg—now you've got Steve Young waiting to get your job. Steve Young actually was the first guest that we ever had here on *CenterStage* five years ago, and he spoke about how he came over from Tampa Bay to San Francisco and how hard it was to be behind you for four years.

JOE MONTANA: It was easy for me. [*Laughter*]

MICHAEL KAY: Were you guys tight, or did you go against each other? Did you like each other?

JOE MONTANA: With Steve Young it was more of a typical competition for a position that I wasn't really ready to relinquish at that time. We were friends, but when you cross that white line onto the football field or that black line onto the basketball court, you're competing for a position. And unless you're willing to sit on the bench and let someone else play, you can't be a friend till you go back on the other side of that line. Every time you walk on the field, it's a competition, and it didn't matter if it was Steve Young or Steve DeBerg or Steve Bono, it was all the same. I wasn't ready to let anybody take my position till I was ready for it.

MICHAEL KAY: Now, that year you guys were on the verge of not making the playoffs, but you end up coming back. You drive them to the playoffs, they go to the Super Bowl. You're down sixteen–thirteen with three ten left, and you end up driving ninety-two yards to win the game. You continue to roll with the 49ers, but then you miss all of the '91 season and all but one game of the '92 season [because of an elbow injury]. And finally Steve Young takes over. Now, you had always wanted to retire a 49er, and it doesn't work out that way. Were you angry that it didn't work out the way you wanted it to?

JOE MONTANA: Well, I was just disappointed that I didn't get an opportunity to at least compete for the job. Typically when a guy gets hurt, he gets his job back [after he recovers]. I understood that Steve was playing well, but the last year that I played was one of the best statistical years I had. When I came back, I said I should at least get the opportunity to compete for the job. And they said that they weren't gonna do that, I was going to have be second team and be quiet. I said okay, then I'd rather go somewhere else and get back on the field.

MICHAEL KAY: So you end up getting traded to Kansas City, and that's what you wanted because you wanted to play. How difficult was it to leave San Francisco?

JOE MONTANA: Oh, it was hard leaving. I had been there my whole career at that point. The organization was great, the owner was tremendous, and the fans were great. We had accomplished a lot. That being said, it came down to two teams—Phoenix and Kansas City. All the money was in Phoenix, but they had no offensive line. That year they went through three quarterbacks with injuries, and my agent said that I might not make it through the year. So Kansas City seemed to be the likely choice because it was another great organization, a great team. And they had a great opportunity to get back to the Super Bowl.

MICHAEL KAY: You were eleven and five. And you play the Bills. If you win that game, you go to the Super Bowl. How disappointed were you that [you lost]? I mean, you could have showed everybody that they made the wrong choice.

JOE MONTANA: The most disappointing thing was that we didn't play in Kansas City with fifty degrees and sunshine, instead of Buffalo and twenty-eight degrees and light rain. I couldn't throw the ball from here to that doorway accurately [in that weather].

MICHAEL KAY: The next year you lose in the wild card to the Dolphins. But that same year you played the 49ers and Steve Young and you won. That was probably very sweet for you, wasn't it?

JOE MONTANA: Oh, it's always good to beat your friends. [*Laughter*]

MICHAEL KAY: After that second year in Kansas City, did you know that that was your final season?

JOE MONTANA: After the season, yes, I knew it was close. All I was thinking about was my kids at that point, and the other injuries. Going to practice became work, and when I'm thinking that way in my mind, it's not the same. And I wasn't preparing the same.

MICHAEL KAY: What do you miss most about playing?

JOE MONTANA: The excitement of the game. I just wish everyone could have an opportunity to experience it, the competition, the challenge.

MICHAEL KAY: Now, what meant more to you, being inducted into the Pro Football Hall of Fame or having your number retired by the 49ers?

JOE MONTANA: The Hall of Fame. I mean, it's great having your number retired. But the Hall of Fame is something that puts you in a pretty elite group of players.

MICHAEL KAY: What do you want your legacy to be, Joe? What do you think it's going to be?

JOE MONTANA: Well, I don't really think about it that much. I just hope people will think, "Hey, there's a guy who enjoyed what he did, who loved playing the sport and was a winner." That's all you can ask for.

MICHAEL KAY: Joe, thanks so much.

JOE MONTANA: You bet, my pleasure.

Bobby Orr

Asked which sport I have the weakest knowledge of, I'd say it's a draw between soccer and hockey. Whenever we book a guest from either sport, I double down on my prep because I never want to insult the guest or embarrass myself. My usual preparation for each show is to read a voluminous amount of material. My producers usually send me five hundred to six hundred pages on each guest, and I try to learn everything I can about him or her. Someone once told me that you should never ask any question in an interview to which you don't know the answer. I don't *totally* buy into that theory because you want to take the conversation to new places. If you only ask questions you know the answers to, then you haven't peeled back the cover to reveal what's new and interesting. But I do agree that your research should be exhaustive so the person doesn't surprise you with something that's already public knowledge.

When we booked Bobby Orr, I got to work. I wanted to give him the respect his incredible accomplishments deserved. This man is one of the greatest hockey players of all time. He spent twelve years in the NHL, ten with the Boston Bruins, where he won two Stanley Cups. It borders on the tragic that his brilliant career light was extinguished at age thirty because of injuries that destroyed his body, particularly his left knee.

But, as you can tell in the following interview, Orr is not one to feel sorry for himself or lament that he might have left something out of his résumé because of the physical toll the game took. He continued to be a major influencer in the sport after retirement, and he began representing other players as an agent in 1996.

For someone with his accomplishments, he was friendly, down-to-earth, and simply a joy to be around. At the end of the interview, we walked offstage together, and Orr put his arm on my right shoulder and said, "I really enjoyed that. I love to do these types of interviews with people I know truly love the sport, and I could tell you do. Thank you for that." I was speechless and almost felt guilty that I'd put one over on this great man, but then it became a source of pride for me and the show's staff that we'd prepped to the point that I came off as a true hockey expert, someone who lived and breathed the sport. My satisfaction had nothing to do with ego, but rather, pride that we'd worked and created a fascinating discussion with one of the greatest to ever play his sport.

The Interview

MICHAEL KAY: Thank you, everybody, and welcome to *CenterStage*. Today's guest grew up on the frozen ponds of Ontario, Canada. He enjoyed fishing and playing baseball, but hockey was his true passion. At the age of fourteen, he left home to begin his journey through junior hockey. And after turning eighteen, he set out to Boston, where he joined the Bruins. He was the NHL's rookie of the year and later helped lead Boston to two Stanley Cup championships. Despite a career cut short due to repeated knee injuries, his impact was great. He used his speed, shooting skills, and playmaking abilities to revolutionize his position. He led the NHL in scoring twice and remains the only defenseman to do so. He also won three consecutive league MVP awards and was the youngest player to ever be inducted into the Hockey Hall of Fame. This ultimate teammate is renowned for his modesty, generosity, and fierce loyalty. As the head of the Orr Hockey Group he serves as a player agent, and as an outspoken adviser on youth hockey. His new book is *Orr: My Story*. Please welcome an athlete who redefined the game, arguably the greatest hockey player of all time, number four, Bobby Orr. Welcome, Bobby.

BOBBY ORR: Nice to see you, nice being here.

MICHAEL KAY: All right, so number four, Bobby Orr, it kind of rolls off the tongue. Did you ask for number four because it rhymed?

BOBBY ORR: Oh, no, no, no, in those days you didn't ask for your number. You would take what they gave you.

MICHAEL KAY: Now, in reading your book, you downplay your achievements hockey-wise. I said you are arguably the greatest hockey player of all time. Some people might say Gretzky, some people might say Howe. Do you say Orr?

BOBBY ORR: [*Laughs*] I don't even think about it.

MICHAEL KAY: Really?

BOBBY ORR: No. I was playing a game, and I was being paid to play a game, and I always looked at it as a game. I never looked at it as work. I was having fun, and it was pretty special. But I don't spend much time thinking about my position on the ladder. It's not that important to me. I wanted to go out every night and, and play my game. I mean, I had a level that I was expected to play at. That's what I tried to do, and you know, we did okay.

MICHAEL KAY: You did more than okay. You were a defenseman, but you were a different kind of defenseman, you scored a lot. Did anybody ever try to change you and say, "No, no, no, that's not the way this position is played"?

BOBBY ORR: It was a lot different back when I was coming up, we didn't have a draft as it is today, so the NHL teams owned junior teams, and they would go around signing players to play on their junior teams, and the Bruins signed me at fourteen. I was offensive-minded, so I went through four years of junior, being owned by the Bruins, their coaches are coaching me, and even into the pros they didn't ask me to change my style. If I had had to change my style, it wouldn't have been any fun. It's how I always played, and they thought I would be most effective continuing to play my style.

MICHAEL KAY: Now, a former teammate of yours, Terry O'Reilly, once described you as a very private, very shy guy who just happened to be the best hockey player in the world. It's been said that all great athletes have a mean streak. Do you have a mean streak?

BOBBY ORR: My wife has often said I'm not easy to live with. [*Laughter*] Early on I was challenged to see if I was going to stand up, and I stood up. And I think that helped. As the seasons went on, they stayed away from me a little more.

MICHAEL KAY: So, it all started in Parry Sound, Ontario. I want to know where exactly is that, and how was life going at 124 Great North Way?

BOBBY ORR: [*Laughs*] Parry Sound is a hundred and forty miles north of Toronto. Winters were tough. We did all our skating on Georgian Bay, the river, parking lots, the school rink, just the guys, no coaches. That's how we learned to play the game.

MICHAEL KAY: What did Mom and Dad do?

BOBBY ORR: Mom and Dad worked two or three jobs. My father was a wonderful man, pretty good hockey player, too, he tells me. But my mother was the rock. The thing they taught us was hard work, and the Orr kids always worked. We didn't have a whole lot. We had a house that was very cold in the wintertime, but there was love in the family, there was support in the family, and my parents worked very, very hard to take care of us.

MICHAEL KAY: Any favorite teams, favorite players, growing up?

BOBBY ORR: I loved Tim Horton, the late Tim Horton. Of course Gordie [Howe] and Bobby [Hull] were just starting, and they were the big guys.

MICHAEL KAY: My research indicates that you were always the fastest skater when you played as a kid, and you were a great puck handler. Were you a big kid?

BOBBY ORR: No. The first year I went to play junior, when I was fourteen, Oshawa and Niagara Falls were the two junior teams that the Bruins owned in the East. I can still remember going by train to Niagara Falls, and when we arrived, we had to get in a line to weigh in and give our position. So I got on the scale, I was a hundred and twenty-five pounds and [playing] defense, and I heard snickering behind me.

MICHAEL KAY: You were a member of the Parry Sound Shamrocks, and your coach had the idea of you playing defense. Why?

BOBBY ORR: I think he wanted me on the ice more. So one shift I would play forward, and the next shift I would go back on defense.

MICHAEL KAY: Did you like playing forward at all, would you rather have played—?

BOBBY ORR: I didn't care where I played. I would have just played anywhere.

MICHAEL KAY: Now, at what point, Bobby, did NHL scouts start to take notice of you, that you knew they were around?

BOBBY ORR: I went to a town called Gananoque, which was east of

Toronto, to play in a playoff series, and the Bruins were there scout-
ing a couple of other players who they were trying to sign for their
team in Oshawa. We happened to be playing them in the playoffs,
and all the Bruins scouts were there, and even the owner of the Bruins was there, because it was one of their teams. So that's how they
found me. It was really a mistake.

MICHAEL KAY: Bobby, explain to everybody what a C Form is and,
and why the fourteenth birthday was so important when you were
growing up.

BOBBY ORR: A C Form was a contract you signed back then, and
once you signed that C Form you were owned by that professional
team.

MICHAEL KAY: At the age of fourteen?

BOBBY ORR: At the age of fourteen. You had to be fourteen. And
when I turned fourteen, I signed a C Form with the Boston Bruins,
and they would own my rights. We didn't have a draft as it is today,
and from that day on I was owned by the Bruins, unless they traded
or sold me or released me.

MICHAEL KAY: I mean, you're fourteen! Did you enjoy your youth?
Did you do birthday parties and kid stuff or—?

BOBBY ORR: Did I enjoy my youth? Oh, absolutely, absolutely. But I
was the happiest when I was on the ice.

MICHAEL KAY: Did you have a concern, Bobby, I mean, you're essentially playing professional hockey at fourteen, and you're just at a
hundred and twenty-five pounds, did you think, "How am I going
to get it done against these bigger guys?"

BOBBY ORR: Never thought about it. I really didn't. The key to my
game was skating, and I could skate. I mean, I was beat-up. I'd go
home Monday morning and I'd have shiners going into class, and
the other kids would go, "Ooh!" Skating was my game, and I could
avoid a lot, but, hey, hockey's a physical game, and you will be hit.

MICHAEL KAY: Now, your second year in Oshawa, you're living away
from home, and you're going to high school and playing hockey
there. Do you ever get homesick?

BOBBY ORR: Oh, yes. I was very homesick, but I never wanted to quit.
We didn't have a lot, so I was only allowed to call home once a week,
and I'd cry most of the time. But that's where I was the happiest. I

mean, I couldn't wait to get on the ice, I couldn't wait to get a stick in my hands. I was lucky in that the team, the players I played with, were wonderful. I was playing against nineteen- and twenty-year-olds, and my teammates were protective, and were very supportive and looked after me.

MICHAEL KAY: Now, I also read that when you were a kid, you decided that you did not want to wear socks under your skates. Did you not want to wash the socks?

BOBBY ORR: There are two things that I'm asked about a lot—my socks, and no tape on my stick. I'd like to tell you two exciting stories. No socks because I forgot them one night in junior hockey. I forgot to put them on, and that was that. The stick, I just like the feel without the tape on my blade. Not really exciting. [*Laughter*]

MICHAEL KAY: How often do you skate now?

BOBBY ORR: I don't play in games. But I will go out and I do clinics with the kids. I don't skate real fast, but as long as I keep my blades on the ice, I'm fine.

MICHAEL KAY: Let's go back just a little bit. When you make the Bruins team, you get your number four, your first professional game was against Gordie Howe. What was that like?

BOBBY ORR: First of all, he's my favorite player. I don't know if we'll ever see another Gordie Howe. I met Gordie when I stood in line for an autograph, and then I went fishing with him, and he said, "Don't forget, kid, if you make the NHL and we play against each other, watch my elbows." And he was right. My first game was against Detroit, I went into the offensive zone, I'm going around, I make a pass, and I'm watching my pretty pass, and next thing you know, I'm laying on the ice. Gordie hit me. [*Laughter*]

MICHAEL KAY: You knew you were an NHL player at that point?

BOBBY ORR: When Gordie hits you, it's great.

MICHAEL KAY: All right, now, first game, you also had your first goal and your first fight. How about the fight?

BOBBY ORR: I was challenged, and I had to stand up, and I stood up.

MICHAEL KAY: There's so much discussion in hockey now because there's so much concern about concussions, that there shouldn't be fighting. What do you think?

BOBBY ORR: I'm really frightened about taking fighting completely out of the game. The fear of getting beat up, in my mind, is a great deterrent to getting silly on the ice. I don't believe we need fighting for the game to survive. I'm just afraid if we take it out completely, there's a lot of guys that are going to get real brave, and I think we're going to see a lot of chippy hockey.

MICHAEL KAY: Prior to your third NHL season, which was '68/'69, you underwent a second knee operation. At this point, Bobby, are you starting to think, "This is going to give me problems, my knees"?

BOBBY ORR: No, it's funny, when you're young, you think you're indestructible. We didn't have the kind of surgery they have today, we didn't have the therapy, the programs that they have now. I thought I was fine. I probably came back too early, without proper rehab. But I wanted to play. It wasn't the team forcing me back, it was me saying, "Hey, I'm playing."

MICHAEL KAY: Now, in that season you suffered a different sort of injury, the only one that you had in your hockey career, a concussion [after being checked by Pat Quinn]. Right?

BOBBY ORR: Well, I was knocked out. But I played the next night. I don't remember having the symptoms, being nauseous or dizzy. I honestly don't remember that. Then we're back in Boston—back then we stayed in a hotel, we didn't stay at home—and I walked in the lobby of the hotel, and there was a rather rough, tough-looking gentleman with a hat, coat, collar up, and he walked over to me and said, "Would you like us to take care of that guy?" And I said, "I'll take care of Pat myself." [*Laughter*]

MICHAEL KAY: Did you take care of him?

BOBBY ORR: We had a little tiff somewhere along the line. But Patty's a friend, we laugh about it a lot today.

MICHAEL KAY: Now, you don't like talking about all the things that you've done. But you've done some very, very special things for people, and you keep it on the down-low. You've done charity work with Boston's Children's Hospital, others that deal with multiple sclerosis as well. I know you're involved now with the Chevrolet Safe and Fun Hockey Program for Kids. What is that and can you tell us about it?

BOBBY ORR: We bring in a hundred kids, or a hundred and twenty kids, their parents, coaches, and so on, and we talk about being respectful, being responsible, teach the fundamentals of the game.

It's been written that kids are very impressionable at an early age, and we're trying to instill good values at an early age, and it's gone very, very well. We are really doing it for the adults as much as the kids, getting the adults to understand their responsibility. We're putting our kids in your hands and it's a great responsibility for you, and you should teach good values. We just think if we instill those good values early, that the kids will remember and carry them with them, whether they're at the rink, ball field, school, at home.

MICHAEL KAY: A lot of athletes aren't very nice, they almost feel like they're above people. Why are you an exception? And why are athletes not that great sometimes with the public?

BOBBY ORR: I'm not a role model, but I happen to believe that we have a responsibility. If we can put a smile on someone's face or raise money for a cause, then I think it's a responsibility we all have. We're not perfect, I'm not perfect, we've made mistakes, we've done some things we wish we hadn't done. But overall we need to try to make things better.

MICHAEL KAY: Bobby, it has been an absolute pleasure, thank you so much.

BOBBY ORR: Thank you.

Paul Simon

When I interview a guest on *CenterStage*, I'm about three feet away from him or her. You can tell by body language if I'm comfortable and if the guest is comfortable. If the guest is leaning back, then all is good, it has turned into a conversation. If the guest is tense and tight, it becomes a fight. I usually lean forward in my chair because I become so engrossed in what's being said, I don't want to miss a word.

When Paul Simon came on the show, I was in awe. This was Paul Simon! He is one of America's greatest singers and songwriters. When he came out onstage, he had a guitar resting on a stand right next to his chair. I wasn't sure if it was there as a visual prop or to serve as a pacifier for Simon during breaks. Instead, he used it as an instrument (pun intended) to tell his stories and relate his process in writing songs.

Simon would be in the middle of an answer and pick up the guitar and start strumming away, adding depth to what he was saying. If you ever watch a tape of this interview on YouTube, you might be able to see the wonder in my eyes. I was this close to Simon as he was singing, and I was daydreaming about how lucky I was to be doing what I was doing. I was sitting a few feet away from musical genius as he was telling his stories. I'd occasionally have to snap myself to attention so I didn't drift too far away and miss following up on what he was saying.

Simon was there because he was a huge Yankee fan and had seen the show on YES and had heard me countless times during games. And, trust me, he's not your typical celebrity fan. He knows everything about the team, and when he comes to a game, you'll see him remain in his seat, no matter the score, for the game's entirety.

His stories about his humble beginnings and the start of Simon and Garfunkel and the subsequent breakups and makeups were a window into modern musical history. This interview is certainly in my top ten list of favorites and is an essential archive for anyone researching the musical genre Simon is a part of.

My only regret about this excellent interview is that we didn't have cameras rolling after the show in the dressing room, where Simon sat down and jammed with former Yankee center fielder Bernie Williams, an accomplished guitarist. Bernie was there to record our next show that day. The two were so comfortable with each other, and the stories and the music flowed so effortlessly. Again, I realized how lucky I was to have this gig.

The Interview

MICHAEL KAY: Thank you, everybody, and welcome to *CenterStage*. Today's guest was raised in Queens, New York, where he began his music career with a high school friend [named Art Garfunkel]. Heavily influenced by the Everly Brothers, as teenagers they scored a minor hit, "Hey Schoolgirl," before drifting apart. They would eventually reunite in 1964, and Columbia Records offered them a recording contract. Together they recorded four highly influential albums before parting ways in 1970. As a solo artist, he continued to make cutting-edge records and enjoyed huge success, incorporating musical styles from around the world. In 1986, he released a landmark album, *Graceland*, which featured the use of African rhythms. He has appeared in movies like *Annie Hall* and wrote the title song for the film *The Graduate*. In 2006, *Time* magazine called him "one of the one hundred people who shape our world." And by the way, he is also a longtime devoted Yankees fan. Please welcome a twice-inducted member of the Rock and Roll Hall of Fame, the legendary Paul Simon. [*Applause*]

PAUL SIMON: Thank you.

MICHAEL KAY: Paul, you were born in Newark, New Jersey, but you grew up in Kew Gardens, Queens. What was it like in the Simon household? What did your parents do?

PAUL SIMON: My father was a musician, a bass player.

MICHAEL KAY: So were you preordained to be a musician 'cause your dad was?

PAUL SIMON: Probably—in the same way I was preordained to be a Yankee fan. [*Laughter*]

MICHAEL KAY: When you were growing up, did you play sports? And were you good?

PAUL SIMON: Yeah, I was good. I was best at baseball. And I played All-Queens Second Team in high school. Then I played a little bit at Queens College. But then I stopped because I was more interested in music, and besides, by the time I got into college the other players were too good.

MICHAEL KAY: Now, was it always the Yankees for you, Paul? And when did it start? How old were you?

PAUL SIMON: Since I was seven. The first Yankee game I went to, it was probably '51, because it was the last year that DiMaggio played. You know, it's a very strange thing, the DiMaggio aspect of my life, because even though I was fan of his, DiMaggio wasn't my all-time favorite player. But then I wrote a famous song that had Joe DiMaggio in it. Then we met, and my life and his became intertwined because of that song. I first met him in a restaurant in New York, and I went over to meet him with some trepidation because I had heard that he didn't like the song. So I came over and I said, "Hi, I'm Paul Simon, and I wrote 'Mrs. Robinson.'" And then we started to talk, and he finally said, "What's that all about? 'Where have you gone, Joe DiMaggio?' I didn't go anywhere." [*Laughter*] Then we met again a couple years later, and he told me that he loved "Mrs. Robinson," but his favorite song was "Old Friends." [*Sings*] "'Preserve your memories / They are all that's left you.'" I ended up writing a piece for the *Times* when he died. And then I sang in center field when they unveiled the monument for him. So I had a lot to do with Joe DiMaggio.

MICHAEL KAY: But you loved Mickey [Mantle], and you were probably too young to really love Joe. So why, when you wrote "Mrs. Robinson" . . . ?

PAUL SIMON: I have no idea. You know, when I wrote the line—and this is true of a lot of my writing—one second before I write it, I have no idea what it's going to be. And then it appears and I say, "Oh, that's interesting." And in that case, I thought, "Well, that's an interesting line, but what does it have to do with Mrs. Robinson and *The Graduate*?" And I thought, "Well, I don't know what it has to do with it, but I like it so much I am just gonna keep it." And you know, it might be the most famous line that I have written so far. But I don't know why I wrote it. I was doing a talk show once, and Mickey Mantle and Whitey Ford came on, and Mickey said to me, "How come you wrote 'Where have you gone, Joe DiMaggio'? Why didn't you write about me?" [*Laughter*]

MICHAEL KAY: Well, it's hard to talk about your career without talking about Art Garfunkel. When did you meet him, at what age?

PAUL SIMON: I was in the fourth grade. And they had a school assembly where they would let kids come up and perform. And Art Garfunkel gets up onstage and he sings this song called "They Tried to Tell Us We're Too Young," and everyone just loved it, they ate it up. I was thinking, "Hey, maybe this is something I oughta try, I wonder if I can do that?" And that's how I started singing.

MICHAEL KAY: Who were your rock-and-roll heroes growing up?

PAUL SIMON: My heroes were Elvis Presley, the Everly Brothers, Chuck Berry. Various doo-wop groups from around the city. . . .

MICHAEL KAY: Did you ever meet Elvis?

PAUL SIMON: I never met Elvis. I saw him sing one of my songs once, but I never met him. He sang "Bridge over Troubled Water." When I think of the people who have sung my songs, it's pretty amazing to me to think that Elvis Presley sang one of my songs, and Ray Charles, and Aretha Franklin, and Frank Sinatra sang "Mrs. Robinson." Actually, I got into a fight with Frank Sinatra. . . . [*Laughter*]

MICHAEL KAY: You have to tell me how that went.

PAUL SIMON: Well, fortunately, as you can see, I'm still here, so it wasn't a literal fight. [*Laughter*] But here's what happened. He recorded "Mrs. Robinson," and somebody rewrote the words for him. And they wrote it in a very Rat Pack kind of style, you know? So it's [*sings*] "Ring ding a ding, Mrs. Robinson, [*snaps fingers*] Jilly loves you more than you will know." [*Laughter*] So at the time I was being a little too full of myself, and I said, "I don't like that, you can't go changing my words. You didn't ask permission, you can't put the record out." Then I get a call from some guy at a record company who says, "Please don't do this to me, man. It's my fault, I did it. Please, *I have a family!*" [*Laughter*] So I said, "Go ahead, I don't care."

MICHAEL KAY: You started writing at fourteen, and in the summer of 1957 you [and Art Garfunkel] cut a twenty-five-dollar demo for a song called "Hey Schoolgirl." And that's your first hit.

PAUL SIMON: Right. There was a place where you could go in and make a record for twenty-five dollars. So we went and we sang our song, Artie and I, and there was a guy waiting to use the demo place next. He had a record company and he heard us and he said, "I would like to sign you." And he signed us and they put the record out. And the most popular show for kids at that point was Dick Clark's *American Bandstand*. They would put up new songs, and then the kids would rate the songs: "Uh, I'll give it a ninety-five. It's easy to dance to, it had a good beat," you know? [*Laughter*] So our song got on the show, and everyone gave it a ninety-five. And we were watching on television, and it was unbelievable. We were in high school! Then we were invited to go down to Philadelphia to be on *American Bandstand*. I mean, that was a big deal, to get on a train and go to Philadelphia. And I'll never forget this, we walk into a dressing room, and sitting in front of the mirror combing his hair is Jerry Lee Lewis.

MICHAEL KAY: Now, you guys were called Tom and Jerry then, right? How come Tom and Jerry, and not Simon and Garfunkel?

PAUL SIMON: Yeah. Well, this is the fifties. Nobody had their real name, and all ethnic names were anglicized. There really wasn't any possibility that you would call a group Simon and Garfunkel. In fact, when we were signed to Columbia Records, there was a big debate about what name they should call us—and this was in the sixties.

MICHAEL KAY: Now, why did you guys separate after that first song? Just went your separate ways?

PAUL SIMON: Well, we graduated from high school. He went to Columbia, I went to Queens College. But then we met again back in the old neighborhood where we were living. I don't remember why it is that we started to sing together again, but we did.

MICHAEL KAY: So how did you get to the Columbia Records deal in 1963?

PAUL SIMON: So I go up to Columbia Records, where there was a man named Tom Wilson. He was producing Bob Dylan at the time, but he also was producing a kind of a pseudo-folk group called the Pilgrims. I had made a demo of "The Sound of Silence" and a couple other songs. And he said, "You know, maybe this would be good."

MICHAEL KAY: Now, is this just you, Paul, or is it also Garfunkel?

PAUL SIMON: No, just me. And he said, "Maybe I could record that song with the Pilgrims." And I said, "You know, I sing with this other guy, and we could do this song. Would you be interested in hearing us do this?" He said, "Yeah, bring him in." So we came in, Artie and I, and we sang the song and they signed us. And [eventually] it became a number one record.

MICHAEL KAY: And you guys end up turning out a lot of hit records. Then you end up writing the soundtrack for *The Graduate*. When you wrote it, did you say, "This is great. This is gonna be a huge hit."

PAUL SIMON: No, I didn't think that. Nor did anybody think that about *The Graduate*. [*Laughter*]

MICHAEL KAY: Well, it became a very big hit. And it kind of catapulted you. It won the Grammy for Record of the Year. Then you have an album, *Bookends*, and you start to work on the final album with Art Garfunkel, *Bridge over Troubled Water*. What happened during this time that made you guys split up?

PAUL SIMON: Well, first of all, we were always arguing anyway, since we were kids. We would argue, and then we would say, "You know what? Let's just move on." But we were arguing a lot. And I think part of the reason was that after *The Graduate*, Mike Nichols's next picture was a movie called *Catch-22*. So he said to us, "I would like both of you guys to be in this movie, *Catch-22*." So we said, "Oh, fabulous, oh, wow."

MICHAEL KAY: Did you want to be an actor?

PAUL SIMON: No, I didn't want to be actor, I just wanted to be in a movie. [*Laughter*] But then over the summer, Mike called me up and he said, "You know what? The script is so long that we have to eliminate your character." So I said, "Well, okay," and he said, "So I suppose that probably means that we would have to eliminate Artie's character." And I say, "No, no, no, don't be silly." So Artie goes off to be in *Catch-22*. I don't even know if I ever told anybody this actually. . . .

MICHAEL KAY: An exclusive *CenterStage* moment. [*Laughter*]

PAUL SIMON: [*Sighs, laughs*] Anyway, so while we were making *Bridge over Troubled Water*, and he was finishing up *Catch-22*, without telling me he took a job in *Carnal Knowledge*. I didn't know anything about it. So when I heard about it, I said to Artie, "Why didn't you tell me?" He said, "Well, I thought if I told you, that you would [be mad at me]." And I say, "What if I was mad at you? I'd be entitled to be mad, if I want to be mad." And it's one of our fights. [*Laughter*] About nothing, you know? Typical. Anyway, we broke up. But we would have broken up anyway. That's the destiny of duos. It's in the nature of partnerships.

MICHAEL KAY: This is a harsh question. Do you just not like him?

PAUL SIMON: No, I love him. I love the guy. But where I was going musically, we would have ended up breaking up shortly afterwards anyway. Because if you look at the next album that I did, my first solo album, it has hits like "Me and Julio Down by the Schoolyard," "Mother and Child Reunion," rhythm stuff, all different grooves and different things. But that wasn't really Artie's interest.

MICHAEL KAY: So why do you keep getting back together?

PAUL SIMON: Well, when we first went our separate ways, from time to time we used to just show up at each other's show and sing a couple of songs. And it was no big deal. It was kinda fun. Then a promoter in New York, a guy named Ron Delsener, came to me and he said, "Would you like to do a concert in Central Park?" And I said, "Yeah, I would love to do a concert in Central Park." At that point, I think Barbra Streisand was the only one that had done it. It was a really big deal. And I decided it had to be a Simon and Garfunkel show. So we get back together, we do the show in the park, and it was such a big hit. But it was typical of us. We come up, we see half a million people out there, and we had never played in front of half a million people. Then we came offstage after it was over, and I said to Artie, "Well, what do you think?" And he said, "Disaster." [*Laughter*] Really, on a certain level, you cannot find two more clueless people in all the world. I mean, really. [*Laughter*] And so then we went off on tour, 'cause it was such a big hit. And of course, we hated it. We hated each other, we were fighting the whole time. So it wasn't fun. But then we did it again, maybe ten years later, we did a show at Madison Square Garden. And then we got into the worst fight of our lives, a really, really nasty fight. A fight that was so nasty that we didn't speak for ten years.

MICHAEL KAY: You didn't speak for ten years?

PAUL SIMON: Yeah. But finally I thought, "This is ridiculous. I have known this guy since I was eleven, and one of us is liable to drop dead, you know?"

MICHAEL KAY: Can I ask you what the fight was about, that caused a ten-year riff?

PAUL SIMON: You can ask, but I'm not gonna tell you.

MICHAEL KAY: All right. [*Laughter*]

PAUL SIMON: So we said, "Okay, let's go and do this one more time." And everyone said, "They'll never last. They'll never be able to make it through." But we were both determined that this was going to be about repairing a lifelong friendship, you know? I'm not saying that there was no tension [*laughs*] during the thing. But it was hilarious. He is hilarious, really. You should be partners with him sometime, you'll know what I'm saying.

MICHAEL KAY: Now, we talked about the solo career. I mean, so many unbelievable, iconic hits. It began in 1972, but let's fast-forward all the way to 1986 and *Graceland*, which was really a groundbreaking album. It went places that people hadn't gone before, and it's still to this day an iconic album. When you were making it, did you know, "This is special, this is going to be received well," or was it just a passion project for you?

PAUL SIMON: I knew it was special. I had no idea whether it was gonna be received well. I was thinking when I made it, "I wouldn't be surprised if this was a really big hit. And I wouldn't be surprised if this was a complete flop." If it was a big hit, I can't say I am surprised because I am in love with this kind of music. And if nobody gets it, I can't say I'd be surprised, you know?

MICHAEL KAY: Now, what's the connection with Graceland, which obviously is Elvis's mansion?

PAUL SIMON: Oh, there is no connection. Well, I shouldn't say there is no connection. It's a subterranean connection, really. When I had the track to "Graceland," I took it home and started to work on it. I'm trying to make up words and make up sounds, and I'm singing [*sings*], "'Well, you know, I am going to Graceland . . . and Graceland . . .'" And of course, I don't use that, because it's got nothing to do with anything. [*Sings*] "And Graceland, Graceland . . ." Well, like, about three months into it, I said, "Man, I can't stop singing 'I'm going to Graceland.'" I said, "I better go to Graceland, because I have never even been there." [*Laughter*] And maybe there is some reason that I am singing this, you know? This is like a mystery. I was in Louisiana, recording a zydeco tune that's on *Graceland*. And I rented a car and I drove from Louisiana, up Highway Sixty-One, heading up to Memphis. Man, it's an adventure. So I went to Graceland and got in line, I didn't tell anybody who I was, I didn't want any special treatment. I walked around, walked through the place, and I thought, "Well, this is not much. It's supposed to be this incredible mansion, but it's not." So I'm not really being impressed at all, and I was a big Elvis Presley fan, as I said. And then I come out and there are the graves of the Presley family. And I'm reading the plaque and it says, "Elvis Presley, whose voice and music touched the hearts of millions of people all over the world." And I just started to weep. It was a profoundly emotional moment for me. And I began to think of the song as a search for some healing state of grace. And so the song became a story and a song, and that metaphor grew in my mind to encompass the entire album.

MICHAEL KAY: What's the best piece of advice anyone ever gave you?

PAUL SIMON: Well, when I was a kid, I had written this song, and it came out and it wasn't a hit or anything, and I was complaining about it, how hard I had worked on it. And my father said to me, "Paul, let me tell you something. They don't give you an A just for effort."

MICHAEL KAY: This has been so much fun. Thank you so much.

Jon Bon Jovi

Jon Bon Jovi appeared on *CenterStage* in January of 2004 to talk about his involvement with the Arena Football League. He was the founder and majority owner of the Philadelphia Soul, which is not bad work when you consider that owning that team was a hobby, a side job. Bon Jovi was, and still is all these years later, a legitimate rock-and-roll superstar, fronting the band that bears his name. The group, out of New Jersey, has sold almost 150 million albums worldwide, and their soaring anthems have served as the backdrop for several generations.

But despite his prolific musical career, Bon Jovi loves sports and has always wanted to buy an NFL team, making it to the final round of bidders for the Buffalo Bills before they were sold to the Pegula family in 2014.

Back in 2004, Bon Jovi's involvement with the AFL was obviously just a stepping-stone to what he hoped would be ownership of an NFL franchise. So far, that has eluded him, but it has been a small speed bump in what has been an amazing life.

Bon Jovi came to the *CenterStage* studio without an entourage and interacted with ease with our entire crew. He was engaging during the interview, telling stories of his prolific career in music, all the while exhibiting an incredible down-to-earth persona that seemed strange coming from someone of such stature.

At the end of the hour you definitely had a sense of what made Bon Jovi go, but you also felt that you had a bond with him. He wasn't just *telling* you his story; he was *involving* you in his story. Simply put, you felt invested in him and got the sense he was invested in you and what you were about.

A few months after the interview I attended an event thrown by the AFL at which the franchises and their owners were presented. I'd been telling my colleagues how great a guy Bon Jovi had been on *Center-Stage*, and a couple of them came to the event with me. They joked that Bon Jovi would have no idea who I was if he ran into me that night. They said they'd give me a hundred bucks if he even acknowledged me with a head nod. I refused to take the bait because I figured someone that famous would never remember everyone who ever interviewed him. My friends called me gutless, but I just thought I was smart.

After the ceremonies onstage, the event turned into a cocktail party where the owners mingled among the guests. I was standing off to the side with my friends when Bon Jovi noticed me, walked over, and said, "Hey, Michael, good to see you again. I really enjoyed the interview we did a couple of months ago. A lot of people told me they thought it was great." We talked a while longer, and I realized he was the same guy we had onstage. In what was perhaps the secret sauce to his success, his on-camera self was no different from his real-life persona.

Had I known that, I would have had a hundred more bucks in my pocket.

The Interview

MICHAEL KAY: Jon Bon Jovi has worn many hats throughout his career, and he keeps adding new ones. For almost twenty years he's headed one of the world's top rock bands, with megahits such as "Runaway," "You Give Love a Bad Name," "Livin' on a Prayer," and "It's My Life." Plus the solo hit "Blaze of Glory" from the *Young Guns II* soundtrack. The band's record sales are at the one hundred million mark. And they've sold out arenas around the world. Jon the actor has also received critical acclaim, including roles in the films *U-571* and *Pay It Forward*, and stints on the TV shows *Ally McBeal* and *Sex and the City*. Those that know him well know that he lives and breathes football, so it's only fitting that he's taken this love one big step further and is fulfilling a dream as co-owner of the Phila-delphia Soul of the Arena Football League. Please let's welcome to *CenterStage* a true Renaissance man. [*Applause*]

MICHAEL KAY: Where did the love affair with football start?

JON BON JOVI: At my house it was a common bond I could have with my dad. There was one thing we had in common, which was the love of the Giants—depending on what year it was.

MICHAEL KAY: Now, tell me about your Giant memories. Anything that stands out?

JON BON JOVI: The suffering. [*Laughs*] And then the memories of the first time I played the stadium, I'm in the house of the Giants, and playing at a Giants game, and being the only band that's ever played at a Giants game at halftime. I've also had a long-standing relationship with some of the coaching staff and got to know a lot of the Giants over the years.

MICHAEL KAY: All athletes seem to want to be musicians, and all musicians seem to want to be athletes. You started out wanting to be an athlete, and then you didn't have that growth spurt. But you once said that when you played your high school dance, it was cooler than being a quarterback. How come?

JON BON JOVI: Well, it's hard to kiss a girl with a face mask on. [*Laughter*]

MICHAEL KAY: Did you get into the music because of the girls?

JON BON JOVI: Yeah. I realized that sports wasn't gonna go very far after my freshman year. I was five-nine at fourteen and stayed five-nine for the rest of my life. But I found music. And you know, at the end of the day you realize that music is a sport, it's a team sport. You're only as good as your weakest link, and we've had the same team now for twenty years and we're still going on.

MICHAEL KAY: Your parents met in the Marine Corps. Did you have a very disciplined upbringing because of that?

JON BON JOVI: No, probably just the opposite. They allowed us to do silly things, like stay out at a bar until three, four in the morning, and I was in high school.

MICHAEL KAY: Your father was a marine, and he was a hairdresser. How does a marine become a hairdresser?

JON BON JOVI: My mother pushed him into it. He was gonna be a plumber like his father.

MICHAEL KAY: Now, he did a lot of your hair. And we have a shot of your high school yearbook. Do you give him credit for that?

JON BON JOVI: Yeah. Or blame. [*Laughter*]

MICHAEL KAY: That's a good look. Does he still do it?

JON BON JOVI: No. No. He's retired now. He plays golf now.

MICHAEL KAY: When the band first started, the hair was a big thing. Was he doing it then?

JON BON JOVI: Yeah, he's to blame for what every kid in the mall looked like. I certainly influenced a few haircuts in my day.

MICHAEL KAY: How many bands did you go through before you got to Bon Jovi?

JON BON JOVI: Not that many. Maybe half a dozen bands prior. They were all cover bands. I had a record deal by the time I was twenty or twenty-one, so this band [Bon Jovi] was formed around that. And I thought it was gonna be for three weeks. Richie [Sambora] was trying to get his own band going and had an independent record out. And Alec [John Such] was making a lot of money in the cover-band circuit. Tico [Torres] was actually in a band called Franke & the Knockouts; they had records out at the time and were on the road touring. And Dave [Bryan] had given it up and gone to school. I called the guys asking them to help me out for a couple of weeks—and now I can't get rid of them. [*Laughter*] A hundred million records later, they're still following me around.

MICHAEL KAY: Did you ever envision this scope of success? What did you want out of it?

JON BON JOVI: My aspirations at that time were to be the Asbury Jukes. They had a nice little career, never had a gold record, they were popular regionally, but not nationally or internationally.

MICHAEL KAY: There are a lot of good bands that don't have twenty-year staying power. What is behind that? Now there are fans who weren't born when you started.

JON BON JOVI: It crossed generations. I'd like to think it's because the songs touch people lyrically—it becomes them and their characters become them. In all honesty there have been years when we weren't as popular in America. So if America turned its back on me, we went to Europe, Africa, Asia. And we didn't follow fads or fashions. When things like rap or grunge came in, I didn't move to Seattle, I didn't get a guy scratching records. We stayed true to what we were. You can dislike it or you can love it. It was up to you.

MICHAEL KAY: You're a good-looking guy. You have a huge rock band. Sold a hundred million records. And you've been happily married to your high school sweetheart [since 1989]. How did that work out?

JON BON JOVI: Penance. That's my penance. [*Laughs*] No, that's the best deal I ever made. It has a lot to do with I don't like change. I don't want to play with other guys, I don't want to change my manager, I've been at one record company for twenty years. And I don't want to lose my wife. My wife is the greatest, I couldn't imagine going on without her. That Hollywood game is so boring: "Who's with who today?" It's so shallow.

MICHAEL KAY: But you guys still think it's cool that you can just walk in and say hello to Heather Locklear.

JON BON JOVI: That doesn't suck, you know. [*Laughter*]

MICHAEL KAY: [*To audience*] Heather is married to Richie Sambora of the band.

MICHAEL KAY: When did you decide to get into acting?

JON BON JOVI: It was an accident. One of Richie's previous loves, in another life, was Ally Sheedy, who was friends with Emilio Estevez. I was asked by Emil if could they use [the song] "Wanted" for the *Young Guns* movie. I said, "I'll write you something like that for the film," and he invited me out to the set. So it was so easy to be inspired on my first movie set. I wrote the album, I just knocked the whole thing out. That was my fifth album, and I wasn't sure if I wanted to continue making records. All I ever knew how to do from the time I was a young kid was sing and play. Eventually I got the courage to go for it, and I won a role in *Moonlight and Valentino*, and on the set I had a good experience. And because of that I subsequently wanted to do others.

MICHAEL KAY: In the future, do you want to do more music?

JON BON JOVI: I do. I see us continuing to make records forever as long as we are relevant. This will never be a nostalgia kind of band. I won't be doing that circuit anytime soon. But we'll do less and less touring. The idea of another club sandwich from room service somewhere at a Holiday Inn just doesn't appeal to me.

MICHAEL KAY: Tell me why you got involved in the AFL [Arena Football League]? We know you're a big fan, but you're investing money in this. How come?

JON BON JOVI: Well, I'm a football fanatic. I've always loved the game.

I go into mourning post–Super Bowl. I was talking with a friend who's a sports agent about the AFL, and initially it was a goofy joke. He says, "Hey, let's buy one of these teams, they're cheap." He misled me, they're not cheap. [*Laughter*] It was gonna be a band endeavor, but one by one they dropped out because the price was completely different than what he had told us. It was in the multimillions of dollars. But when I did my homework, I loved the idea. Part of the AFL fan bill of rights is that the players stay on the field and they interact with these kids, so they're accessible, and tickets are affordable. And it's the pure love of the game that inspires these guys to play, because they're certainly not making a lot of money. Some of them are on the cusp of getting into the NFL, or going back to the NFL, and others know that their playing days are coming to an end, and that they're gonna start another chapter in their lives. But when you see that—the pure love of the game—it's energizing. I was out in San Jose last week for our first ever scrimmage game. I was in the stands and the arena is empty, and we don't even officially keep score, but I wrote it down, and we lost by a touchdown. I went in the dressing room afterwards expecting to see all these guys who are trying out for the team listening to music, laughing it off, no big deal. But you would have thought we lost the Super Bowl. They were so devastated that they even lost a scrimmage game.

MICHAEL KAY: How is AFL any different from the NFL, for those that don't know?

JON BON JOVI: Eight guys a side, not eleven. Twenty-four-second play clock instead of forty seconds. Twenty-one-man squad. It's a fifty-yard field instead of a hundred. The goalpost is nine feet wide instead of eighteen. It's a high-scoring, very energetic game.

MICHAEL KAY: Now you own the Philadelphia Soul. You obviously want this to do well. But would you mortgage your soul to buy the Giants?

JON BON JOVI: I could probably buy a small country for less money than I could buy the Giants. [*Laughter*]

MICHAEL KAY: Over the years there have been a lot of things written. And we took some factoids off fan websites. I just want you to tell me if they're true or false. Your guilty pleasure—cartoons.

JON BON JOVI: False.

MICHAEL KAY: You're a junk-food fanatic.

JON BON JOVI: False.

MICHAEL KAY: Your wife, Dorothea, has a black belt in karate.

JON BON JOVI: True.

MICHAEL KAY: Does she ever kick your butt?

JON BON JOVI: Absolutely. Nothing wrong with a good spanking once in a while.

MICHAEL KAY: Your mom bought you your first guitar when you were seven and you threw it away.

JON BON JOVI: I threw it down the basement stairs. I wasn't gonna practice. At seven, I was still swinging a baseball bat.

MICHAEL KAY: You had a hundred and nine absences during your last year at War Memorial High School.

JON BON JOVI: Possible if not probable.

MICHAEL KAY: Your mom was a Playboy bunny.

JON BON JOVI: True. She worked in the restaurant, she wasn't in the magazine.

QUESTION FROM AUDIENCE: Where do your ideas come from for most of your songs? And when you come up with an idea, what actually motivates you to sit down and write the song—other than money?

JON BON JOVI: [*Laughs*] You know, I don't know where it comes from. Sometimes it doesn't come. Richie and I were writing last week and it stunk. So you say to yourself, "Today is just not the day for it. And tomorrow will be." But everything around you is a story as long as you're ready to accept it. You can shut yourself off to it and miss the moment. But a lot of times your eyes open wider and you get it and you go, "Bang! There it is." Every so often it's lightning in a bottle, and I don't know where that magic comes from.

MICHAEL KAY: When you think something is going to be a huge hit, is it sometimes a clunker?

JON BON JOVI: More often than not. [*Laughter*] I didn't want to include "Livin' on a Prayer" on the *Slippery* record, and I thought "It's My Life" was the most self-indulgent song I could ever write. You get songs like that, and then bang, zoom. Who knew?

QUESTION FROM AUDIENCE: What was your most embarrassing moment onstage?

JON BON JOVI: I've split my pants more than once. [*Laughter*] I remember recently on this tour feeling a breeze and looking down and going, "Oh, wow!" [*Laughter*] You have those moments. It's not choreographed, it's not overly rehearsed. Anything can happen. And if you fall down, you get up.

QUESTION FROM AUDIENCE: How do you get and stay in shape for your rigorous touring schedule?

JON BON JOVI: I wish I could tell you I do something great. The truth is, I smoke and I drink, then I feel bad in the morning, so I go to the gym. It hurts, so I go, "Oh God, I'm not gonna do that anymore." Then the next night I see Richie. My wife always says, "The devil's not gonna be red and have horns. He's gonna look just like Sambora." [*Laughter*]

MICHAEL KAY: Did you ever think you'd have four kids, when you were growing up?

JON BON JOVI: I'm from a family of three, and [my wife] is from a family of four. Ever since we got together, we always talked about the idea of four. Kids are great. No wonder people have been having them for thousands of years.

MICHAEL KAY: Do your kids know how famous you are?

JON BON JOVI: I think that my kids have a pretty good idea of it now. On television they don't like the fan kind of stuff. It sort of freaks them out.

MICHAEL KAY: Can you walk into your favorite diner in New Jersey without [being bothered]?

JON BON JOVI: Absolutely. It's a great misconception about show business. People think you can't do things. One of my most vivid memories is watching Dylan walking down the street with a guitar case in his hand, all by himself. It's a big misconception.

MICHAEL KAY: Can you even imagine being seventy years old?

JON BON JOVI: I have to say that at twenty I didn't know what it was gonna be like to be forty, and at forty I'm having the best time of my life now. So I can only imagine that it continues to get better. As long as you have your health and good relationships, the rest of it is gravy. So if I have that, then I'd love to still be doing this at seventy. Why not? Sinatra did it.

MICHAEL KAY: So you can see Bon Jovi playing at sixty-five, like Mick Jagger?

JON BON JOVI: As long as we're relevant, as long as we were making music that we feel is relevant and we're doing it on the level that we have grown accustomed to. But I won't be doing the state-fair circuit and clubs.

MICHAEL KAY: You said in the past you never want to be the fat Elvis. In twenty years, where do you see yourself, what do you think you'll be doing? You think you'll be a big movie star?

JON BON JOVI: Well, I don't know if I'll ever get the shot in Hollyweird. But I'd like to continue to make records, and I'd like to continue to make movies, and it's been a great ride this far. And I have no intention of getting off it. The book isn't finished being written yet.

MICHAEL KAY: Thank you. I had a great time.

JON BON JOVI: Me, too. Thank you, everybody!

Steve Young

Steve Young was booked for January 19, 2002, as the first ever *Center-Stage* guest. It was unusual since the first time the YES Network would air was March 19, 2002, broadcasting a spring-training game between the Yankees and the Cincinnati Reds, so Young was going to be interviewed for a show that had never aired on a network that had yet to deliver any programming. Young had only agreed because of his relationship with John Filippelli, from their days together at ABC Sports. January 19 was a day of NFL playoff games, and Young was slated to be on ESPN's *NFL Countdown* before making his way down to the YES studio in Manhattan from Bristol, Connecticut, the home of ESPN.

Mother Nature had other ideas, pelting the Northeast with a snowstorm. The show was to be taped at 3:00 p.m. since Young got off the air at noon in Bristol. We had a full studio audience waiting for the taping.

But with the snow blanketing the city and the surrounding areas, we feared Young was going to cancel, and we felt that would have been reasonable on his part. But the Hall of Fame Super Bowl champion wouldn't cancel and tried to make his way into Manhattan despite dangerous conditions. We were in constant contact with him since the going from Bristol was extremely slow. We heard he was going to be an hour late. Then two hours. Then three hours. We were afraid that if he finally arrived, we wouldn't have a studio audience. To guard against that, we kept ordering pizza and rolled in a couple of large-screen TV sets so the crowd could watch the NFL playoff games. Like true New Yorkers in a storm, they made it work, and the constant flow of pizza didn't hurt.

Young finally arrived a little over three hours late and was charming, funny, and engaging. That evening, he showed himself to be one of the nicest famous people you'd ever meet.

Because it was my first show, I was obviously nervous, and I became even more panicky as the wait grew longer and longer. But Young was so easy to talk with, and his story about his date with Marie Osmond was the hit of the afternoon, putting me at ease and winning over the crowd.

As I walked out of the studio that night, I felt we'd put together a solid first show, but I never dreamed that we'd still be rolling two decades later. No matter how many guests I end up interviewing, I'll always remember my first and the weird circumstances behind our conversation.

The Interview

MICHAEL KAY: I'm Michael Kay, and this is *CenterStage*. Hello, everybody. On *CenterStage* is a man whose trials and tribulations may not be all that familiar to those on the East Coast, although he's one of Connecticut's own. Yet his story is one of the most dramatic in football history. He's former San Francisco 49er and future Hall of Famer Steve Young. Let's check out his résumé. Steve is in a group of about ten of the greatest quarterbacks of all time. He was an undisputed brilliant runner who later proved he could be the best passer in the league. He threw for a record six touchdowns in San Francisco's 1995 Super Bowl win against San Diego, earning an MVP award. Young retired two years ago as the highest-rated quarterback in football history. Steve's friend and the coach of the Denver Broncos once said of Steve, quote, "He could do it all. He had a great sense of timing. He could make all the throws. He was a great competitor. He had that burning desire which only the great ones have." End quote. Yet Steve Young's single greatest accomplishment may always be that he was a quarterback who followed Joe Montana. Please welcome our guest on *CenterStage*, Steve Young. [*Applause*]

MICHAEL KAY: Steve, it must be kind of nice to hear your eulogy while you're still alive.

STEVE YOUNG: I'm thinking to myself when it goes that long, usually my mom wrote it. [*Laughter*]

MICHAEL KAY: She phoned it in for us.

STEVE YOUNG: You know, "retired"! I hear that all the time now. It's really hard to retire and feel like, "Wait a second, I'm a young guy. I'm not retired—I'm thirty." Well, I'm actually forty, but it's really a crappy feeling being retired at a young age. I mean, surgeons get to go till they're sixty-five. Taxi drivers get to go to their midsixties.

MICHAEL KAY: Let's start at the beginning and see how it all began. You were all-everything [at Greenwich High School] in Greenwich. And then you ended up going to BYU. Now, your dad had played at BYU as well. Did that decision have anything to do with the fact that they turned out quarterbacks?

STEVE YOUNG: Well, I think mostly it was because they turned out quarterbacks. When I left Greenwich, Connecticut, I told my friends I was going to BYU, and they're like, "What? Where's that? You know, it's in the middle of nowhere." I said, "No, it's in Utah. I mean—tepees and Indians and cowboys and stuff." [*Laughter*] No, that was a hundred years ago. They got buildings now. But I went there because I really wanted to be like my hero, Roger Staubach. I wanted to be a quarterback.

MICHAEL KAY: You were one of the gutsier, toughest players in the NFL, but few people know that you almost gave up the game your freshman year at BYU.

STEVE YOUNG: Well, I was, like, eighth on the depth chart, eighth string, and I was getting sick of getting beat and no one knew my name, the coach didn't care about me. I called home and said, "Dad, I'm out of here, this is ridiculous." He said, "Hey, you can quit, but you can't come home." I was out of money, I couldn't go anywhere else. I stuck in there mostly because he wouldn't take me back. [*Laughter*]

MICHAEL KAY: Now, you sat two years behind Jim McMahon, and as you said, you were the eighth-ranked quarterback, and they wanted to turn you into a defensive back. Did you know all that going in?

STEVE YOUNG: Yeah, they recruited me as an athlete. They said, "Look, you're fast, you can do a lot of things, maybe you don't want to play quarterback. Play safety or DB or something." But I refused to play any other position. I said, "I'm playing quarterback."

MICHAEL KAY: Now, I can't think of two more different people than Jim McMahon and you. You're supposed to be one of the nicest guys in the world, and, well, Jim McMahon is Jim McMahon. How tough was it to be behind him for a couple of years?

STEVE YOUNG: Yeah, he was a nutty guy. I mean, he did crazy things. But as far as quarterbacking, that's truly where I learned to play—I copied Jim McMahon. If you watch me play and you watch him play, you say, "Holy cow, those guys look a lot alike." Off the field he was a little crazier, but, you know, it was more hype than anything. He's still a family man. He's got kids and a nice wife. He's not that crazy.

MICHAEL KAY: You come from BYU and you're a straightlaced guy. One of the nice guys and all that. You do everything right. And then you go to the USFL. I mean, that is totally against what Steve Young is all about. Why did you go to the USFL?

STEVE YOUNG: I shook people up on that one. USFL was a league that at that time they were signing everybody out of college. If you were a top draft pick, you were gonna get a bid from the USFL. I thought to myself, well, the LA Express sounds crazy, but Sid Gillman, the great Sid Gillman, was gonna be my coach, and right off the bat I'd play. I thought I'd play for a couple of years, get good, you know, and then I'd be a free agent, I could go anywhere.

MICHAEL KAY: They threw a lot of money at you. How much did that have to do with it?

STEVE YOUNG: You know, it was funny, I was the forty-million-dollar man. [*Laughter*] That was supposed to be the highest amount of money paid to anyone at that time. But at that point it was all kind of funny money, in my head, anyway. I thought if I played a lot, I would be more credible coming out of USFL into the NFL. And that's how it worked out.

MICHAEL KAY: All right, then you go to Tampa Bay for two years. And then you end up going to San Francisco, where one of the greatest quarterbacks of all time is manning the position that you play. What's your thinking there?

STEVE YOUNG: Well, okay, so I'm in Tampa Bay, and things aren't going real well. We had fights in the locker room, and it was just a horrible situation. Bill Walsh came to me during the off-season, and he said, "Look, Joe Montana has a horrible back, it's gone out on him, he's had surgery, he is literally on his last leg. He won't play much longer, and we would like you to come in and play quarterback for the 49ers." Now, what would you do? The only guy that they didn't check with was Joe, because Joe's like, "Hey, my back's not that bad." [*Laughter*] So I kind of got suckered into that one a little bit. I spent four years watching Joe play the greatest football you could ever see. I was always thinking, "Holy cow, I gotta follow this? This is insane!" But, you know, when it's all said and done, I got an opportunity to play with the greatest offense, with the greatest guys. It all worked out in the end. But it was a hard four years.

MICHAEL KAY: Now, a lot of people say that you had such a healing effect on Montana because he saw this great quarterback ready to take over for him. He was getting out of a hospital bed pretty quick.

STEVE YOUNG: Well, it was very competitive. I was just this brash young kid who didn't know anything. Joe had already won Super Bowls and had been playing for seven, eight, nine, ten years. So I was way behind. But I hated being second string, I hated *watching* people play football. So that was what was so hard.

MICHAEL KAY: You're thirty-one years old. You've been sitting on the bench four years in San Francisco. The sands through the hourglass of your career are running out. What are your thoughts at that point, and are you saying, "I gotta get out of here"?

STEVE YOUNG: Well, I needed to play. And it was getting worse every year. At that point I really didn't care about where. And ironically that's when Joe got hurt and I was able to play for an extended period of time, and I really never left the field after that. Obviously Joe would have loved to have played on for many, many more years, but for me it happened at a pretty good time.

MICHAEL KAY: Now, I've heard from some people—I don't know if it's true, that's why I want to ask you—that you two didn't like each other. I mean, there's a picture of you hugging Joe at his retirement, but I've seen a picture of Lou Gehrig and Babe Ruth hugging, and they hated each other's guts. So what was the deal with you two guys?

STEVE YOUNG: Actually we never had a cross word, ever. Never had an argument in all the years that we were together, no animosity whatsoever. In fact, for the most part we laughed and had a good time. Except for the fact that, look, I'm here, I want to play, and you're a legend and you want to play, and what can we do about this?

MICHAEL KAY: Now [Coach Mike] Shanahan calls you one of the top five quarterbacks of all time. Some people call Montana one of the greatest quarterbacks of all time, maybe the greatest. You had the closest view, what do you think?

STEVE YOUNG: [*Laughs*] I think that Joe had a unique quality, as if he was an old soul. He had a maturity and a patience and a peace about how he played football. It seemed like the bigger the game, the calmer he was. He was just Joe Cool. I tried to take as much as I could from Joe and use it in my way, [and I tried] the best that I could to emulate Joe. Because I was learning from the best.

MICHAEL KAY: One thing that we've read a lot about you is your social life. You're a great-great-great-grandson of Brigham Young, you're a Mormon, you did not get married till later in your life [at the age of thirty-eight]. And in San Francisco, a lot of people concentrated on that. Was that a little bit odd that people were so concerned over who you were dating?

STEVE YOUNG: You know, my great-great-great-grandfather Brigham Young once said if you're twenty-seven years old and not married, you're a menace to society. And I was like, "Well, I must be a real menace to society." [*Laughs*] But for me it's about love, and we can get into all that mushy stuff later, but I found the right girl and I'm glad I waited. So it worked out great.

MICHAEL KAY: It's so strange, I've covered sports for a number of years of my life, and I'm not knocking every athlete, but, I mean, what you see on the road is—debauchery at its best or worst, whatever you want to say. Drinking, carousing, a lot of people cheat on their wives. And then there's nice clean Steve Young. How did you fit in with your teammates? Was that a little uncomfortable?

STEVE YOUNG: Well, first of all you must be talking about basketball or baseball. [*Laughter*] Yeah, money and fame has its price, and everybody understands that. I don't know, my dad was a pretty straightlaced guy, and I just found it [easier] to stay with what I really believed and what I thought was really important. So it was very meaningful for me to try to maintain a real straight regimen. I wasn't trying to prove a point or anything. It's just that's who I was.

MICHAEL KAY: Back to football. The 49ers fell right on their faces after you left. You're probably a nicer guy than me, but I would love the fact that they stunk after I left.

STEVE YOUNG: [*Laughs*] Well, I think that's human nature. I feel like I bled and died for the 49ers, and when you leave, you want it to have been meaningful. You want to have it feel like it mattered that you left. That you left a little bit of a hole. So it's like it's catch-twenty-two. You want everyone to do well because they're all your friends. But you're kind of like, "You miss me, right?"

QUESTION FROM AUDIENCE: Would you like your son to grow up and play football and follow your same steps?

STEVE YOUNG: That's a nice question. I think you choose whatever you want to do, but you can't quit. That was my dad's big thing: have a passion for it and don't quit. And if you find that you lose that passion over time, then you move on to the next thing. But you stick with whatever you do. I don't care if it's football or tiddlywinks or piano or saxophone or whatever it is. Football's a great game, and I wouldn't be mad if [my son] played, and I wouldn't be mad if he didn't play. But I love sports. For young kids, it teaches them lessons about teamwork and all the rest of that stuff. I would encourage him to play sports just because of what it teaches you.

QUESTION FROM AUDIENCE: What's going through your head the second before you know you're gonna get sacked?

STEVE YOUNG: Some of the greatest experiences I ever remember were throwing balls that I threw blind because I knew that Jerry Rice was there. I threw it right on time, and I got hit right afterwards—*boom!* And you're on the ground and your face is in the dirt and the guy is squeezing you down, and you look to the sidelines and all you see is the crowd, and you can tell by the crowd reaction that it worked. But you didn't ever see it. I think those are some of the greatest memories of playing quarterback. You're not ever thinking, "Oh my gosh, I'm gonna get hit." You just dream of letting that ball go right at the last second, taking a hit, and having something great work out.

MICHAEL KAY: Well, speaking of taking a hit, let's go to the moment that ended your football career: 1999, third game, Cardinals, Aeneas Williams absolutely flattens you. And that's the last play you ever have in the NFL. We have a shot of you right after the hit. You don't look like you're in that much of a good-time mode. What's happening right there?

STEVE YOUNG: It never happened to me before where I actually got knocked out on the field. But I was knocked out for a few seconds. I look back at that time and it was just too bad, because you can tell the passion I have for playing football. Certainly that's not the picture of how I want to remember me playing football. But the truth is football is a very violent game, and you're gonna run into some of those situations. You play long enough, you'll find yourself in a bad spot.

MICHAEL KAY: That was your fourth concussion in three years. Eight overall. Did you ever think, "Gee, I might be getting brain damage here, this might not be worth it."

STEVE YOUNG: Not really. Because those official numbers of concussions, I don't think they really ever know. Because you know more than anybody, and it's tough to really track. If I had a concussion or something that felt like that, I would usually wake up the next morning and be kind of tired. And I always did rest and I took the time to get well. I never had any of the stuff that you hear about, like I can't remember where my keys are or I can't taste hot and cold. If I would ever have had that, I would have sprinted away from the game. I wouldn't have even hung around because that would scare me to death. When I look back on my career, the hits to my head weren't nearly as tough as the hits to my soul when people doubted me over the years. I don't remember the physical beatings really as much.

MICHAEL KAY: Now you've become a broadcaster.

STEVE YOUNG: Yes, it's almost like you're playing a little bit because you're talking about it and it feels like you're part of the game. Clearly you're not—it's not even close. But I do enjoy the sport very much, so it's fun to watch the games and analyze, especially the quarterbacks. As the young guys try to come up, I find myself saying, "I remember being there, I remember that lap on the track of life." So broadcasting has in a way brought me back to the game to help other guys. And I like that.

MICHAEL KAY: When you become old and gray, how do you want to be remembered?

STEVE YOUNG: I want to be remembered as a football player at some point, you know, "Yeah, he was a pretty good football player." But I'd really like to gain some expertise in other things, in new things, in new challenges. At the end of my life I want to say I was really good at maybe two or three things. And one was football.

MICHAEL KAY: We thank you so much for joining us.

Chris Evert

Chris Evert is full of life. When she walks into a room, she gives off an energy, drawing you into her vibrant orbit. That's the vibe she brought onstage in 2002. She was willing to talk about anything and everything.

She spoke freely about her somewhat demanding upbringing, in which she almost seemed to be *programmed* to be a tennis champion. She also talked about her many loves and her long-scrutinized relationship with the seemingly volatile Jimmy Connors.

She was brutally honest in conceding that, for a stretch in her long-time rivalry with Martina Navratilova, Chris came onto the court knowing she was going to lose, and she was also frank in admitting that, even in her prime, she wouldn't have been able to beat Serena Williams.

Nothing was off-limits for this winner of eighteen Grand Slam singles championships. She was sharp, quick, and self-deprecating, and her verbal volleying was as impressive as the racket strokes she displayed on the court.

This conversation focused on one of the greatest careers any American athlete has ever had, and it's a must-read for any serious student of the game.

The Interview

MICHAEL KAY: She was a teenage wonder on the tennis court. Known for her two-handed backhand, her nearly flawless baseline game, her intense concentration on the court. She won eighteen Grand Slam singles titles, including six US Opens, seven French Opens, and three Wimbledon championships. She was a rare unanimous selection to the International Hall of Fame. Since her retirement from the game, she's become a TV tennis commentator and is the publisher of *Tennis* magazine. Please welcome one of the greatest tennis players in the history of the sport, Chris Evert. [*Applause*]

CHRIS EVERT: Thank you. Good to be here.

MICHAEL KAY: Chris, if you had never picked up a tennis racquet in your whole life, what would you be?

CHRIS EVERT: Stupid. [*Laughter*] I get asked that question a lot. Because it's like all I knew was tennis. But I probably would be in some sort of psychology area. I'm always trying to analyze why people react, what they do in certain situations and under stress. So I think definitely I would have thought about getting into psychology.

MICHAEL KAY: When did you know you wanted to play tennis? You've said you first picked up a racquet when you were five years old. Did you know right away?

CHRIS EVERT: No, I didn't know I wanted to play at five years old. My father knew I wanted to play at five years old. It was the sort of situation where I was definitely pushed into the game. My father had won numerous tournaments, then he got drafted [in World War II], went to war, then he came back and had to earn a living. So he was a tennis professional, he gave lessons and coached. There were five kids in our family, and he wanted to teach every single one of us. It was sort of a great thing, in the sense that the whole family was together every day. But it took me away from [some childhood things], and at times I was very resentful.

MICHAEL KAY: Was there a point where you could tell your dad, "Hey, that's it, I'm not doing it."

CHRIS EVERT: Not at five years old. [*Laughs*] I just went along for the ride because in those days you didn't rebel against your parents. You just did what they told you to do. Then I started liking it and I started getting good, and then it was a whole new ball game.

MICHAEL KAY: At what point did you start to like it?

CHRIS EVERT: At about eight years old. I was starting to enter tournaments and doing well in the ten-and-unders. And I was starting to win matches and I was able to travel—even if it was an hour travel to Coral Gables or Miami or Palm Beach. And I realized that I liked it, that tennis was my showcase. I could really express myself on the court.

MICHAEL KAY: Is it ever too early to start a kid on tennis? Is there an age at which you shouldn't be forced into it?

CHRIS EVERT: I think nowadays they try to make it fun for the kids. I have my own tennis academy, and when we have kids who are five, six, seven years old, we sort of play peewee tennis with them, where we play with big soft balls. If you make it fun for kids, if you make it like a game, they're not going to resent you for it. We didn't have that in our day.

MICHAEL KAY: The two-handed backhand. How did that come about?

CHRIS EVERT: When I started playing, we didn't have children's racquets in those days, and I was using my dad's racquet—and at five years old I could barely pick it up with one hand. So I just naturally held it with two hands and started hitting the ball.

MICHAEL KAY: Did your dad try to change it once you got big enough?

CHRIS EVERT: When I was about eleven or twelve years old, he said he still felt the one-handed backhand had better reach, better technique, you could be a little more versatile. And I said I didn't want to relearn the game all over, from square one. And it was my best shot. So we both decided, if it's my best shot, keep it.

MICHAEL KAY: You're playing in competitions at nine years old, and there's a lot of emphasis on winning. Did you ever feel that "I better win this or Dad's gonna be upset"?

CHRIS EVERT: No, I never felt that. My parents never put pressure on me. I put pressure on myself. My dad only got mad at me once in my whole career, and that was because I tanked, because I gave up. I was playing the Nationals and I was losing. And I came off the court and said, "Dad, I've got a stomachache," and all these other excuses. And he saw right through that and chewed me out, and that never happened again.

MICHAEL KAY: Did you feel that you had a good childhood?

CHRIS EVERT: Oh, absolutely. I had a very normal childhood. I went to school, I graduated from high school, I wasn't pulled out of school to play tennis. I went to a prom, I went to dances. But I was sort of the one who was hiding behind a pillar, just petrified that somebody would ask me to dance and I would have to get out there and move.

MICHAEL KAY: Now, you were known as a beautiful woman—you still are—and you were very feminine on the court. And at the time women's tennis might not have been that way. Did you think you engendered any change?

CHRIS EVERT: Oh, I'm gonna get in trouble with this answer.

MICHAEL KAY: That's why I asked you. [*Laughter*]

CHRIS EVERT: Thank you. I get in trouble with Billie Jean King every time I answer this question. When I came on the scene, there was Billie Jean and Margaret Court [and others], and they were jocks. They were great athletes, and they didn't worry about ribbons in their hair and nail polish and jewelry. And I did, because I was a sixteen-, seventeen-year-old girl who liked boys and wanted to catch their eye. So being feminine was an important part of my life.

MICHAEL KAY: Was there any animosity from the other girls because you were pretty hot when you played?

CHRIS EVERT: Yeah, there was. They hated me.

MICHAEL KAY: Really?

CHRIS EVERT: I remember I was on the cover of *Newsweek* magazine when I was seventeen, and the headline was "The Women Take Over." I was on the cover, but it was really largely due to Billie Jean. She was the one that had the vision, ninety percent of the women's game is due to her, and there I am on the cover of *Newsweek*. I remember I played Billie Jean once in Houston, Texas, and there's a whole box seat right in the front [and all the other women players] were cheering her on. Then when I went in the locker room, they were throwing champagne parties because Billie Jean beat me. And I remember I went into the bathroom stall and started crying. Because it was very hurtful. But you know what? It was fine. I was the first young player to do well and take away some of their limelight and their glory. But Billie Jean had a talk with the girls and she said, "You know, she's putting money in our pockets, she's getting women's tennis out there in the newspapers. Let's embrace her instead of avoiding her."

MICHAEL KAY: Do you get along with Billie Jean now?

CHRIS EVERT: I've always gotten along with Billie Jean. We're alike in a lot of ways.

MICHAEL KAY: You said a long time ago that when you were younger, you were a robot—wind her up and she plays tennis.

CHRIS EVERT: I think in the early years I was pretty mechanical in the way I played tennis. I didn't have a lot of flair and pizzazz, I was pretty technical, pretty precise—like a metronome. I think I was like that in the beginning of my career, but I don't think I ended up like that.

MICHAEL KAY: In sports they always say that in order to be really great you have to have a great opponent. And for you Martina Navratilova was that opponent. How did that come about, how did the rivalry start? Because I know you dominated at the beginning.

CHRIS EVERT: Yes, I dominated at the beginning. I was eighteen or nineteen, she was sixteen or seventeen. And when she came over from Czechoslovakia, she was this heavy little Czechoslovakian, an emotional kind of whiner. She would literally cry on the court if things weren't going her way. But she had enormous talent and a big serve, a big forehand, and she was a very dangerous player. After the first time I played her I thought, "Boy, if this girl ever gets herself in shape, and if she ever gets her emotions under control, she's gonna be tough."

MICHAEL KAY: So you knew right at the beginning that she could be the ying to your yang?

CHRIS EVERT: Yeah, I knew. We were so different in every way. We were different on the court, our style of play was different, we were different personalities, we came from different parts of the world, we had different philosophies on life. We were very different in every way, shape, and form, and that's what made the rivalry so great.

MICHAEL KAY: The crowds mostly loved you, though.

CHRIS EVERT: I think in the beginning they did. And then she came out and said she was gay, and she did a lot of good things for special causes. She's a very giving person, a very good person, and I think people started to really appreciate her.

MICHAEL KAY: Do you think that hurt tennis or helped tennis when she came out and said that she was a lesbian?

CHRIS EVERT: I don't see how it could have hurt tennis. I don't like any kind of prejudice of any kind. I grew up with some of the women on the tour being gay. It's a fact of life, in every aspect of life, and also in sports. I look at people as people, instead of looking at their sexual preference.

MICHAEL KAY: I think you [and Martina] played eighty matches, and it was almost even at the end of your careers. Was it especially tough for you to lose a match to her because the competition was so fierce?

CHRIS EVERT: Yeah, it was tough. There was a period of two years when she beat me, like, thirteen times in a row. And during those times I walked on the court knowing I was gonna lose. She was so dominant in the early eighties. And she was so cocky and arrogant about it, she knew she had my number. That's one of the reasons why she won. She had a confidence about her, and once she started winning, she'd steamroll over you. But once I broke that streak, I beat her at the French Open the next two years, and we got back to being on equal terms again.

MICHAEL KAY: Your long-running rivalry with Martina was great for tennis. And then there was you and Jimmy Connors. He's this hotheaded guy on the court, and you were known as the Ice Queen, and yet you were engaged. When you were together, it was like a white-hot spotlight.

CHRIS EVERT: Opposites attract, yeah.

MICHAEL KAY: Well, how did it not work out eventually [that you didn't get married]?

CHRIS EVERT: We would have killed each other. [*Laughter*] Well, no, I shouldn't have said it quite that way. Jimmy was great, and I saw a side of Jimmy that nobody else saw. He was a different guy around me than when he was on the court. It worked because I calmed him down, and he revved me up. And it was a great first love. But on the other hand, I'm so happy I never ended up with him, and he's happy he didn't end up with me, either. I mean, gosh, I was nineteen, he was twenty-one. Nobody should get married till they're thirty. That's my advice to everybody out there.

MICHAEL KAY: Are you guys friends now?

CHRIS EVERT: Friendly, yeah. I'm friendly with all my exes. [*Laughter*]

MICHAEL KAY: You have three boys [with Olympic downhill skier Andy Mill]. Are they athletic? You think they're gonna be tennis players?

CHRIS EVERT: I know they're not. My husband was an Olympic skier, he was a daredevil, he rode motorcycles, and he did all the danger sports. So for my kids, tennis is boring. I've tried. I even offer them money. I'll say, "I'll give you twenty bucks if you go hit with me for half an hour," and my ten-year-old goes, "I want twenty-five," and my six-year-old goes, "I want thirty." [*Laughter*] And finally I'm paying them, like, fifty bucks to hit with me. And I'm like, "What's wrong with this picture? Shouldn't they be paying me?" But I end up paying them and I feel so good for that half hour. And I say, "See, isn't this sport fun?" And they say, "No, it's boring." [*Laughter*]

MICHAEL KAY: I have a quote from John McEnroe I want to read about you. He said, "She was an assassin who dressed nice and said the right things, and meanwhile she'd just cut you to shreds." [*Laughter*]

CHRIS EVERT: Well, he meant on the court, right?

MICHAEL KAY: I would hope. But do you think that's true? Were you an assassin?

CHRIS EVERT: Yeah, I had that killer instinct, but it wasn't toward the person I was playing. It wasn't anything personal. I wanted to win. I didn't want to lose.

MICHAEL KAY: What did you do before a match to get ready?

CHRIS EVERT: Nobody could talk to me for an hour. I just focused in my head on what would happen. I would just think about the match for about an hour.

MICHAEL KAY: So you weren't fun to be around before a match?

CHRIS EVERT: You wouldn't want to be around me.

MICHAEL KAY: Chris, people might not know this about you because they used to call you the Ice Queen on the court, and the all-American girl off the court. But your personality was actually a little raunchy, am I right?

CHRIS EVERT: Absolutely. I think I surprised a lot of the girls in the locker room because they expected me to be very straightlaced and very serious. But after matches, to let off steam, I'd come into the locker room and just start telling dirty jokes, and they'd be, like, shocked. I kind of got a reputation for that.

MICHAEL KAY: Really dirty jokes?

CHRIS EVERT: Funny dirty. And as I got older, they got dirtier. [*Laughter*]

QUESTION FROM AUDIENCE: In your prime, how would you have done against the Williams sisters [Venus and Serena]?

CHRIS EVERT: Okay, I'm five foot six, and they're what, six foot two? [*Laughter*] In my prime I could have been in a match with them, but I wouldn't have beaten them. I'd play anybody but the Williams sisters. Because they hit the ball so hard and they move so well, the power and the mobility would be overwhelming to me.

QUESTION FROM AUDIENCE: Hi, Chris. Do you think that power has kind of replaced finesse in the men's and women's game? And if so, do you think that it has hurt the popularity of the sport?

CHRIS EVERT: That's a good question. I think it's helped women's tennis because I think women's tennis could have used a little more power to match the men's. When I watch Venus and Serena hitting, they hit as hard if not harder than the men at the baseline. You know, they really do.

MICHAEL KAY: What was your favorite moment in your career?

CHRIS EVERT: My favorite moments in my career were my first US Open when I was sixteen, and the last French Open that I won—because I beat Martina and nobody thought I could do it.

MICHAEL KAY: Chris, this has been a pleasure, thank you so much.

CHRIS EVERT: Thank you, I enjoyed it.

Lindsey Vonn

Lindsey Vonn is one of the greatest skiers of all time. From Saint Paul, Minnesota, she began skiing when she was able to stand and has been competing at the highest levels since.

Although her career has been spent speeding downhill, success has forced her to do a lot of climbing. Greatness doesn't come easily even if you're blessed with incredible talent. The amount of work and sacrifice necessary to reach the top of the mountain robbed Vonn of a lot of her childhood. But amazingly, she doesn't show any bitterness toward her journey. Vonn seems totally well-adjusted and happy and had the *CenterStage* crowd smiling and laughing throughout the hour.

And why *should* she be bitter since she has established herself at the top of her sport? Check out the résumé: eighty-two World Cup victories, which is a women's record, and four World Cup overall championships. She has also won Olympic gold and bronze medals in her sparkling career. Her medals and records are far too many to list.

But with the pros come significant cons. She has suffered through some horrific injuries and has had the perseverance to rehab, battle back, and make herself one of the best again. Her single-minded purpose makes her one of the finest skiers—female or male—to ever race down a mountain.

It's stunning to consider all that has gone right and wrong for Vonn since she appeared on *CenterStage* in 2010. The heartbreaks and the bone breaks have highlighted a competitive instinct and drive that explain her all-time greatness. When you get the opportunity to interview so many accomplished people, you tend to spot one thing that separates each from their peers. With Vonn it's simply an inability to give up.

Vonn finally retired in 2019, on her own terms and *not* on the advice of a surgeon. After you read this interview, you'll realize that she would never have allowed herself to be forced out. She alone had to make the call.

The Interview

MICHAEL KAY: Thank you, everybody, and welcome to *CenterStage*. Today's guest is a Minnesota native; she began skiing at the age of three and was placed on the fast track to competitive skiing early. By the age of sixteen she made her World Cup and Olympic debuts, but just prior to her second Olympics in 2006 she suffered a horrific crash while training in Torino, but returned in time to compete. Her dedication earned her the US Olympic Spirit Award. In 2008 she became only the second American female to win the overall World Cup championship. And she's repeated that again the past two seasons. Leading up to the 2010 Winter Games in Vancouver, she became the cover girl and the face of the US Olympic team, and despite the many pressures and expectations, she delivered a gold and a bronze medal. A combination of beauty, grace, strength, maturity, and competitiveness, this is one athlete who knows the need for speed. Please welcome the most successful American female skier ever, Lindsey Vonn. [*Applause*]

LINDSEY VONN: Thank you, thank you. [*Applause continues*]

MICHAEL KAY: You had so much hype coming into the Olympics in Vancouver. How much pressure was on you?

LINDSEY VONN: It was really intense. Everyone was saying, "You're gonna win five gold medals," and that was just ridiculous. [*Laughs*] My goal was to try to get one medal of any color. I was ecstatic with one gold [in the downhill] and one bronze [in the super giant slalom].

MICHAEL KAY: Did you embrace the pressure, or did it affect how you skied?

LINDSEY VONN: It's really hard to compete when all eyes are on you and everyone's expecting so much of you. But we kind of secluded ourselves in Vancouver, we stayed in our condo, I didn't watch any TV or read any newspapers or go online. I just did my Facebook and hung out with my husband. I think that really helped clear my mind and just stay focused on my skiing.

MICHAEL KAY: Now, how fast do you go typically in a downhill race?

LINDSEY VONN: Anywhere from seventy to ninety miles an hour.

MICHAEL KAY: And there's no fear? I mean, if I'm going ninety miles an hour in a car, I'm getting a little nervous. [*Laughter*]

LINDSEY VONN: No, I love going fast, I always have, and I always want to go faster. I like to kind of keep pushing the envelope as much as I can.

MICHAEL KAY: Because you like speed on the slopes, do you also like speed in real life? Do you drive cars fast and everything?

LINDSEY VONN: Yes.

MICHAEL KAY: What's the fastest you've ever driven in a car?

LINDSEY VONN: [*Laughs*] I think I've gone, like, one hundred and fifty miles an hour.

MICHAEL KAY: I'm gonna ask you a weird question. After the downhill race, you're at the end of the course, and you've won [the gold medal], did you ask yourself if it was worth all the work?

LINDSEY VONN: No, it was worth it. It was definitely worth everything. It was worth missing the prom and not having many friends growing up and just being on the road all the time. It's worth all the hours on the bike and in the gym. Standing there up on that podium and hearing our national anthem play was so incredible, and I'm just really thankful.

MICHAEL KAY: So it all started out with Lindsey Kildow in Saint Paul, Minnesota, which is a really nice place. And your parents put you on skis at three. Why so early?

LINDSEY VONN: That's a good question. [*Laughs*] Right around the time I started walking, my parents had this cool little harness that they put me in, and they put little skis on me. I really wasn't skiing by myself.

MICHAEL KAY: When did you realize, Lindsey, that "Okay, this is my passion, I want to do this"?

LINDSEY VONN: I think it was when I was about eight or nine. I met [American skier] Picabo Street at an autograph signing in Minneapolis, and I just was in awe of her. I'd never really thought about having ski racing as my career until I met her, and it kind of just opened my eyes to the possibilities of having ski racing as a career. I was like, "I want to be an Olympian just like her," and I went full steam ahead to try to be an Olympian. Later my family moved out to Vail, Colorado, so that I could be in the mountains more, and then I made the US Ski Team shortly after that—and it was just an amazing ride. But it all started with meeting Picabo Street. She was just an amazing person, someone that I could look up to, and a very good role model for me.

MICHAEL KAY: So by seven you're spending your summers training in Oregon, by the age of nine you're training in Europe. Was there any time to be a kid? To play with Barbie dolls? Did you ever feel that you were cheated out of being a kid?

LINDSEY VONN: I had a really good Barbie collection, actually. [*Laughter*] But, no, I had a great time, you know, doing what I wanted to do, I got to see a lot of things that I wouldn't have normally gotten to see. So I feel really lucky to have gotten those experiences. I did miss out on the prom, which I was disappointed about. [*Laughs*]

MICHAEL KAY: Did you have a date for the prom if you could've gone?

LINDSEY VONN: Not really. I was kind of a dork.

MICHAEL KAY: Ohh, I'm not believing that. . . . You know what's weird, Lindsey, is that when you hear about child actors, and they miss everything, too, they don't go to the prom and stuff, and a lot of them are really fouled up. You don't seem that messed up. [*Laughter*] How'd you avoid that?

LINDSEY VONN: Thank you! [*Laughter*] My family has just been really good to me, and my brothers and sisters have always been so supportive. I haven't changed, I'm the same person that I was, and my family doesn't treat me any differently. I just have really good people around me, and I think that's really important.

MICHAEL KAY: You make your World Cup debut shortly after turning sixteen, at Park City, Utah, in 2000. That's the big leagues. Were you nervous?

LINDSEY VONN: Very nervous. I was totally out of my element, I didn't really know what to do, and there are all these amazing athletes. So I just was like, "Okay, I'm gonna go out there and try my best," and I ended up being thirty-first, which was one place outside of qualifying for the second run. But I was happy with that, you know, it was a good start.

MICHAEL KAY: Now, in the 2002 Winter Olympics in Salt Lake City, you compete in the slalom and the combined. What was that initial Olympics like for you? And how'd you do?

LINDSEY VONN: It was really fun. Having the opening ceremonies in your home country was so amazing, and I did the opening ceremonies with the whole team, and it was one of the coolest and most patriotic moments of my career.

MICHAEL KAY: Now, in December 2004 you climb up on the World Cup podium for the first time [after a third-place finish in down-hill]. How are you feeling about your career at this point? Do you think, "Okay, we are right on pace"?

LINDSEY VONN: At that point, I felt like I belonged. I felt like, "Okay, the work that I am putting in now is making a big difference. I am in shape, I am focused." Mentally, I felt like I was so much more mature and prepared at that point, you know?

MICHAEL KAY: Prior to the 2006 Winter Olympics in Italy, you are on a practice run doing max speed—which you tell me is about ninety miles per hour—and you have this horrific crash. Tell me what happened.

LINDSEY VONN: It was awful. I was having a great run and then I kind of caught a little bit of air with the tips of my skis, and one edge caught out, and I literally did the splits going like eighty miles an hour. So I landed on my back, it was excruciatingly painful, and I was helicoptered to the hospital. And I literally thought my career was over. They were saying that most likely my back was broken, and most likely my pelvis was broken—you know, "You are done." Picabo Street actually met me in the hospital, and she was the first person that I saw. And I was just laying there, in a neck brace, and we just started crying. We didn't have to say anything, it was just a really emotional moment. Then I went through all the tests—the CAT scans, the CT scans, the MRIs, everything—and I got the word that nothing was broken. And I was like, "Okay, when can I ski again? [Laughs, laughter] Can I get back out there? The race is in, like, forty-eight hours." I can't walk, I can't move, but I am gonna get out there. So we did some therapies, and it worked [and I was able to ski]. I knew that the Olympics were over for me as far as getting a medal, but I just wanted to go out there and give it my best, I didn't want to give up, even with that injury. I got eighth place, but it didn't matter. I was out there at the start and I had a huge grin on my face. I had never experienced anything like that, where I thought that my career was over, and it made me appreciate every single day that I have. I cherish every day that I get to be on the mountain doing what I love. It's the best job in the world. And honestly, I think that injury was the best thing that's ever happened to me in my life.

MICHAEL KAY: Then you win the US Olympic Spirit Award for representing the best Olympic spirit. What did that mean to you?

LINDSEY VONN: That meant a lot. It's voted on by the public and by the press [and your teammates and former US Olympians]. It meant that even though I didn't win anything, people still recognized the work and the effort that I was putting in. The Olympics isn't just about winning the gold medal, you know? It's about representing your country and setting a good example for young kids. And it's about the spirit of doing what you love and dreaming as high as you can. That's what the Spirit Award meant to me. So it was very emotional, and a cool award, and I was really thrilled about that.

MICHAEL KAY: Now, you would win your first "big race," in quotes, uh, with a silver medal in the downhill super G in the '07 World Championships in Sweden. But you had a training crash, causing an ACL sprain to your right knee, to end your season. Now, people might be thinking, "Wow, she falls down a lot." [Laughter]

LINDSEY VONN: [Laughs] Well, crashing is just part of our sport. Everyone crashes all the time, it's just that sometimes you are lucky enough not to crash during the moments where it really counts. But when you're pushing the limits, when you are always trying to go faster, and trying to find that fine line just short of being completely crazy, you are gonna crash. But that's the only way that you can be fast.

MICHAEL KAY: When you were a kid and you watched Wide World of Sports, did you ever feel sorry for the "agony of defeat" guy who was tumbling on his skis?

LINDSEY VONN: [Laughs] Definitely.

MICHAEL KAY: Okay, it's a disappointing '06 Olympics with the crash. In '07 you get married [to former US Ski Team member Thomas Vonn]. Then in '08 you start to take the skiing world by storm. Are you feeling good about things at this point?

LINDSEY VONN: Yeah, that was my first season being Lindsey Vonn. And it was kind of funny, because on Swiss television, they are like, "These Americans, I don't know where they come up with all these young great skiers. There is this new girl, Lindsey Vonn, and she is winning everything." They have no idea that I was [the former] Lindsey Kildow. [*Laughter*] But everything was just fitting well together.

MICHAEL KAY: The 2010 Winter Olympics are on the way, and you are on the cover of the 2010 *Sports Illustrated* Swimsuit Edition, and inside there were pictures of you in a bikini. How cool was that?

LINDSEY VONN: [*Laughs*] Well, it was cool. I wasn't really anticipating that, nor everything that followed it, but I was definitely very honored to be on the cover. I think what meant the most to me was the headline that said, "America's Best Woman Skier Ever." That was really special to me.

MICHAEL KAY: I never got to those words, I just [looked at the pictures]. [*Laughter*] I think you are blushing, Miss Vonn.

LINDSEY VONN: [*Laughs*] Yes, I'm getting red.

MICHAEL KAY: Now, a lot of people look at you as a sex symbol. Are you happy with that?

LINDSEY VONN: No. I hope that people watch my sport and enjoy watching my sport and enjoy skiing themselves. I don't want to be known as a sex symbol. I just want to be known as me.

MICHAEL KAY: We are so-o-o-o different. [*Laughs, laughter*] Now, most Americans who compete in the Olympics, they think, "Well, that's it. After it's over, that's it." But [after the 2010 Winter Olympics] you went on and you won the World Cup, right?

LINDSEY VONN: Yeah, it was really difficult actually. After the Olympics I got straight on a plane and went back to Europe and had two of the most important weeks of the season. All the titles were on the line, and I have to admit, I was really, really tired after the Olympics. It was a tough two weeks, but I made it through.

MICHAEL KAY: The 2010 US Olympic Ski Team won eight medals. It was very successful. Are you happy with the way the US Ski Team is going? Are you happy with the management and everything like that?

LINDSEY VONN: Yeah, it's great. As a team, we are doing a really good job, not just in alpine but in cross-country. Everyone is working really hard and doing a really great job.

MICHAEL KAY: The final thing, and I have always wondered this. You have an Olympic gold medal. Do you ever walk around in pajamas with it around your neck? [*Laughs, laughter*] Or do you ever look at it anymore?

LINDSEY VONN: [*Laughs*] Yeah, I do. I do look at it. It's a great way to keep things in perspective—things like life and how hard you need to work. It's a reminder to keep going and keep following your dreams.

MICHAEL KAY: It was very cool to meet you. [*Applause*] And it was fun.

LINDSEY VONN: Thank you.

David Halberstam

David Halberstam, a native of New York City, was one of the greatest writers this country has ever produced. His genius output included the brilliant book about the origins of the Vietnam War *The Best and the Brightest*, and his comprehensive look at the American media, *The Powers That Be*, but he wrote a number of sports classics as well, such as *Summer of '49*, *October 1964*, *Playing for Keeps*, and *The Teammates*, a heartwarming story about a trip Dominic DiMaggio and Johnny Pesky made by car to visit their former Red Sox teammate Ted Williams, who they knew was dying.

Sports brought Halberstam to *CenterStage* when he was promoting his book about Patriots coach Bill Belichick, *The Education of a Coach*.

When we booked Halberstam, I was anxious to talk about everything he'd done in his amazing career. He was a willing subject. Although there to promote his latest book, Halberstam took us through his life and how he dealt with the hard elbows when he covered things outside "the garden of sports," as he put it.

In the hour we spent together, Halberstam was brilliant. He didn't carry himself in the elitist way you might expect from a Pulitzer Prize winner; instead, he easily moved from subject to subject, explaining his exacting process and how he arrived at the finished product.

Midway through the interview, we were talking about his reporting on Vietnam and how he'd clashed with the Nixon administration, and I asked him if he'd ever been audited. He laughed heartily and said he'd been audited every year. When we went to break at the end of that segment, he leaned over to me and whispered, "In all my years being interviewed, I've never been asked if I was audited. Never. What a great question." To me, it remains one of the great compliments I've ever received.

Two years after our talk Halberstam died in a car accident in Menlo Park, California, as he was driving to do an interview for a book about the 1958 NFL title game between the Giants and the Colts. He was seventy-three and obviously had so much more to give.

The Interview

MICHAEL KAY: Today's guest has become a legendary figure in American journalism; he has faithfully chronicled the profound changes in America over the last fifty years. His writings have won numerous awards, including the Pulitzer Prize for his reports from Vietnam in the early 1960s. His book *The Best and the Brightest*, about the origins of the Vietnam War, was the first of fourteen bestsellers. His writings about sports like *The Summer of '49*, *October 1964*, and *Teammates* have also been critical successes. His latest book is *The Education of a Coach*, the story of Bill Belichick. *Newsweek* has called him very simply "one of our greatest reporters." Please welcome David Halberstam. [*Applause*]

MICHAEL KAY: When did you know you wanted to be a writer?

DAVID HALBERSTAM: Well, I wasn't good at anything else. [*Laughter*] I went to Harvard in the early fifties and I was in the bottom third of my class. I had what they now call attention deficit disorder, but we didn't know ADD then. In grade school if I had a teacher I didn't like or a subject that was not being well taught, I would fly out the window in boredom. And the one thing I was good at in college was the *Harvard Crimson*, the undergraduate newspaper. I was really good at it. And like a lot of ADD people, there's so many other things you can't do that when you find the one thing you can do, you home in on it. Journalism was my ticket, and I knew it was probably the only ticket I was going to get. I wasn't going to be a doctor, and I wasn't going to be a lawyer, the textbooks were too big. So I thought, "I'd better not screw up on this."

MICHAEL KAY: Now, you grew up in the Bronx and you were a Yankee fan. You obviously had a love of sports, so when you got to Harvard, did you play any sports?

DAVID HALBERSTAM: Well, I would've liked to have played basketball, and I could've made the freshman team. But I had a [part-time] job, and I was trying for the *Crimson*. I kept falling asleep in the library, and I made this decision that I better put the *Crimson* ahead of being the number eleven player on a freshman basketball team. That was a critical career choice. [*Laughter*]

MICHAEL KAY: Now, after Harvard your first reporter's job is at the *Daily Times Leader* in West Point, Mississippi.

DAVID HALBERSTAM: Yeah. It was the smallest daily in Mississippi. It was 1955, a year after *Brown vs. Board of Education* [which outlawed segregation in public schools], the civil rights movement was about to begin, and I thought, "Well, why not go down to Mississippi?" But the newspaper's editors were very nervous about having someone who was just out of Harvard, Northern, Jewish, and I was writing for some liberal magazines, so I got fired after ten months. The editor told me, "David, you're free, white, and twenty-one, it's time for you to go, and I've hired your replacement and you have to be out of here today." Then I went to Nashville for four years on a very good paper, the *Tennessean*, and then I went to the *New York Times*.

MICHAEL KAY: When I read stories of that time and the civil rights movement, it makes your stomach roll. And, going through it, could you believe what was happening?

DAVID HALBERSTAM: It was terrifying. I was a young reporter, first there then for the *Tennessean* covering these things, and then again after two years in Vietnam for the *New York Times*. This was in 1964, the summer that the three young civil rights activists were killed in Philadelphia [Mississippi]. I was more scared in Mississippi that summer than I had been in Vietnam. You were a target if you looked different because the entire state was like a beehive that someone put a baseball bat into, everybody was buzzing and angry, and you'd be driving at night and there'd be a pickup truck with a whiplash radio and a shotgun in the rack, and they'd be following you. It was very scary. I was surprised that more people weren't murdered that summer because there was no law of the land, the local FBI was passive and essentially on the side of the rednecks, and the police and judicial apparatus were all pro-segregation. You had no protection in your own country, and that was terrifying.

MICHAEL KAY: So in 1960, at the age of twenty-six, you get a job with the *New York Times*, as a foreign correspondent.

DAVID HALBERSTAM: I didn't actually start as a foreign correspondent. I was hired to the Washington bureau, but when I got there, the Congo was blowing open. And it was a very dangerous place; the Belgians were pulling back their colonial presence, and the *Times* didn't have any young reporters with a lot of experience who were single, and I'd covered the civil rights movement for five years, so they thought, "Send him." Of course I was so hungry, I was delighted to go, and I found out that I could do it, that I could deal with the fear thing in order to get the story. You're balancing your ambition with the risks, and the excitement of the story, and I found out I could do that. I did about a year of that, and then in 1962 Vietnam was clearly just about to develop into something, so I volunteered for that—and they didn't have any other volunteers. So I was the first full-time *New York Times* permanent correspondent in Saigon, starting in '62.

MICHAEL KAY: What was your initial thought, first of the country and then of our war effort?

DAVID HALBERSTAM: Well, I first thought, *This'll be terrific*, because I had all the conventional anti-communist attitudes of that time; we were going to help a country to save itself. And I loved the country, the country and the people are really lovely. But the war didn't work. I would keep going out in the field and I would see young American or not-so-young American advisers—in those days we were not full combat, we were in an advisory-and-support mission, we were teaching a country to fight for itself. And wherever I went, they said, you know, "It doesn't work, we can't get it done." So that's when I began to write pessimistic stories, which greatly angered Washington and put me in a confrontation with the Pentagon, the White House, the State Department, and it culminated with President Kennedy asking the publisher of the *New York Times* to pull me from Saigon [which the *Times* refused to do]. Kennedy wanted to get through his first term and then deal with Vietnam in his second term, and here I was, saying on the front page of the *New York Times* that Vietnam was a failure. And then [after the Kennedy assassination] Lyndon Johnson called me and my young friend Neil Sheehan traitors to our country. It got very heated. It was not fun.

MICHAEL KAY: Did you ever get audited?

DAVID HALBERSTAM: Oh, yeah. [*Laughter*] I must've gotten on some big-time list, because [I] was getting audited every year. [*Laughter*]

MICHAEL KAY: Now, because of your work in Vietnam, you end up winning the Pulitzer Prize at the age of thirty. What did it mean to your career?

DAVID HALBERSTAM: At the time it meant a lot because I had been under so much pressure to conform and give a conventional optimistic version of events. And when I didn't, I became the enemy. So when I won the Pulitzer, it was like the Supreme Court of the journalistic world had voted in favor of me, so that was very nice.

MICHAEL KAY: Have you ever been able to just totally trust your country since then, and the people that run it?

DAVID HALBERSTAM: I have great faith in this country, and I have great faith in its resiliency, in democracy, that a democracy creates the nobility of ordinary people.

QUESTION FROM AUDIENCE: Mr. Halberstam, should a reporter's first duty be to the truth, or to his country's best interests?

DAVID HALBERSTAM: I think the truth *is* the country's best interest, that this country is a democracy, and the more truth it gets, the better decisions it makes.

MICHAEL KAY: In 1967, after six years you leave the *Times*. I mean, you're a big shot at the *Times*, so why'd you go?

DAVID HALBERSTAM: Well, I was thirty-three years old, I had spent five years in the South, a year in the Congo, two years in Vietnam, and a year in Eastern Europe. I wanted to use the wonderful education that I'd been given in a different way and just write longer magazine pieces and books.

MICHAEL KAY: Nineteen seventy-two, *The Best and the Brightest* comes out, which was a stunning success. Why'd you write that book?

DAVID HALBERSTAM: Something ached in me. When the Kennedy people first came into office, they were dazzling, each was brighter than the next. Robert McNamara, McGeorge Bundy, Dean Rusk, General Maxwell Taylor—they had these great reputations, and Washington was overwhelmed. So the question that prompted the book was, how could men who on paper seemed to be the ablest men to serve the country in a generation, how could they have been the architects of the worst tragedy since the Civil War? I wanted to answer those questions that had torn me and many of my generation apart.

QUESTION FROM AUDIENCE: Do you think the rise of twenty-four-hour news channels has been good or bad for journalism?

DAVID HALBERSTAM: It's a very good question. I think essentially it's been bad because it has diminished the editing, and the verification part of the process. There's really not that much that you need to know instantaneously, but because it's all the time, everybody's racing, and the verification process has really suffered, I think. The pressure to get it out first is overwhelming, and I don't think it's a healthy thing for a democracy trying to make wise decisions.

MICHAEL KAY: David, you've written about so many things—wars, presidents, the civil rights movement. But when I read your stuff on sports, there seems to be an innate joy about it. Tell me why.

DAVID HALBERSTAM: Well, it's a lot nicer working in the garden of sports than it is working on Vietnam, the decision making, the anger, the contradictions, or the world of politics or the world of high media. Most of the people I've met in the world of sports I generally liked, and for me one of the nice things about each book is that I've ended up with a friendship that's endured. When I did one of the first of them, *Summer of '49*, I was finally meeting all these guys like Tommy Henrich and Charlie Keller and Allie Reynolds who'd been great heroes to me when I was a kid. Tommy Henrich had been my favorite player, and I went down to see him in Arizona, and it was a lot of fun. I really enjoyed doing that book.

MICHAEL KAY: Why was that summer important to you?

DAVID HALBERSTAM: Well, I was fifteen years old, it was the year before my father died, the last year of me really being a kid, and I was holding on to baseball. I wasn't a very successful teenager, so I glommed on to the Yankees that year. DiMaggio was having this exceptional year where he'd come back from missing the first fifty or sixty games, and he went up to Fenway, hit four home runs, and knocked in nine runs and won a three-game series. And years later it struck me that that was the last year of a certain era in America, when baseball essentially was white, even though Jackie Robinson had already broken in. They were playing in the daytime, traveling by train, no expansion teams yet, the owners in complete control in terms of salary. It was a slower, different America, and that pulled me to it.

MICHAEL KAY: You know, a lotta people say that sports is the toy store of the newspaper. Do you feel like that?

DAVID HALBERSTAM: No. Because sports is a reflection of who we are as a society, in race and so many other things. If you want to understand the changes in politics and culture, it tends to happen first in sports.

MICHAEL KAY: Did sports play a role in furthering the civil rights movement in the South?

DAVID HALBERSTAM: Oh, sure. There's a great story about when Bear Bryant's [all-white Alabama team] played the University of Southern California, and [USC] had [the black player] Sam "Bam" Cunningham at fullback, and he scored two touchdowns. It was later said that in just sixty minutes Sam "Bam" Cunningham did more for integration in the Deep South and particularly in Alabama than Martin Luther King had done in the previous ten or twelve years. Because people finally realized that [Southern black athletes] were native sons, they were talented, they were owed the chance to play—and besides which, if you didn't let them play, you could no longer compete nationally. Up till the 1960s the great black athletes from the South were going into the Big Ten and other schools, and now for the first time they began to stay home. And it's not surprising that today the Southeastern Conference is probably the best all-around football conference in the country.

MICHAEL KAY: Your new book is called *The Education of a Coach*, and it's about Bill Belichick, the head coach of the New England Patriots. How did you get Bill Belichick to agree to cooperate on a book? I mean, this is not exactly an outgoing man.

DAVID HALBERSTAM: No, he's wary of the media. I'd been interested in him for twenty years, because I started picking up on him when he was the young defensive coach for the Giants. He has a house in Nantucket and I have a house in Nantucket, and we had never met, but a mutual friend suggested that Belichick was thinking that he ought to have a book. And we sort of made contact, but then he pulled back for two reasons: one, he'd have to promote it during the season, and he doesn't wanna give up a *minute* during the season. And then secondly, he was afraid it would be an ego thing, you know, "Look at me!" And then I said, "Well, what about a book on the education of a coach? The people who taught you? Who teaches a coach? How do you put it together?" And that interested him, he really liked the idea, and so we sat down and talked about it. He had enough trust that if I said I was going to do that, that's what I was going to do. He never got to check the manuscript, it's my book, but obviously he sort of knew the direction it was going in.

MICHAEL KAY: What's your advice to a young writer, a young reporter, somebody who wants to get into this business, what would you tell 'em?

DAVID HALBERSTAM: Work hard, treat people with respect, and always try and do one more interview.

MICHAEL KAY: David, it's really been a pleasure, thank you.

PART THREE

THEY MADE US LAUGH

Lorne Michaels

Lorne Michaels is quite simply one of the greatest content producers in the history of television. His creation and longtime production of *Saturday Night Live* has created a comedic time capsule for almost half a century. His keen eye for talent uncovered some of the greatest comedy minds and performers in history. He has been in the catbird seat and watched and launched the careers of John Belushi, Dan Aykroyd, Chevy Chase, Bill Murray, and Gilda Radner in the beginning of *SNL*'s run while recently nurturing the genius of Jimmy Fallon, Will Ferrell, Seth Meyers, Kate McKinnon, and Tina Fey, to name just a few.

There has been triumph and heartbreak while he has been at the helm of *SNL* and I was totally pumped to have his full attention for an hour. Oh, the stories he could tell.

After sitting down with Michaels, we found out what the loss of Chevy Chase to the ensemble cast meant to the franchise and who he felt was best able to fill in for the transcendent star and the sudden departure. He also revealed who he felt was the most talented cast members over the years. Just think about that: everyone who has ever watched *SNL* has a favorite and debated with friends who was the one who transcended the others. It was riveting to get the take of the man who found and discovered and promoted the talent. The following might actually settle some arguments that friends have had over the years.

But the most amazing thing you get from this journey with Michaels is that he has built an assembly line of greatness. He has become the Henry Ford of comedians, churning out comic geniuses rather than Model Ts.

It can't be easy, but Michaels has made it look that way. *SNL*'s timeline mirrors the timeline of this country, from the performers to the subjects that they tackled.

This was easily one of the interviews I was most eager to conduct, and you'll realize the eagerness was warranted.

The Interview

MICHAEL KAY: Thank you, everybody, and welcome to our one hundred and first *CenterStage* program. Our first guest in our second century is Canadian-born Lorne Michaels. He moved from the Great White North to Los Angeles and began as a comedy writer in the late 1960s on classic shows like *Laugh-In*. In 1975, working with an NBC executive, he formulated a new program that continues to entertain today. It began as *NBC's Saturday Night* and shortly thereafter was renamed *Saturday Night Live*. Since its premiere, *SNL* has been a trendsetter and groundbreaker in American humor for over thirty years. It has influenced American music, politics, manners, and even fashion. Performed in front of a live audience, *SNL* established a reputation for being cutting-edge and unpredictable and launched the careers of some of entertainment's most successful comics. The list is seemingly endless. It includes Chevy Chase, John Belushi, Dan Aykroyd, Bill Murray, Eddie Murphy, Mike Myers, and Adam Sandler. Additionally, *Conan O'Brien*, *30 Rock*, and the recent film *Baby Mama* were brought to life and succeeded under his guidance. Please welcome the creative force behind television's wittiest programs, the legendary writer and producer Lorne Michaels. [*Applause*]

LORNE MICHAELS: Thank you.

MICHAEL KAY: It's been over thirty years of *Saturday Night Live*. Has it gone quickly?

LORNE MICHAELS: Well, it's a very intense week when we are doing the show. But when we're not doing the show, time moves at the same pace as it does for everyone else.

MICHAEL KAY: Now, obviously, politics seems like it's great fodder for comedy. How important do you think *SNL* is in an election year?

LORNE MICHAELS: I think we're just one of the voices, sometimes with more impact than others. The show tends to pique an interest both for the audience and for us when it's an election year. I think that's because the show came on just after Watergate, it's just part of what we always did. We were always interested in American politics—and in election years more so. But our job is to find a way into it that's funny. I mean, we are, first and foremost, a comedy show.

MICHAEL KAY: You obviously have likes and dislikes when it comes to politicians. Do you let that spill over?

LORNE MICHAELS: No. It won't play if it's partisan or if we are just doing it because we like or dislike someone.

MICHAEL KAY: Is it tough? Because you run in circles where you might meet these people the show skewers. Do they like it?

LORNE MICHAELS: No. But I think everybody understands what we do. I doubt you can be in public life and worry about us.

MICHAEL KAY: I would think that the stress level has to be enormous. I mean, you have to come up with an hour and a half of live television on Saturday.

LORNE MICHAELS: When I was younger, I think I worried all the time. Now I just worry more selectively. I think experience teaches you when to worry.

MICHAEL KAY: Anything off-limits that you won't make fun of?

LORNE MICHAELS: Oh, yeah, yeah, lots of things.

MICHAEL KAY: Like what?

LORNE MICHAELS: I have no idea. [*Laughter*]

MICHAEL KAY: All right. What was your comedy influence? How did you get into it?

LORNE MICHAELS: I don't know. My grandparents owned a movie house, and I used to go there when I was little. But I think television was the biggest influence.

MICHAEL KAY: And what was your favorite TV show, comedy show?

LORNE MICHAELS: It depends on what stage of my life. But I loved the *Sergeant Bilko* show when I was growing up.

MICHAEL KAY: Now, as a teenager at camp, you were directing plays? That's pretty early, right? How did that come about?

LORNE MICHAELS: I did it at school as well. I kind of liked it. And I liked being in the plays. I sort of went back and forth. I don't think, when I was young, that I had any one interest, you know? I kind of liked sports. I kind of liked movies. And I kind of liked lots of things. So, I think it was just something that I drifted into that I liked. But I didn't think, at any point when I was young, that it would be something I would end up doing the rest of my life.

MICHAEL KAY: What kind of sports did you like and play?

LORNE MICHAELS: Well, we played a lot of baseball, and we played a lot of touch football and a lot of hockey and a lot of ball hockey as well. I grew up in the kind of school where, in October, November, they would put up boards in the schoolyard and we didn't play with full equipment, just skates and sticks.

MICHAEL KAY: Down-in-the-dirt hockey.

LORNE MICHAELS: Yeah.

MICHAEL KAY: What was your first job out of college?

LORNE MICHAELS: I worked with another guy in radio. We were comedy writers and performers. Then we worked for some stand-up comedians. And then we got offered a job in Los Angeles in 1968. And we went out there and I was a comedy writer on a bunch of television shows.

MICHAEL KAY: The old saying is "Dying is easy, and comedy is hard." Why is comedy so hard?

LORNE MICHAELS: Because with comedy, there is just such clarity about it. When it doesn't work, it's completely evident. You can go to a drama, and some people are moved and some people aren't. If there is a story, people want to stay till the end of the story to see how it turns out. But comedy, if they don't laugh, it's very clear it's not working.

MICHAEL KAY: You did *The Beautiful Phyllis Diller Show*. And *Laugh-In*. *Laugh-In* must have been an unbelievable place to work.

LORNE MICHAELS: Yeah, it was. I was twenty-three, one of the youngest people working there. It was 1968, '69. It was fun.

MICHAEL KAY: In the mid-seventies, you wrote for Woody Allen, Dick Cavett, Lily Tomlin, Joan Rivers.

LORNE MICHAELS: And my impact on any of their careers was, to say the least, minimal. [*Laughter*]

MICHAEL KAY: Of all those people that you worked with, who was the biggest influence on you?

LORNE MICHAELS: Lily Tomlin was an enormous influence because, first and foremost, 'cause she was the first person to go to an American network and say, "I would like to have him as a producer." She just had really high standards and, and was prepared to fight to make sure that the show was everything she wanted it to be.

MICHAEL KAY: Well, all of this led up, obviously, to *SNL*. It's 1975 and NBC green-lights a new TV show and they call it *NBC's Saturday Night*. And what did they say they wanted from you? What was the basic concept? Did they say what they were looking for, or did they say, "Just give us something to fill that time on Saturday night"?

LORNE MICHAELS: There was an opportunity to do a show in late night, where the standards were lower than in prime time and you didn't need as many people. And I thought then that if I could do a show that *I* would watch, that it would work. So I took everything I was interested in, comedy and music and politics and films, and threw it all together. I had the ingredients, but I didn't quite have the recipe. But [NBC executive Dick Ebersol] was incredibly supportive and pretty much interested in the same things. So I was given the opportunity to put together a group of people to do it. I was hired on April first, 1975, and we didn't go on till October. So I used the first three months to find the people that I wanted. I met with lots of people and, and sort of narrowed in on the people that I thought were exceptional in some way.

MICHAEL KAY: Now, the names. Everyone knows Chevy Chase, Belushi, Aykroyd, Radner, Curtin, Morris, Laraine Newman. What did you think was exceptional about these people?

LORNE MICHAELS: Dan Aykroyd I knew from Canada. Gilda Radner I knew from Canada, from shows there. Chevy Chase I met on a movie line in LA for a Monty Python film. Laraine I had worked with on the Lily Tomlin shows. Jane came out of an audition. Garrett was hired originally as a writer, and then I moved him into the cast. And John had worked with Gilda at Second City, and with Chevy in a show called *Lemmings*, which had run here in New York.

MICHAEL KAY: Did you ever dream it could become this?

LORNE MICHAELS: I never thought there were limits, no.

MICHAEL KAY: Now, the first show—October eleventh, 1975. Do you have any, like, visceral memories of that day?

LORNE MICHAELS: There was lots of stuff that worked. The big fight that weekend was about George Carlin, the first host. Someone at the network wanted him in a suit. He felt we would lose the affiliates if Carlin didn't wear a suit. And Carlin wanted to wear a T-shirt. And so the compromise was, he wore a suit with a T-shirt. [*Laughter*]

MICHAEL KAY: Were you aware when the show started that you were kind of groundbreaking, and changing the way people think and thinking about television? Changing an era of television?

LORNE MICHAELS: You never get up in the morning and go, "I feel like groundbreaking today." But there was a feeling we were doing a show that was true to ourselves. And we were sort of excited by it all. That part was intoxicating.

MICHAEL KAY: Now, the first season is over, and the show is obviously a hit. And at the time you had said that there was a loss of innocence after that first year. What happened?

LORNE MICHAELS: We were beat up when we first came on, critically, and then that sort of changed somewhere in the middle of the year. And then the industry was very supportive of us. And that year we had won a bunch of Emmys. So suddenly we were under a different level of scrutiny. And people who only marginally had been in show business six months before now had agents and managers and, and were being pursued. So I think that there just became a consciousness that was different. In the beginning we were just doing a show for ourselves. It was just sort of state of grace. All that mattered was the show—and I don't think anybody thought of careers at that point. And then, career—as it always does—comes up.

MICHAEL KAY: Was there jealousy amongst the cast members when Chevy was on the cover of *Time* magazine?

LORNE MICHAELS: I think it altered things a little, yeah.

MICHAEL KAY: Now, Chevy leaves after the first year. Did that tick you off?

LORNE MICHAELS: He and I were very close, and I knew how hard it was for him, because he was being offered all sorts of things that he wanted to be doing. When he left, I was definitely fearful of what would happen. But I sorta felt we would be all right.

MICHAEL KAY: And you end up hiring Bill Murray kind of to replace him. Did you realize that he was going to be that big? That he was that good?

LORNE MICHAELS: Yeah. He was one of the people that I wanted originally.

MICHAEL KAY: So he was on your radar?

LORNE MICHAELS: Yeah. But the audience wasn't there for him right away because it was all about Chevy leaving. But by the end of that second season, John and Gilda were sort of preeminent, and Bill was doing amazing work. We were still a winning team.

MICHAEL KAY: And with every good thing, there has to be something bad. There were rumors of drug abuse on the set. Was that unsettling to you? Was it something that you could stop, or try to stop, or was it part of the creative thing?

LORNE MICHAELS: I think that it was not so much a problem *on* the show. But people began pushing boundaries, yeah.

MICHAEL KAY: And did you think that it was in your purview to stop it?

LORNE MICHAELS: Yeah, when it intruded on the show. I think the value system then was sort of, whatever gets you through the night. And as long as it didn't get in the way of the work, then people could live their lives the way they wanted to. It turned out that value system was wrong, but it's what we believed in.

MICHAEL KAY: Did you have a lot of problems with censors?

LORNE MICHAELS: Yeah. There is a natural thing in comedy to keep pushing, and we would keep bumping up against things. The standards department is there to protect advertisers and, and the general public—and to make sure that there are boundaries. And I am a big believer in creativity coming within boundaries. There are certain things you can't do. You have to figure out things in a cleverer way.

MICHAEL KAY: Of all the great hosts that you had, do you have a favorite?

LORNE MICHAELS: Well, Steve Martin redefined the show, particularly after Chevy left. He became a big part of where we were.

MICHAEL KAY: Any host that was a disappointment?

LORNE MICHAELS: I am sure there are people like that. . . . [*Laughter*]

MICHAEL KAY: Now, in '84, you, you created a new sketch-comedy show, *The New Show*. Dave Thomas, Buck Henry, but it didn't hit. How disappointing?

LORNE MICHAELS: Well, when it's not working, it's never much fun.

MICHAEL KAY: Do you ever have any self-doubt and go, "Well, hey, maybe I don't have it anymore"?

LORNE MICHAELS: I have had that thought every week. [*Laughter*]

MICHAEL KAY: Now, when you went back to *Saturday Night Live* [in 1985, after a five-year hiatus], that first season was not one of the best seasons. Again, are you thinking, you know, "What's wrong here? Why didn't I turn it around?"

LORNE MICHAELS: No. I decided to drop down a generation, and it was Joan Cusack and Anthony Michael Hall and Robert Downey Jr., and Jon Lovitz was in there. I knew the part of the show that was working, and I sort of kept that nucleus and then added to that, and then we were all right up there.

MICHAEL KAY: Phil Hartman, Dana Carvey, Kevin Nealon.

LORNE MICHAELS: And Dennis Miller. Nora Dunn. Nora was in the '85 cast.

MICHAEL KAY: And then you add Mike Myers, Chris Rock, Chris Farley, Adam Sandler, David Spade. When you are hiring these people, are you going, "All right, this guy is gonna be like Dan Aykroyd, and this guy is gonna be my Chevy Chase . . ."?

LORNE MICHAELS: No. You try not to have two people that do the same thing.

MICHAEL KAY: Chris Farley was unbelievably funny. But did you look at some of the same signals that you got from Belushi? Did you try to save Farley from that fate?

LORNE MICHAELS: I want to make the point about John, that he didn't run into that problem *while* doing *Saturday Night Live.*

MICHAEL KAY: And how sad were you that it . . . that [he and Farley] couldn't be saved ultimately?

LORNE MICHAELS: I loved them, so it's heartbreaking, you know? Both of them were thirty-three when they died.

MICHAEL KAY: Is there a member of a cast that you would say that your breath was taken away by how talented they are, or were?

LORNE MICHAELS: Yeah. I mean, Bill Murray, in his time. Dan Aykroyd, in his time. You know, Chevy. There is no one that you are gonna stay with who doesn't just blow you away.

MICHAEL KAY: Thirty-plus years of *SNL*. There has to be a moment that jumps out at you—good or bad—where you just go, "Oh my goodness, that . . . that, that was amazing" or "That was terrible." What was that moment?

LORNE MICHAELS: You know, I could never answer these questions. There's, like, seven hundred hours of stuff, you know?

MICHAEL KAY: Why hasn't anybody been able to successfully copy-cat *SNL*? I guess 'cause *you* are at *SNL*, right?

LORNE MICHAELS: Right, yeah. [*Laughs*]

MICHAEL KAY: You are just a megagiant in your industry—

LORNE MICHAELS: Awww.

MICHAEL KAY: —and you created this unbelievable lasting image, which will be around as long as television is around. Do you ever go, "Wow, this is special, what I have been a part of"?

LORNE MICHAELS: Yeah. But I tend to feel it while it's happening.

MICHAEL KAY: Oh, so you don't reflect? How come?

LORNE MICHAELS: Because I am not a reflective person? [*Laughter*]

MICHAEL KAY: It's been a nice run, though.

LORNE MICHAELS: Oh, yeah. It was a very, very nice run. It's not most people who go to the same office for thirty-four or thirty-five years—and get to laugh.

MICHAEL KAY: Thank you so much.

Billy Crystal

Billy Crystal is another rare two-time *CenterStage* guest. His appearances were separated by ten years, the first occurring in April of 2002.

He makes the two-timer list because he's an exceptional storyteller. He has enough material to fill ten shows, and he was gracious enough to grace our stage twice and was brilliant each time.

He's also a legitimate Yankee fan and knows the game inside out. Of all the incredible things he has accomplished in his show business career, getting the chance to lead off for the Yankees in a 2008 spring-training game ranks as one of his top moments.

As you will tell by our conversation, Crystal is a master comic and actor but, at heart, a wannabe Major League Baseball player. But things certainly turned out okay for this native New Yorker.

When you sit down and interview someone such as Billy Crystal, you realize his immense gift of being able to tell a story and make it conversational, but all the while displaying impeccable timing and delivery. With someone of lesser expertise you'd feel you're in the middle of a show and not having an exchange, but Crystal is the rare genius who can put on a show while also showing you who he is. In the two conversations I had with Crystal, I was in awe of his amazing recall of facts and punch lines, all made to look effortless.

In the years I've done this I've realized that those who deliver effortless-seeming performances are the ones who put the most effort into making them appear that way.

Crystal has spent a lifetime honing his craft and sharpening his delivery—so it comes off as natural and easy. To be a part of that journey for a couple of hours is an amazing experience that I'm thrilled you can now share.

The Interview

MICHAEL KAY: Thank you, everybody, and welcome to *CenterStage*. Today's guest is a Yankees favorite who grew up in Long Beach, New York, playing baseball, listening to jazz, and learning comedy routines. In the early 1970s, he worked the local comedy clubs and rose to prominence as Jodie Dallas on the groundbreaking TV series *Soap*. In 1984, he joined the cast of *Saturday Night Live* and later made memorable films like *When Harry Met Sally*, *City Slickers*, and *Analyze This*. Known for his quick-witted humor, he has hosted the Academy Awards nine times and received six Emmy Awards for those efforts. And for decades he has worked tirelessly to help eradicate homelessness in America. In March of 2008, he signed a one-day minor league contract with the New York Yankees, which produced a respectable at bat in a Major League Baseball spring-training game. His new film is *Parental Guidance*, where he stars with Bette Midler as grandparents to Marisa Tomei's children. Please welcome a true Yankees fan, and only the second person to make a second appearance on *CenterStage*, actor, comic, writer, producer, and former Yankee DH Billy Crystal. [*Applause*]

MICHAEL KAY: I was worried that you wouldn't show up.

BILLY CRYSTAL: Why?

MICHAEL KAY: The Yankees released you.

BILLY CRYSTAL: Oh, yeah. Well, you know, I was supposed to retire—

MICHAEL KAY: [*Laughs*]

BILLY CRYSTAL: —and that was the deal, the one at bat, which was thrilling in itself. And I said to [Yankees general manager] Brian [Cashman], "Then I'll retire. I'll have a press conference and announce my retirement." And he released me. He is cold. It was on my birthday, too.

MICHAEL KAY: That's just wrong.

BILLY CRYSTAL: It was the greatest day of my life, I really have to say.

MICHAEL KAY: You did the movie *61** about Mantle and Maris. And you later became friends with Mickey Mantle. It must mean so much to you that your film *61** was put into the Hall of Fame. How cool was that?

BILLY CRYSTAL: Yeah, it was the fiftieth anniversary of Roger [Maris's] sixty-first home run. And the movie really is the only dramatic document of it besides the newsreels and everything. I worked so hard to make it realistic. And when we were honored at the Hall, I had trouble getting through the speech 'cause I thought I would always get there as a player. [*Laughter*]

MICHAEL KAY: And your friendship with Mickey Mantle?

BILLY CRYSTAL: It was crazy that I got to know him as well as I did. The first Yankees game I went to was May thirtieth, 1956, a Memorial Day doubleheader, and they played the Washington Senators. Mantle batted lefty off Pedro Ramos that day and hit the ball off the facade, and at that time it was the longest home run ever hit in Yankee Stadium. And that's the first time I saw him. Then [years later] we become friends. And it's strange to be with somebody that you loved and admired your whole life, and then suddenly there you are, talking with him. Many is the night that I spent with him, when he'd been drinking, and Bob Costas and I would actually put him to bed at the Regency Hotel. And we became really close and talked all the time. And then, when he was fading, Bob called me and said, "He's not gonna make it through the weekend." I flew to Dallas, and after Mickey had passed, Bob and I sat up late at night in the hotel and we wrote his eulogy together, which Bob so eloquently delivered, about this man who was so idolized but so flawed at the same time. And at the funeral I just sat there in front of the casket with the number seven in flowers, and I just lost it. I just started sobbing because I realized that my childhood was really over. [*Sighs emotionally*]

MICHAEL KAY: Now, people don't know this, but you were actually born in the Bronx, and then you moved to Long Beach. So for the geographically challenged, where is Long Beach?

BILLY CRYSTAL: Long Beach is a little barrier island on the south shore of Long Island, right near Jones Beach. It was the greatest place in the world to grow up.

MICHAEL KAY: All right. So what came first: passion for baseball, appreciation of music, or talents as a comedian?

BILLY CRYSTAL: Oh, I was a comedian, right from the beginning. 'Cause it was a great era of television then, really the golden age of TV comedians. Ernie Kovacs, Phil Silvers as Sergeant Bilko, Sid Caesar. Every Sunday night, somebody would be on *Ed Sullivan* doing stand-up. So my whole world was that. And my dad had a great eye for comedy. We had this little music store on Forty-Second Street, which was the family business, and he'd bring home the comedy albums—Nichols and May live on Broadway, Bob Newhart. And then the greatest of all was Cosby, 'cause Bill spoke to us. He had brothers, I had brothers. He went to Temple, I belonged to a temple. So . . . [*Laughter*]

MICHAEL KAY: Now, in high school you were voted Most Popular, which is a very nice thing. I had read that you had a memorable performance at a high school show. Do you remember it?

BILLY CRYSTAL: Yes, I did Bill Cosby's "Noah," and it was a smash, and everybody thought I wrote it. Years later, people come up and say, "You know, this guy Cosby is doing your stuff." [*Laughter*]

MICHAEL KAY: So when you were in college, you were in shows and things like that, did you have a plan? 'Cause you were married at that point. Did you have a plan how to support a family?

BILLY CRYSTAL: Uh, no. I was married at twenty-two, and I will be married for forty-three years in June. [*Applause*] But somehow I always thought it was gonna happen [professionally], that things would work out. I graduated from NYU, from the film school as a directing major, I thought I was going to direct films. And I thought, "Well, if the directing thing didn't work out, I have to have something solid to fall back on—like acting." [*Laughter*] Then I got a call from a friend, who was at NYU in a ZBT [Zeta Beta Tau] fraternity, and he said, "Listen, we need a comedian for a party. Do you know anybody who could do twenty minutes in front of the folk singer?" And I said, "I could do it. How much?" Twenty-five dollars. So I went, and I was supposed to do twenty minutes, but the singer didn't show up, so I did, like, an hour.

MICHAEL KAY: Did you get laughs?

BILLY CRYSTAL: Yeah. Big! Then these management guys, they produced all of Woody Allen's movies, they came to see me, and it worked, and they said, "Let's go to work." And I never looked back. And that's how it started, as a stand-up.

MICHAEL KAY: So you started in the comedy business. We have had so many comics on the show who talk about that moment when they are first on [*The Tonight Show* with Johnny] Carson. What was it like? That was in '75 for you, right?

BILLY CRYSTAL: Yeah. I worked up very quickly about a year after that fraternity-house party, and I get my first *Tonight Show*. I literally laid in bed that whole day till it was time to go to NBC. If Johnny liked you, he'd have you back—hopefully—and something would happen, a sitcom would happen, something—that's how powerful that show was. And so I get there and, and I'm backstage and I'm really nervous. And they're about to open the curtain, and I hear him, I hear that voice: "Here is a new kid, and what he does is kinda different and blah blah blah." And I did my routine, which was not a classic stand-up routine, it wasn't jokes. It was about a late-night comedian who worked like a singer would, and he did jokes in the style of, like, a Buddy Greco or something. It was very moody. It wasn't jokes, it was more attitude and timing. And Johnny never called anybody over [to the guest couch] unless he was thrilled. Before the show, the stage manager said to me, "Listen, when you are done, if I put my hands up like this [*motions*], just stand there and take your bow. But if I give you one of these [*motions*], get your ass over to the couch." So I finish my thing, I look over, and the [stage manager] goes like this. So I walk over to the couch and I shook Johnny's hand. And I sit down and he said some lovely things, like "It's great when a young guy comes out here and does something different. And I really think that's great." And it was a little awkward, 'cause my feet didn't touch the floor. [*Laughter*] I feel like I'm getting a haircut when I'm six. [*Laughter*] I get emotional when I think about it. Johnny Carson was the greatest superstar I have ever been around. And I found myself just staring at him. He wasn't the greatest stand-up comedian, but he was the greatest host ever. And his power was really incredible. He was an awesome guy. I ran right to the dressing room when it was done, and I called [my wife,] Janice, who was back in New York, and I don't know if it was a wail, or a sob, or what it was, but it was like, "He liked it! He really liked it! He is so cool-looking!" It was very emotional.

MICHAEL KAY: Now, your [Muhammad Ali] impression is famous. Did you become friends with Ali?

BILLY CRYSTAL: Yeah. He was being honored as the Man of the Year for *Sport* magazine, he had just beaten [George] Foreman in

Africa, and they were doing a local special from the Plaza Hotel. The late, great Dick Schaap was the editor of *Sport* magazine, and he had called my agent, looking for Robert Klein, 'cause Bob does great sports stuff. Bob wasn't available, but [my agent] said, "But I got this new guy, and he does this really good Ali imitation." So I'm doing this thing, I'm sitting on the dais, Ali is in the middle. And Ali is looking around, and he is looking at me going, "What is Joel Grey doing here?" [*Laughs, laughter*] So I get up to the microphone, and I go right into the Howard Cosell part of it, with Howard in Zaire in the ring with Ali. [*Imitating Cosell*] "We are in Kinshasa, Zy-ear, Z-A-I-R-E. Some would pronounce it 'Zair,' but they are wrong! Muhammad, come over here. Muhammad, may I call you Mo? Get over here!" [*Laughter*] [*Imitating Ali*] "Howard, I am announcing tonight that I am changing my name because I got new religious beliefs." [*Imitating Cosell*] "What do you mean, new religious beliefs?" [*Imitating Ali*] "Now I'll be known as Izzy Yiskowitz. I am now an Orthodox Jewish boxer. You don't hit the other fighter, you just make him feel guilty. [*Laughter*] I get in a clinch with Foreman, I say, 'When is the last time you called your mama?' He goes, 'Well, I don't know.' Voom, I give him a spritz and he is out!" [*Laughter*] And everybody in the audience went crazy. And afterwards Ali called me "little brother," which is what he calls me still to this day. I see him a few times a year, and he is an astounding man.

MICHAEL KAY: You were friends with Cosell, right?

BILLY CRYSTAL: Yes, Mr. Cosell and I were very close. He and I were really good friends, we spent a lot of time together. And when Howard passed away, at his memorial service I end up sitting with Ali. Now, they were partners, you know? Howard, for all his crassness, was a very dear man and a very principled man. He was the first journalist to stand up for Ali when he refused induction into the armed forces. Together they fought through these things, and they were very devoted to each other. So I am sitting next to the champ, and the casket is closed up there, and Ali whispers to me, "Little brother, do you think he's wearing his hairpiece?" [*Laughter*] So I go, "I don't know. Why?" And Ali said, "Well, if he's not, how will God recognize him?" [*Laughter*] So I said, "Once he starts complaining, God will know who he is." [*Laughter*]

MICHAEL KAY: In 1984, you are in a movie, *This Is Spinal Tap*. Then you worked with [director] Rob Reiner again when you did *When Harry Met Sally*. I'm curious about the Meg Ryan [fake orgasm] scene in the deli. [*Laughter*] How many times did she actually do that?

BILLY CRYSTAL: She was supposed to do it a few times, but then I started screwing up my lines on purpose so I could hear it again. [*Laughter*] That was a tough scene for Meg to do, and she was phenomenal.

MICHAEL KAY: So in 1984 you join the tenth season of *Saturday Night Live*.

BILLY CRYSTAL: Yeah, it was Christopher Guest, Marty Short, Harry Shearer, and myself, we came as a group. I had hosted the show twice the season before, and Dick Ebersol, the producer that year, called me up over the summer and said, "Would you think about coming and doing the year with us?" And it took me a second to go, "Yes." 'Cause I knew that's where I wanted to be. I was already thirty-six years old, I wasn't really having the career I wanted to be having. So we all moved to New York, and it was phenomenal.

MICHAEL KAY: After the *SNL* season, mid-eighties, your film career really begins to take off. *Running Scared*, with Gregory Hines. *The Princess Bride*, another Rob Reiner film, *Throw Momma from the Train*. Which one did you like the most of those?

BILLY CRYSTAL: I loved working with Gregory in *Running Scared*. That was really my first big movie. And *The Princess Bride*. I worked three days, and I was in the movie for four minutes.

MICHAEL KAY: Tell me about *City Slickers*, with Daniel Stern and Bruno Kirby. And then Jack [Palance] ended up being the funniest guy.

BILLY CRYSTAL: Jack Palance was an amazing guy to work with. I smile thinking about him. The first movie I ever saw him in was *Shane*, and Jack plays Wilson, the bad guy who Shane finally kills in the end of the movie. And he terrified me for years. That big back, that angular face. He was scary. When I first had the idea for the movie and wrote the first story, I was sitting home and I just started writing: "Three guys, city slickers, go on a fantasy cattle drive, and the crusty trail boss dies"—and I wrote, "Jack Palance." He only worked two weeks on the movie—two weeks!—and he won the Oscar. I was hosting that year, and he did the one-arm push-ups. That was the greatest setup any host could ever have—a seventy-year-old guy doing one-armed push-ups. We ran with jokes about it the whole night. Every time I came to the podium, I had something different to say: "And Jack just won the New York State primary." Big laugh. "Jack just bungee jumped off the HOLLYWOOD sign." Big laugh. There was a musical number with thirty or forty kids from the movie *Hook*, and I followed it with "You know, Jack is the father of all of those kids." [*Laughter*]

MICHAEL KAY: Johnny Carson hosted the Oscars. Bob Hope hosted the Oscars. What did it mean to you?

BILLY CRYSTAL: It was awesome. I walked out and Jack Nicholson was in the audience, and I went right after him. It was after the first *Batman*, and he had made a huge amount of money, something insane. So I went, "Jack is so rich, Morgan Freeman drove him here tonight." And "Jack is so rich [former celebrity hairdresser-turned film producer] Jon Peters still cuts his hair." So I had an eighteen-minute break in the middle of the show, and they're redoing my makeup, and there's a knock at the door, and I go, "Who is it?" And I hear, "It's Jack." I had never met him before. I open it up, and it's not only Jack, it's Warren Beatty. And they say, "You are just doing such a great job and we just want to tell you." It was so gracious. Here are these two iconic stars taking the time to make me feel good. It was amazing.

MICHAEL KAY: Now, you had a seven-year hiatus from doing the Oscars until 2012. Why such a long hiatus?

BILLY CRYSTAL: I had had enough. I had done it eight times, and I just said, "Oh, that's enough." Then I was in Atlanta making *Parental Guidance*, and Brian Glaser called me. They gave me overnight to decide if I wanted to do it again. Then I hit on a couple of ideas in the middle of the night that woke me up and put a smile on my face. I wrote 'em down and said to myself, "If I am still smiling in the morning, I'll do it." And it was fun.

MICHAEL KAY: You are nine away from Bob Hope. Do you think you can tie him?

BILLY CRYSTAL: I don't know what'll happen, but I know I'm not gonna do it nine more times. But I do love my relationship with the Academy, and it's been a lot of fun. We came up with new ways to be the host, and I'm proud of that. When you run out of new ideas, then it's time not to do it anymore.

MICHAEL KAY: We thank you so much for coming on again.

BILLY CRYSTAL: Michael, it is a pleasure.

Adam Sandler

Booking big-time stars for a show such as *CenterStage* is never easy, and getting Adam Sandler was a big chore. It seemed like a lost cause until, well, Adam Sandler stepped in.

The journey began when I ran into Adam at a Yankee game. He was friendly and so easy to talk with. He mentioned how he loved *CenterStage*, and I immediately seized the chance to ask him to come on and be interviewed. He said he'd love to do it and that our staff should contact his people and he'd get it done.

Well, we have an amazing group of people, starting with our lead booker, Steve Bernie, who immediately went to work to nail down a time and place. Steve kept running into roadblocks, though. Adam's people simply wouldn't make it happen. After a while we just figured it wasn't meant to be.

Once again, I ran into Adam at a Yankee game and he came up to me and said, "I thought we were going to do *CenterStage*." I told him we'd been trying but couldn't get past his people. He laughed and said, "Yeah, that's kind of their job, to make it difficult to get to me, but I thought they knew I wanted to do the show." I said, "I guess they *didn't* know." Adam then said, "Have your guy call and we'll make it happen."

Adam was true to his word. When my booker Steve talked to Adam's PR people, they quickly agreed to make him available the next time he was in New York.

Adam's movies have earned billions, but he couldn't be more down-to-earth. The sweet, almost innocent nature that comes through on film showed up right there on our set. He laughed easily and told great stories about his life and improbable rise to superstardom. I also joked with him that he could fulfill one of my lifelong dreams by getting me cast in a movie. This throwaway line was meant to get a laugh. He simply said, "Done."

After the show I never gave that promise a second thought until I received a phone call about eight months later. "Michael," the caller said, "Adam Sandler here. I wrote a small part for you in *Grown Ups 2*, which we'll be filming in Boston. I'd love for you to do it. I will send you the script and have someone contact you to make arrangements." I was stunned. Somehow he'd tracked down my number and kept his promise.

I flew to Boston one summer day and was picked up at the airport and escorted to a trailer to be fitted for the role of Coach Romey, a high school football coach. After I received my hoodie, another person came in the trailer and said, "Adam would love for you to come say hi." When I got to his trailer, Adam and his production crew started peppering me with questions about the Yankees. They acted as if I were the star and couldn't have been more gracious.

When it was time for my scene, Adam stood right off to the side as I spoke my lines. He kept feeding me new lines, writing on the run. He came up with an off-color line, and before I could say it, he said, "No, let's not do that. You're the voice of the Yankees—it wouldn't be cool for you to say that in a movie."

I was blown away by Adam's kindness, consideration, and generosity. The movie was released and made hundreds of millions at the box office. I'm just shocked that Adam never followed with a Coach Romey spin-off.

The Interview

MICHAEL KAY: Thank you, everybody, and welcome to *CenterStage*. Today's guest hails from Brooklyn, New York, but was raised in Manchester, New Hampshire. He began a stand-up comedy career at the age of seventeen and later attended NYU. In 1990 he was hired as a writer by *Saturday Night Live* and became a featured player the following season. There he created several memorable characters as well as penning "The Chanukah Song." In 1993 he released the first of five successful comedy albums, and two years later he wrote and appeared in *Billy Madison*, which began a string of successful film releases. And a 1998 release of *The Waterboy* made him one of the hottest names in Hollywood. His latest film, *Just Go with It*, has him in the enviable position of starring opposite both Jennifer Aniston and Brooklyn Decker. He is not only an actor, comedian, singer, screenwriter, musician, film producer, but he is genuinely an all-around really, really nice guy. Please welcome Adam Sandler. [*Applause*]

ADAM SANDLER: Thanks, thank you. Hello, everybody! This is great. Thank you!

MICHAEL KAY: We have been wanting to do this for years, we're glad we can finally connect. You grew up as a Yankee, Jets, and Knicks fan, but you lived in Manchester, New Hampshire, which is kind of close to Boston. So did you get beaten up a lot?

ADAM SANDLER: Yes. [*Laughter*] I moved to New Hampshire when I was five. My dad was an electrical engineer, he had worked in Brooklyn and in Jersey, and then he got a nice job in New Hampshire, and he said, "All right, we gotta move there." But the family is all New York, everybody, grandparents, uncles, aunts, me, my father, who's a crazy Yankee fan. I just did whatever my father told me to do. So when I went to school the first day, in the first grade, I had a Yankees hat on, and I was like, "What's going on, why do they all hate me so much?" I thought it was anti-Semitism, but they just hated the hat. [*Laughter*] But I refused to take it off, and there was just year after year of people hating the Yankees hat. That was my life back then.

MICHAEL KAY: A Jewish kid from Brooklyn living in New Hampshire. That sounds like one of your movies.

ADAM SANDLER: No, I grew up great, in a nice town, except that there weren't many delis and the Chinese restaurants served bread. That would always get my father crazy. "What is with this bread?" [*Laughter*] "How dare they!" And he didn't like the color of the lobster sauce. So we would take the four-and-a-half-hour drive to New York and eat some knishes.

MICHAEL KAY: Were you funny even as a kid?

ADAM SANDLER: I tried to make the family laugh. There were four kids in the house, and if Dad was in a bad mood, they would definitely want me to try to get him to break that mood and be happy again.

MICHAEL KAY: Did everybody appreciate your humor, or did some people not like it?

ADAM SANDLER: When I was a child, critically I wasn't accepted. I was getting bad reviews when I was eight! [*Laughter*] No, I actually did pretty good at home.

MICHAEL KAY: Now, did any one or two people in your life shape the comedy that you did, that made you funny?

ADAM SANDLER: Well, it all goes back to the old man. When I was a kid, he would wake me up if there was a good Marx Brothers movie on, or Martin and Lewis, the Three Stooges, that kind of stuff. And then in high school I got into Rodney Dangerfield, I memorized all his albums, and I used to do Rodney jokes for my dad.

MICHAEL KAY: Did you have interest in other things? Did you have interest in sports, did you play at all?

ADAM SANDLER: Sure. I was into baseball the most. I was pretty good at first, I made the all-star team when I was eleven. Then all of a sudden, at thirteen, everybody else started getting bigger, and I was like, "I've got to get into comedy quick."

MICHAEL KAY: You have mixed comedy and music throughout your career. When did music come in? When did you learn how to play the guitar?

ADAM SANDLER: My father taught me how to play guitar. He had an acoustic guitar that he used to play Johnny Cash tunes on, and he showed me some chords, and then I wanted an electric guitar, and Daddy bought me a Stratocaster. My first time singing onstage was when my sister Elizabeth got married, at a nice temple in Manchester, New Hampshire, when I was ten. I sang, "You're Sixteen," and I crushed it, and the crowd went crazy. And I was like, "Oh, I like this!" And then, I sang "Yesterday," and the crowd was like, "All right, one was enough." [*Laughter*]

MICHAEL KAY: Now, how did it get to the point that all of a sudden you were going to Boston comedy clubs? Were you a rousing success right away?

ADAM SANDLER: No, no, I was pretty bad. I was seventeen. I didn't have much to talk about. I didn't even prepare at all. And then I got there, and I saw all these comedians onstage, killing, and I was like, "Oh my God, I gotta go up there now? I remember the other comedians just going, "What is this moron doing here?" So I go up there and no one liked it. There was a nice guy in the front row who was giving me mercy laughs. He was like, "Yeah, yeah, good one." But the rest of the place was like, "Please don't do this anymore." [*Laughter*]

MICHAEL KAY: And you weren't discouraged?

ADAM SANDLER: I was crazy. I swear to God, when I was young and I started pursuing this stuff, I didn't understand what doing bad even meant. Crowds would walk out on me, and I was like, "What, these guys don't get this? What's the matter with these people?" I didn't ever think it was me.

MICHAEL KAY: When did you decide, "Okay, this is how I'm going to make a living"?

ADAM SANDLER: I'm seventeen, I'm about to apply for colleges, and [on the forms it said], "What do you want to major in?" I had no idea what that even meant. I was pretty dumb. I talked to my brother, said, "What do I want to major in?" My sister was a dentist, my brother was going to be a lawyer, and I said, "What am I going to be?" And my brother said, "Why don't you be an actor?" And I said, "Oh yeah, yeah, yeah, let's do that!" So I applied to NYU and studied acting there.

MICHAEL KAY: Now, you're doing a lot of stand-up in New York and you're at NYU. Do you study at all? I mean, are you going to class?

ADAM SANDLER: My mother thinks I did. [*Laughter*] No, I did, I actually did. Also, I got on *The Cosby Show*, four episodes, when I was, like, a junior at NYU, and NYU gave me a few credit points for it. So that was pretty good.

MICHAEL KAY: That was one of the most successful shows in the history of TV. Could you believe you were on that show?

ADAM SANDLER: Yeah, and I was dumb enough to think I belonged there.

MICHAEL KAY: So in the eighties you moved to Los Angeles. Why?

ADAM SANDLER: I had just gotten out of NYU, I was twenty-two, I was at Catch a Rising Star, and I had a pretty good night, and Budd Friedman was in the audience. He ran the Improv out in California. I got offstage, and he said, "What's your name?" We talked for a second, and he said, "You should come out to California, that's where the movie projects and television projects are." It was that quick.

MICHAEL KAY: In 1989 our research has you making your film debut, *The Unsinkable Shecky Moskowitz* [later rereleased as *Going Overboard*]. What was that about?

ADAM SANDLER: That's not the best movie, but it was a good experience for me. I just got to California, I think it was my third night onstage, I get offstage, did pretty good, and the director of the movie said, "Hey, we're doing a movie. Would you like to star in it?" And I said yeah. They said, "We're shooting in a week and a half, and it's on a cruise ship going to Mexico, and we're just going to shoot the movie on the boat." And I said, "That sounds good." I was just excited about making a movie.

MICHAEL KAY: When you watch that movie now, what do you think?

ADAM SANDLER: Skinny. Every old movie of mine, I go, "Well, God, I was skinny there." It's *Billy Madison*, I know I weighed one sixty-eight; *Happy Gilmore*, I got up to one seventy-five; *Wedding Singer* about one seventy-nine; then after that over two hundred every movie.

MICHAEL KAY: Well, in *Zohan* you were buff.

ADAM SANDLER: I did that for the Jews. I said, "Let me get in shape for the Jews." [*Laughter*]

MICHAEL KAY: All right, so in 1990, *Saturday Night Live* calls. How does that come about?

ADAM SANDLER: Dennis Miller saw me do stand-up, I got to know him a little bit, and he thought I had some funny stuff. And he told them about me, and then Lorne Michaels and a couple of other members of the show came to Chicago, and me and Chris Rock and a couple other really good comedians auditioned that night. We did, like, eight minutes each. Lorne liked my material, but he didn't think of me as being [on camera] on the show, so they hired me as a writer.

MICHAEL KAY: Was that a letdown? Did you want to be on the show?

ADAM SANDLER: Yeah, yeah, yeah. I was shook up for a minute, but I said, "All right, I'll just write myself onto the show."

MICHAEL KAY: And that's what you did. Your *Saturday Night Live* on-camera debut was December 9, 1990, in a sketch with Tom Hanks. Do you remember it?

ADAM SANDLER: It was about an Israeli Home Shopping Network. That's how I snuck on the air: I was one of the few guys who could look like an Israeli. And I'll never forget, just total fear, and hearing the countdown, okay, "Ten, nine, eight . . . ," and just my head spinning, like, "Just don't faint, don't faint." I felt like I was going to faint the whole time. I said to Hanks, "I feel like I'm going to faint." And Hanks goes, "Well, don't."

MICHAEL KAY: Now, you end up getting on the air full-time, they hire you as a cast member. What was that like?

ADAM SANDLER: There was pride, something that felt great, watching the opening credits was a big deal, and Don Pardo says your name and it's official. . . . [But] they weren't using me a lot in the beginning, when I started getting on the air. And I remember sitting with Lorne saying, "You guys gotta get me on more." Again, I was just very dopey, I had no idea how to conduct myself. I was just aggressive. I'd say, "I'm telling you, I'm going to be Eddie Murphy big, Bill Murray big." I would say that out loud! If I had met me back then, I would have punched me square in the face. I would have hated me, but that's who I was.

MICHAEL KAY: Now, in the '94–'95 season on *Saturday Night Live*, "The Chanukah Song" comes about.

ADAM SANDLER: Yes. That was a just a lucky idea. I was walking down to *Saturday Night Live*, and I thought it would be funny to write a song and list a bunch of Jewish people. There weren't a lot of Chanukah songs.

MICHAEL KAY: So the '94–'95 season, you're one of the biggest stars, you and Chris Farley, but you don't return for the next year. I've heard different stories, but lately you've said that you were let go. So what's the truth?

ADAM SANDLER: The truth is I'm not a hundred percent sure what happened. There were new people running NBC, they thought the show was getting too youth oriented, saying that we're trying to hit the young kids too much, and I didn't feel I was getting invited back. And my manager kept encouraging me to quit. . . .

MICHAEL KAY: Before you got fired.

ADAM SANDLER: Exactly. So I don't know if I was fired, or I quit, or what happened, but I [didn't come] back.

MICHAEL KAY: Those five years, then, do you recall them fondly?

ADAM SANDLER: They were the best. I would walk to work so happy, I couldn't believe I was on that show.

MICHAEL KAY: All right, so in 1994 you begin working on *Billy Madison*. You wrote that with Tim Herlihy. Your fans embraced it, they loved it, it did very well at the box office, but you kind of alluded to this at the beginning: the critics were not kind to you. Did that bother you?

ADAM SANDLER: That's the only one that bothered me, because I didn't expect it. And it's the only one when I actually read the stuff. I read the reviews saying it's abysmal, that Adam Sandler's sophomoric, with a moron attitude, and blah, blah, blah. Yeah, it hurt, but I got over it real quick. I felt bad for my family, that's who I felt bad for. I felt bad that my grandmother had to read this stuff. But then *Happy Gilmore* came out, and I remember not reading the reviews, but calling Herlihy and saying, "Did you read the reviews?" And he said, "Yeah." And I said, "Should I read them?" And he said, "No." [*Laughter*] And so I said, "All right, maybe I just won't read them ever again." And that's basically what I do.

MICHAEL KAY: Now, you were also very, very successful with the comedy records you put out, so after *Happy Gilmore* you did a concert tour, and then you began working on *The Wedding Singer*. What was the genesis of that, where did that come from in your soul?

ADAM SANDLER: Boy, oh, boy, I just thought it was a neat idea to have a guy who got his heart broken and had to be around weddings all the time, so he became a bitter guy about weddings.

MICHAEL KAY: With *The Wedding Singer*, right before the release of that film, Chris Farley passes away. How much did that affect you?

ADAM SANDLER: It was my first time having a friend die, and so it affected me greatly. We all loved him, he was the funniest guy, the one guy that when he walks in, it's guaranteed to make you happy. That's how Farley was. So, yeah, it was definitely painful. But we saw it coming.

MICHAEL KAY: You did?

ADAM SANDLER: We told Chris to calm down, constantly, everybody did. I went over the conversations we had, and he was definitely clean on one call, and then the next phone call you could tell he was not clean. I always encouraged him to stop, I'd play hardball with him, but he would just laugh off the hardball and go, "Wow, look at you getting all serious." He didn't want to hear it. Everybody tried, his brothers tried, his mom, his dad. But it just happened.

MICHAEL KAY: Do you ever sneak in the theater in a disguise to watch the everyday people watch [one of your movies]?

ADAM SANDLER: I do this move sometimes: I'll walk into a theater with my wife or whoever I'm hanging out with that helped make the movie. I'll just walk down, look up at the crowd, and see if they're smiling or not, or if they're only staying for five minutes. If they're laughing, I'm in a good mood. If it's off a little, I'll run to the projectionist and say, "You gotta turn it up a little bit!" Or something. I'm a little nutty sometimes.

MICHAEL KAY: What do you think it is about you that connects with the audience?

ADAM SANDLER: I don't know, I don't have a formula. [If] I have a movie coming out, I don't know if people are gonna go to it or not. I just hope that we're doing something that's making people happy. You know, they're PG-13 movies, they're not kids' movies, it's not for an eight-year-old. But I do love fathers and mothers saying, "Hey, I watched your movie with my kid the other day, and we had the best time." I do try to make movies that the whole family can have a good time watching.

MICHAEL KAY: I'm gonna be very forward here. What's the chance of me getting a shot in one of your movies? I don't mean playing a sportscaster, I mean getting a real meaty role?

ADAM SANDLER: Well, the only problem is, you make me look short.

MICHAEL KAY: Final thing. Do you ever sit back, when you're alone, and just go, "Wow, this is just awesome!"

ADAM SANDLER: When I do have those moments, I'm very, very happy and very appreciative. Like I told you, when I was a young guy starting out, I was a driven kid, and now that all my dreams have come true, I am very thankful.

MICHAEL KAY: This was so much fun, thank you so much.

ADAM SANDLER: Thanks, man. [*Applause*]

Yogi Berra

It's refreshing when the überfamous act as if they're the complete oppo-site. That's the way Yogi Berra carried himself. You can make the argu-ment that Berra was one of the most famous faces on the planet. He was one of a kind, but he never acted as if he were better than you. He was a gentleman in every way.

We had Berra on the show in July of 2005, and he was as sweet and gentle and real as anyone who'd ever taken that stage before him and anyone who ever followed.

We have a comedian named Pete Dominick who warms up the audi-ence before the show. Great guy. He brought his father to the Berra tap-ing, and I walked him in to meet Yogi before the show. Yogi made him feel comfortable and joked with him as if he had known him a lifetime. Pete has told me that interaction with a hero was so special for his dad, and he never stopped telling people about it. That was Yogi.

From his beginning on the Hill in St. Louis, to his participation in the Normandy invasion, to his ten championships with the Yankees, Berra's life had a Zelig quality to it. There's a picture of him shaking hands with Babe Ruth and another of him laughing and joking with Derek Jeter. Across baseball generations, Berra served as a human connector.

His life is extraordinary in its simplicity of purpose. He never tried to be anything but a great, dependable player, but his fame superseded his ambition. Everything he touched throughout his life seemed destined to turn to gold, from his involvement with a drink called Yoo-Hoo to buying a big plot of land in central Florida that turned out to be smack-dab in the middle of what would become Disney World. Forget the golden touch, Berra's was platinum.

Even his malapropisms ended up making total sense and becoming part of the lexicon.

Berra was a devoted husband, father, grandfather, and mentor to a generation of ballplayers. When he'd walk into Yankee Stadium, you'd see the excitement in the eyes of the game's biggest stars. They loved being around him and they adored his company. You could never get enough Yogi.

Yogi passed away ten years after our *CenterStage* conversation took place, but he grabbed as much life and happiness out of his ninety years as anyone could. High on the list of great American stories is the life of Yogi Berra. He shared some of that life in this interview.

The Interview

MICHAEL KAY: Welcome. Today's guest is an American success story. His parents came to this country from Italy to make a life and raise a family. One of their sons became a Major League Baseball catcher and joined the Yankees at the age of twenty-one. He stayed there for eighteen seasons, winning ten World Series and fourteen pennants—the most by any player ever. In fact, he holds four all-time World Series records. His unique phrases like "Ninety percent of the game is half mental" are legendary. He was elected to the National Baseball Hall of Fame. He had his number retired by the Yankees. And he was selected as a catcher on Major League Base-ball's All-Century Team. He is one of those amazing people who no longer requires a last name. Please welcome number eight, Yogi. [*Applause*]

YOGI BERRA: Thank you. Oh. Oh, great. Really great.

MICHAEL KAY: Great to see you. Now, Yogi might actually be the most famous nickname in sports. How did that come about?

YOGI BERRA: Well, Lawrence was my name, but my mom called me Lawdie. Then when I played in American Legion ball, we never had dugouts, we sat on the ground, and I always sat with my legs crossed, and my arms crossed. Then Bobby Hofman, who later played with the Giants, he played on the same team, he told me, "Lawdie, you look like a yogi [a guy who does yoga]." And they called me Yogi ever since.

MICHAEL KAY: Does your wife call you Larry or Yogi?

YOGI BERRA: When she calls me Lawrence, I'm in trouble. [*Laughter*]

MICHAEL KAY: Now, your mom and dad were from Italy, and they settled in the Hill, [a working-class] section of St. Louis. What did your mom and dad do for a living?

YOGI BERRA: My mom did all the housework, and my dad worked in the brickyard.

MICHAEL KAY: He did not like you playing baseball, right?

YOGI BERRA: No. He liked me playing soccer. You know, coming from Italy, he loved soccer. Baseball didn't mean anything to him.

MICHAEL KAY: Let's go to the beginning of your baseball career. In 1942 there's a tryout for the St. Louis Cardinals, and you and your friend [Joe] Garagiola are there, and they signed Garagiola for five hundred bucks. What did they offer you?

YOGI BERRA: Two hundred. [And I said] no. I wanted the same thing Joe got. And [later] George Weiss, the Yankee general manager at the time, said, "[We should] sign this kid. He is a good player." And I signed the contract.

MICHAEL KAY: And you got the five hundred dollars you wanted?

YOGI BERRA: I got it . . . and ninety dollars a month.

MICHAEL KAY: Now, this is in World War Two.

YOGI BERRA: Yeah, I had turned eighteen, I was in Norfolk, Virginia, and I got drafted there, but they let me finish out the season. Then I joined the navy, and I volunteered for rocket boats, and I was at the D-Day landing at Normandy. The rocket boats were little thirty-six-footers, with six men and an officer. They had a twin .50-caliber [machine gun] and twelve rockets on each side, and we went in before the soldiers landed and fired the rockets from three or four hundred yards off the beach.

MICHAEL KAY: Were you afraid?

YOGI BERRA: No, I thought it was like Fourth of July. I was very fortunate. We didn't run into much at our beachhead.

MICHAEL KAY: Now, in '46 you get discharged from the military, and you go to the Yankees minor league team in Newark, and in '47 you make the team. What's it like, sitting in the same clubhouse as Joe DiMaggio?

YOGI BERRA: Getting to see Phil Rizzuto, Joe DiMaggio, Tommy Henrich, Charlie Keller, all those guys, it was great.

MICHAEL KAY: Bucky Harris was the manager when you got there in '47. And he said he wanted you to "think more at the plate." What did you tell him?

YOGI BERRA: I said, "I can't hit and think at the same time." [*Laughter*] But Bucky was a good manager. I liked him. Then Casey [Stengel] came in, and I got to like Casey, too. You know, a lot of guys thought he was crazy, but he knew what he was doing.

MICHAEL KAY: In '47, what was the deal with your catching skills at the time? They didn't think you were that good of a catcher yet?

YOGI BERRA: No. I was terrible catching. My first few years I was terrible. But I had a good arm, and Casey worked me hard, taught me how to catch and everything, and I became a pretty good catcher. I owe him a lot.

MICHAEL KAY: In July of that year, when you play the St. Louis Browns, they honor you [with a ceremony] in Sportsman's Park, and you came up with your first "Yogism," right?

YOGI BERRA: Well, yeah. I didn't want to make a speech, but they said, "Just tell 'em you are very happy to receive this," and all that. So I come up to the microphone and I said, "I want to thank everybody for making this night necessary." [*Laughter*]

MICHAEL KAY: Now, for seven straight years you led the Yankees in RBIs. What made you so dangerous?

YOGI BERRA: Well, they all say I was dangerous at the end of the game. Maybe I got the pitcher when he was tired. [*Laughter*]

MICHAEL KAY: Nineteen fifty-one, the third straight World Series, you were league MVP. But you actually took a job at a Newark clothing store. You guys didn't make enough money? What were you making that year?

YOGI BERRA: At that time, we didn't make that much. Nineteen thousand dollars I was making that year.

MICHAEL KAY: That's tipping money now.

YOGI BERRA: Oh, I know it.

MICHAEL KAY: How important were the World Series checks to you? What were they, five thousand dollars?

YOGI BERRA: The first big one, when we played the Giants, in '51. I think we got about nine thousand or ten thousand dollars for that one. It came in handy.

MICHAEL KAY: I bet. In 1961, what was it like watching Mantle and Maris in the home run chase?

YOGI BERRA: That's where I got the "It's déjà vu all over again," watching those guys hit home runs. [*Laughter*] I was pulling for both of 'em. I know that a lot of people thought Mickey was mad at Maris, but they were close friends. You know, if Mickey didn't get hurt, maybe they both coulda hit sixty-one home runs that year.

MICHAEL KAY: Could the 1998 Yankees have beaten the '61 Yankees?

YOGI BERRA: I don't know. It'd be close, maybe.

MICHAEL KAY: The Yankees won the Series, in '61 and '62. They lose to the Dodgers in '63, and fittingly, your last at bat as a Yankee was in the World Series.

YOGI BERRA: Yeah. I lined out to right field, off of [Dodgers pitcher Don] Drysdale.

MICHAEL KAY: You played eighteen seasons, with fourteen pennants, ten World Series. Does it ever hit you how unbelievable that is? That you won ten World Series championships? You are one of the greatest winners in the history of sports.

YOGI BERRA: Well, I was lucky. I was born at the right time. [*Laughter*]

MICHAEL KAY: We're up to 1964, and you become the Yankee manager. Did you know you wanted to manage?

YOGI BERRA: No. In spring training in '63, [manager] Ralph Houk asked me, "How would you like to manage?" I said, "Manage who?" And he said, "The Yankees." And I said, "Why? Where are you going?" And he says, "I'm going upstairs, to the office, but don't let nobody know it [just watch how I do it]." And that's where I got "You can observe a lot by watching." So then I became manager, and we won the pennant.

MICHAEL KAY: Now, were you afraid about managing guys that you were friends with, your teammates? And all of a sudden you were their boss?

YOGI BERRA: No. I respected them. And they respected me. I think they did.

MICHAEL KAY: Everybody knows the story, but I want to hear it from you. The Phil Linz harmonica story. What happened?

YOGI BERRA: Well, Linz starts playing the harmonica, in the back of the bus, after a tough loss to the White Sox. And I told him to "stick that thing up your . . ." And Mickey [Mantle] was back there, and Linz asked him, "What'd he say?" And Mickey said, "He said, play it louder!" [*Laughter*] And Linz started playing again, and I went back and I slapped the thing out of his hand and said, "Don't you ever do that again," and I fined him two hundred dollars. But everything came out good. It made him famous.

MICHAEL KAY: Now, you won the pennant, by one game. But here is the part where it got weird in '64. You guys play the World Series, against the Cardinals, and you lose. [And then the Yankees fired you.] Were you upset?

YOGI BERRA: Well, a little bit after that, yeah. But that's baseball, you know? They wanted to give me an office job, and I said, "No. I want to be on the field." I was too young to get off the field. And that's when Casey called me over to coach with the Mets. And I said, "That's great, I'm home again," you know?

MICHAEL KAY: All you had known your whole career was winning, winning, winning. How tough was it to lose almost every day [with the Mets]?

YOGI BERRA: Well, it was tough for a little bit. But I enjoyed it over there. I really did.

MICHAEL KAY: How exciting was it [for the Mets] to win the World Series in '69? 'Cause they had been bad for so long?

YOGI BERRA: It was great. Even better than winning [with the Yankees].

MICHAEL KAY: And then in 1972 you became the manager of the Mets. And you were also inducted into the Hall of Fame, and the Yankees retired your number. What did that mean to you?

YOGI BERRA: The Hall of Fame? For a kid from the Hill? Are you kidding? It was great. It was great! And I still love going up there. Every chance I get, I go up.

MICHAEL KAY: Now, in '73 the Mets are struggling, and you actually say it for the first time.

YOGI BERRA: "It ain't over till it's over."

MICHAEL KAY: And it wasn't. What did it mean to you, to get to the World Series with that team?

YOGI BERRA: Well, I lost [the Series] in seven games, but it was good.

I managed for five and a half years, and I won two pennants. So, not bad.

.MICHAEL KAY: You rejoined the Yankees in 1976 as a coach for Billy Martin. What kind of manager was he?

YOGI BERRA: Billy was a good manager. He beat you any way he could beat you. He didn't miss a trick.

QUESTION FROM AUDIENCE: When you were catching, did you do a lot of talking to the hitters that came up?

YOGI BERRA: Yeah. I loved to talk to 'em. A lot of guys think I talked to 'em when the ball was on the way, but I never did that, I talked to 'em before the pitch was made. I had a lot of fun with Ted Williams, but he would get mad at me. He liked to go fishing, and I would say, "Where are you going fishing, uh, this year?" and all that. And he would tell me to shut up. [*Laughter*] He wanted nobody bothering him with that.

MICHAEL KAY: You had been involved in every major Yankee thing in fifty-five years. And you were there the night at the Copacabana [nightclub] in 1957, there was a famous fight [involving] Mickey [Mantle] and Whitey [Ford] and Billy [Martin] and [Hank] Bauer. What happened?

YOGI BERRA: Well, it was Billy Martin's birthday, and we went to Danny's Hide-A-Way for dinner, then we went over to see Sammy Davis Jr. at the Copa. And this one guy was getting on Sammy Davis Jr. [shouting racial epithets]. We told him to shut up, you know, and he said, "Make me!" And we said, "Come on downstairs." [*Laughter*]

MICHAEL KAY: So who made him, Hank Bauer?

YOGI BERRA: Hank Bauer went down. But Hank didn't hit the guy, the bouncer hit him.

MICHAEL KAY: Didn't [general manager] George Weiss ask you what happened? And you said—

YOGI BERRA: I said, "Nobody did nothin' to nobody." [*Laughter*] But we all got fined two hundred dollars, and Billy got traded because they thought he was a troublemaker.

MICHAEL KAY: In 1984, George Steinbrenner asked you to become the [Yankees] manager. Was that something you wanted to do?

YOGI BERRA: Well, I had nothing else to do, so what the heck. [*Laughter*]

MICHAEL KAY: Then in '85, three weeks into the season, you get fired. You were really ticked off. Tell me why.

YOGI BERRA: Well, George didn't call me to fire me. Everyplace I got fired, at least the owner called me, and he never did. I don't mind if you tell me I'm fired, but I want to hear it from the owner.

MICHAEL KAY: And you said you were never coming back [to Yankee Stadium]. How tough was that? That was your family, the Yankees.

YOGI BERRA: I can be a rock head sometimes. It was tough, but I still watched the games. I still pulled for the Yankees, and the Mets. I watched both of them. I rooted for both of them. I root for both of them right now.

MICHAEL KAY: So in 1998 you open up the Yogi Berra Museum and Learning Center on the campus of Montclair State University [in New Jersey]. It's been a neat thing for you, right?

YOGI BERRA: Oh, yeah, it's been great. We got a lot of kids come through there. It's kind of nice, a kid from the Hill has a museum. A friend of mine said, "You're lucky you're alive to see it. People who have museums named after 'em, they're usually dead." [*Laughter*]

MICHAEL KAY: Now, the museum was actually the site where you and George Steinbrenner patched things up. Did it mean something to you that George Steinbrenner came out there [and admitted mishandling your firing in 1985]?

YOGI BERRA: Yes, it did, it really did. The grandkids hadn't seen Yankee Stadium or anything, so [after fourteen years] it was time. We're pretty good friends now. At least, he hasn't said anything bad about me.

MICHAEL KAY: Do you watch games with him when you're at the stadium?

YOGI BERRA: Yeah, but he's tough to watch with. He makes you sit next to him, but if we don't score in a couple of innings, he moves. [*Laughter*]

MICHAEL KAY: Then in 1999 you and your grandchildren and your family go back to Yankee Stadium for Yogi Berra Day and you get all that love. Do you realize how much you're loved? I mean, look, this is the biggest crowd we've ever had here [in the studio]. Do you realize how much people love Yogi Berra?

YOGI BERRA: Aww, I don't know. But I owe a lot of things to baseball. And I always say, "Where could anybody make that much money for working three hours a day and having fun?"

MICHAEL KAY: Thank you so much for coming. It's been an honor, it really has.

Charles Barkley

Charles Barkley is a born entertainer. Although voted one of the top fifty players in NBA history, Barkley is perhaps even better known as a broadcaster and commentator on the human condition. You wonder if Barkley has a legitimate editing valve. He seems to say whatever comes into his mind, and he also has a protective force field whereby if he crosses the line, no one gets too upset. The thinking is "Well, that's Charles being Charles." It's a splendid escape hatch for someone who's not "gotten the memo" from the PC police of the world.

Also helping Charles to say what he thinks no matter whom it might rankle is the twinkle in his eye and his general light spirit.

That gift has made him a star on TNT's coverage of the NBA. His playful asides and his pointed criticisms of players and coaches have made him the absolute best at what he does. Every network executive with a pre- and postgame show in every sport has spent endless hours trying to re-create the magic of *Inside the NBA*, but the only thing they can't re-create is the genius of Barkley. It's almost impossible to be him because he's an original. He might not come our way again.

When he appeared on *CenterStage* in 2006, it wasn't exactly heavy lifting. On some shows you have to work to get the guest to open up. Not with Barkley. Sure, you have to be prepared because he can quickly go off the tracks and must be brought back, but he's a natural entertainer with a storytelling gene that is unmatched. That was very much on display in our hour together.

The Interview

MICHAEL KAY: Today's guest was named one of the NBA's fifty greatest players, selected to eleven NBA All-Star Games, won two Olympic gold medals, and the NBA MVP trophy. On and off the court, he was competitive, outrageous, entertaining, and often controversial. When he retired, he continued to make headlines as a basketball analyst for TNT, and a commentator for CNN. He has written a great book about racism in America called *Who's Afraid of a Large Black Man?* Please welcome one of the all-time NBA greats, the Ninth Wonder of the World, Sir Charles Barkley. [*Applause*]

MICHAEL KAY: You say that you are not born into racism, you learn it. You were born in the Deep South, and your grandmother and mother made it a point that you weren't racist toward whites.

CHARLES BARKLEY: My mother was a maid, and the white family she worked for treated her fantastic. My mother and grandmother taught me, "You're gonna judge every person on their own individual merits." And I appreciate that probably more than anything they ever did for me in my life. Because I think it's immoral to be racist, to dislike anybody because of their color of their skin.

MICHAEL KAY: You were one of three kids, three young boys, no dad, growing up in the small town of Leeds, Alabama. Your mother and grandmother raised you. But you have said you never really wanted for anything, that you never really felt "poor."

CHARLES BARKLEY: When kids are poor, they don't know they're poor until they grow up and realize, "Wow, everybody else has got stuff."

MICHAEL KAY: I heard that you were shy as a kid?

CHARLES BARKLEY: I was really quiet and shy. My mother and grandmother used to think I was crazy. They know me as the little kid who didn't say anything growing up. And then Philadelphia happened to me. Philadelphia is a very difficult place. When I first went to the 76ers, I was this nice, quiet kid from Alabama. Then when I got to the NBA, I would say something, and I would get all these phone calls, and all these letters, with people telling me "You are wrong" or "You suck" and things like that. So I figured out, no matter what I say, half the people are gonna like it, and half the people are gonna dislike it. That's just the way the whole thing works. So one day I said, "From now on, I'm just gonna be straightforward and honest, I'm not gonna sugarcoat it." And then my personality kinda took off from there.

MICHAEL KAY: Is it true that as a kid you weren't super-athletic?

CHARLES BARKLEY: Not the least athletic. Short little chubby kid. [*Laughs*] And I am big and chubby now. [*Laughs*] I was a chubby five-ten backup point guard, so I never really played, I never got in the game. And then suddenly I grew from five-ten to six-five in one year. People always say, "He came out of nowhere." No, I just had an amazing growth spurt.

MICHAEL KAY: Your high school team ended up being the best in Alabama, and you were offered a scholarship to Auburn. Did you have any other offers?

CHARLES BARKLEY: When you are a five-ten point guard, you are not getting offers. So at first I was only getting letters from smaller schools. Then a guy from Auburn just happened to come to look at another kid on my team, and by that time I was, like, six-five, about two hundred and thirty. So Auburn said, "Let's try him." And they played me at center.

MICHAEL KAY: Sonny Smith was your coach at Auburn. Is it true that he said, "Do you want to play basketball, or do you want to get a degree?" Like it was mutually exclusive?

CHARLES BARKLEY: That's not to knock on Auburn. The travesty of college sports is they are not graduating these kids. I don't think it's fair to ask an eighteen-year-old kid if he wants a degree, or he wants to stay eligible. 'Cause every kid just wants to stay eligible.

MICHAEL KAY: Did you say you wanted the degree, though?

CHARLES BARKLEY: Up until after my freshman year, I did. Then I realized I could play. [*Laughs*]

MICHAEL KAY: In college they had a lot of nicknames for you because you were [relatively] short and could still rebound. "Ton of Fun," "Good Time Blimp," "Round Mound of Rebound." And none of them bothered you or insulted you?

CHARLES BARKLEY: No. It probably fired me up more than anything. I didn't take it personally.

MICHAEL KAY: You leave Auburn after your junior year and decide to go into the NBA. A tough decision? Did anybody advise you?

CHARLES BARKLEY: I knew that I was ready. I knew I was gonna go in the top five or six in the draft. It was time. I had been poor my whole life. I had always been the man of the house. It was time for me to make life easier for my mother, my grandmother, and my two brothers.

MICHAEL KAY: Did you ever get your degree?

CHARLES BARKLEY: I did not.

MICHAEL KAY: Does that bother you? You could still go back.

CHARLES BARKLEY: I could. [*Laughs*] But then I wouldn't be able to gamble and play golf all the time. [*Laughs*] Now I'm a Vegas guy. I like to gamble, I love to play golf. Right now I'm getting ready to learn Spanish. I like challenging myself.

MICHAEL KAY: Julius Erving, Dr. J, was on that 76ers team. Tell me what he meant to you.

CHARLES BARKLEY: I remember the night before training camp, I was up all night wondering what was I gonna call Dr. J. Do I call him Dr. J or Mr. Erving? I was just a young kid. But he just walked up and said, "Hey, I'm Doc." And it was fantastic. He and Moses [Malone] were the two most influential people in my NBA career. Moses because halfway through my rookie year I'm not getting to play, and I said, "Moses, why am I not getting to play?" He says, "Hey, big fella, you fat and you lazy and you out of shape." So he took me under his wing and got me in shape, and that was great. It was an amazing transformation because at that point I'm probably two-eighty. He got me to two-seventy, I started playing better, and then I got to two-sixty and I started playing really good. As for Dr. J, he helped me financially, because young kids are stupid when they're poor and suddenly they get all this money. I bought, like, seven cars, and Dr. J says, "Young fella, you're not gonna play basketball forever. Take them cars back. Save that money. You're gonna need that money in ten, fifteen years. You don't know how long you're gonna play." Dr. J was a fabulous businessman, he had all these different things going on. That was a most valuable lesson, and that's what I share with these young guys today. Cut the bling, cut the cars, get one vehicle, save your money. Because you might play for ten, fifteen years. But you might not play for even five years. If you wasted all that money on bling and cars, you're gonna be sad. Because no matter how much money you make, it's only a short period of time in your life.

MICHAEL KAY: Was the NBA lifestyle weird for you? Was too much thrown at you?

CHARLES BARKLEY: No, because you are so consumed with the game. People talk about all the extracurricular stuff, but when you play a professional sport, you're tired all the time, especially your rookie year, you're tired. That's the hardest time, your rookie year. The other stuff they talk about, that stuff happens when you're a veteran. When you're a rookie, you're drinking milk at night. [*Laughs*] And I'm taking Dr. J his newspapers in the morning. So you ain't got time.

MICHAEL KAY: You ended up being the star in Philadelphia. Because by '87, Doc is gone. Malone's gone. And you're twenty-three years old and you're the star. Were you ready for it?

CHARLES BARKLEY: I was ready for it my third year. But the Sixers screwed up [with bad trades and draft decisions.] I was very fortunate that they gave me Rick Mahorn and Mike Gminski one year and we were able to win the division. But overall they didn't do a good job of putting players around me. And unfortunately a star is gonna get the blame.

MICHAEL KAY: Was the media really tough in Philly?

CHARLES BARKLEY: Philadelphia and New York have the worst media because controversy is going to sell. That's just how it is. And that goes back to being a star. You're either gonna win the championship or you're gonna get the blame. I think it's unfair.

MICHAEL KAY: Nineteen ninety is a great season for you. But you finish second in the MVP to Magic Johnson.

CHARLES BARKLEY: I should have won it.

MICHAEL KAY: Do you think you rubbed the media the wrong way? Maybe it cost you votes?

CHARLES BARKLEY: I know it did. I get frustrated with the media because they ask me questions and I'm honest. I don't think I'm right all the time, but they should respect me for being honest and not hold it against me.

MICHAEL KAY: Did you think you treated them rudely?

CHARLES BARKLEY: Never, but I ain't gonna say what they want me to say. I have never been mean to a media guy. I'm gonna be honest and I'm going to be fair, and I hope they respect that, but some of them don't. They go on TV and kill me for being controversial and outspoken, then they go on TV and kill Michael [Jordan] and Tiger [Woods] for never saying anything. It's like you can't win.

MICHAEL KAY: So was it worth it being open if it cost you an MVP?

CHARLES BARKLEY: It's always worth being honest. I love Magic Johnson, I respect him and admire him, but it bothered me.

MICHAEL KAY: Now, in that season, in late '91, things are starting to fall apart in Philly for you.

CHARLES BARKLEY: It was miserable for me.

MICHAEL KAY: And there was an incident in Jersey, you're getting heckled. And you went to spit on the guy, and you ended up spitting on a little girl [and getting suspended for one game and fined $10,000].

CHARLES BARKLEY: It was a stupid thing to do, but I think it probably saved me. I had always played angry, with a chip on my shoulder, and you can't play like that because it's just a matter of time before you're gonna fall off the cliff. When I was suspended, I decided, "I've got to control myself."

MICHAEL KAY: But isn't that a delicate balancing act? Because maybe playing angry made you great. How do you stay great without that intensity?

CHARLES BARKLEY: You got to channel it. It is a delicate balancing act, but you gotta do it or something bad is gonna happen, and it's gonna keep happening. I had to calm down, I had to be so intense in my game that I wouldn't worry about what somebody was shouting at me in the stands. That thing saved me. The one thing about fame and television, if you do one thing stupid, it's there forever. And you don't get to take it back. But that was the turning point for me. Like, "Hey, man, you've got to step back. There' s a lot at stake here." And that was a blessing.

MICHAEL KAY: The 76ers end up trading you to the Phoenix Suns. And your first workout in Phoenix, they have ten thousand people show up—for a workout. Did it freak you out a little bit?

CHARLES BARKLEY: It was great because they just appreciated me. At that time Phoenix didn't have baseball, they didn't have hockey. The Suns ruled Phoenix. We would sell out every game, and there was a waiting list to get tickets. We were the Beatles.

QUESTION FROM AUDIENCE: In a Nike commercial you once stated that you're not a role model, that parents and teachers should be role models. As an inner-city schoolteacher, I can say that like it or not, celebrities are role models. Why do you think that statement that you made was so controversial?

CHARLES BARKLEY: I knew it was gonna be controversial. When I went to Nike, I just wanted to start a dialogue. People see black kids as brainwashed. They think they can only play sports and be entertainers to be successful. They don't think about being doctors, lawyers, engineers, firemen, teachers, policemen. We have to address that. And the problem has gotten worse since I made the commercial. It's really interesting when I go speak at schools. If I go to an all-black school and I ask, "How many of you want to play in the NBA?" every kid raises his hand. But when I go speak at white schools, less than ten percent of the kids raise their hand. They say they want to be doctors, lawyers, engineers, firemen, teachers, and things like that. For the black community that's a problem.

MICHAEL KAY: You've had some public confrontations, and it's usually with people that are drunk. You don't travel with bodyguards, and you do go out in public, while a lot of superstars just stay in their rooms. Do you think it's worth it?

CHARLES BARKLEY: It is. I've probably been arrested six or seven times [for fighting], and that's unfortunate, but I meet great people. And this has been the greatest time of my life. Being Charles Barkley has been fantastic. I've met kings, queens, presidents, I've been all over the world. I've met the most amazing people. Why would I sit in my room like a fool and not enjoy my life?

MICHAEL KAY: You had one of the great lines. You threw a guy through a window, and when the judge asked you if you had any regrets, you said—

CHARLES BARKLEY: "I regret we were on the first floor." [*Laughter*] What happened was, I was sitting at a table with three or four guys, three or four girls, and the guy throws a drink on me. And he's standing probably ten feet away and he's laughing. So I chase him, and by the time I catch him I'm in front of one of these big windows, and I throw him through it, and I get arrested. I don't wanna fight, but I'm not gonna let somebody threaten me or hit me just because I'm in the limelight. Of course I'm gonna swing on them. And I never lost one of those cases.

MICHAEL KAY: Let's go back to your basketball career. After Phoenix you end up going to Houston. And then the last year you were playing, you suffer a really tough injury, and you're walking off the court and there's another great line by you. You said, "Just what America needs, another unemployed black man." [*Laughter*] Do you worry when you say stuff like that, that the politically correct police might say it's the wrong thing to say?

CHARLES BARKLEY: I never worry about them. I always joke on the show. Like I'll say, "I get nervous when I see white men dancing." [*Laughter*] But I'm just joking. If people can't take a joke, I'm not gonna let them dictate to me. People gotta have a sense of humor. Every time somebody says something about race, it's not racist. There's a difference. Like I'll say, "The greatest white man ever is Colonel Sanders [*laughter*]. Because any white man who cooks chicken like that, you gotta love him." If some jackass reporter wants to make me out to be a racist for that, I can live with it. The politically correct police have gotten way out of hand. You know when somebody's being racist or not. I trust the people at home to be sensible.

MICHAEL KAY: Let's talk about the dress code that the NBA has instituted. I thought it was bordering on taking away somebody's identity. A lot of these kids are from the inner city, and they think they're getting dressed up with the baggy jeans and the throwback jerseys—they don't think they're being sloppy.

CHARLES BARKLEY: They are being sloppy. I think a dress code is fantastic. The reason I like it is because young black kids can't dress like that and get jobs. An NBA player who's making fifteen million dollars a year, he can dress like that, but they set the style for all of these young black kids today. When those black kids go out on a real job interview, they're not gonna get a job. Every other job in the world has a dress code. Young black kids, they dress like that, they can't get jobs. There's a lot more to being black than throwback jerseys and pants showing the crack of your ass. Blacks have always been a strong group, but our level of pride and self-esteem has dropped. We don't have respect for each other. And I think we've done a great disservice to older black people. Because I always say older black people did all the heavy lifting. They put us in a situation where we could be successful, and we have squandered it. I feel bad for all older black people when they see us killing each other, when they seeing us dress certain ways. We have done them a disservice.

MICHAEL KAY: You're in your forties now. Do you think you're gonna live to see a change in attitudes about race? Is it gonna happen in your lifetime?

CHARLES BARKLEY: Oh, I think it's gotten a lot better in my forty years. But we've still got a long way to go.

MICHAEL KAY: Charles, it's been great.

CHARLES BARKLEY: Thank you.

Seth Meyers

Seth Meyers doesn't act like a star. He could be anybody's next-door neighbor. He's totally unassuming, doesn't seem to have much of an ego, and is quick with a smile or a kind word.

You'd think the star of NBC's *Late Night* would be someone who'd stick out his chest and announce to the world all of his accomplishments. But the person who showed up on *CenterStage* in July of 2015 exhibited none of that attitude. It's always interesting to see how a guest interacts with the crew, the backbone of any endeavor but the segment of the workforce that doesn't get much notice. Meyers was gracious and friendly to everyone and also exchanged easy comments with the audience during breaks. Without an entourage or any handlers whatsoever, he'd arrived at our set right on time before he had to head to NBC to start work on his show.

Meyers came to prominence when he joined the cast of *Saturday Night Live* in 2001, although he didn't get the amount of screen time that creates a breakout star. But in 2006 he became co–head writer on *SNL* and then became the coanchor of the coveted "Weekend Update" slot alongside Amy Poehler. After Poehler left to go out on her own, Meyers became sole anchor. In that role he exhibited incredibly sharp writing skills, an easy delivery, and the ability to stay there forever and never get stale. He racked up an impressive eight-year run behind the desk, anchoring until 2014.

Meyers got a huge break when Jimmy Fallon left *Late Night* to become host of *The Tonight Show* in 2014 and Meyers was named to take over the 12:30 a.m. vehicle.

A lot has happened since Meyers appeared on *CenterStage*. He and his wife, Alexi, have had two sons, Ashe, who was born conven-

229

tionally in a New York City hospital, and Axel, who was delivered in the lobby of the couple's apartment building. Axel's special delivery inspired *Lobby Baby*, Meyers's razor-sharp stand-up special on Netflix that started streaming late in 2019.

It's really hard *not* to root for Meyers, and after you experience his career arc and his upbringing in this interview, you'll realize that he's won you over as a fan, if you weren't already.

The Interview

MICHAEL KAY: Today's guest grew up in New Hampshire and later attended Northwestern University, just outside Chicago. He began his comedy career while in college making people laugh, and he later spent time in the Netherlands honing his craft. His breakthrough came as a member of *Saturday Night Live*, where he spent thirteen seasons. His most notable role was as the anchor on "Weekend Update." He was named one of *Time* magazine's one hundred most influential people and succeeded Jimmy Fallon as host of *Late Night* on NBC. Seth Meyers. [*Applause*]

MICHAEL KAY: You made your chops as a comedian. What made you think you wanted to be a talk show host, and what made you think you could do it?

SETH MEYERS: I didn't put any thought into it. [*Laughter*] I was very happy at *SNL*, but I often thought at some point I'm gonna have to come up with an exit strategy. Then Jay [Leno] left *The Tonight Show* [in 2014], and Jimmy [Fallon] moved up as *Tonight Show* host, and there was an opening at *Late Night*. I was on the road doing stand-up, somewhere in southern Illinois in a Red Roof Inn, and my boss, [*SNL* and *Late Night* producer] Lorne [Michaels], called. Lorne sort of convinced me I could do it, and I have a lot of faith in Lorne, and so far so good.

MICHAEL KAY: The *Late Night* legacy is pretty awesome. You've got Letterman, you've got Fallon, you've got Conan O'Brien. Is there a lot of pressure?

SETH MEYERS: Anytime you start comparing yourself to the past or worrying that you're not keeping up that high standard, that doesn't bring out the best work in you. It's probably best not to think about the past too much and mostly focus on your present.

MICHAEL KAY: How have the critics treated you?

SETH MEYERS: You don't get reviewed that much with this show. I feel like overall people are fairly positive. We want to keep getting better obviously. Certainly there are always gonna be people on Twitter who don't think the show is very good. But I'm on an eight-day streak of not checking Twitter, and it's the happiest I've been in five years. [*Laughter*]

MICHAEL KAY: You were raised in Bedford, New Hampshire. What was life like in the Meyers household?

SETH MEYERS: Life was really good. My parents and my brother were my best friends. [*Laughs*] My parents were really supportive of my brother and me. My mother was a theater major at Northwestern, and my dad is the funniest person I know, and I think that combination always made us sort of drawn to performing. They introduced me and my brother [actor Josh Meyers] to comedy. We were listening to Richard Pryor at an age that was probably age inappropriate. Steve Martin albums, Woody Allen movies, Monty Python, *SNL*, at a very young age, so we had this real high sort of comedy understanding at a really young age.

MICHAEL KAY: Was it always comedy, did you like sports growing up?

SETH MEYERS: I'm one of those heartbreaking stories. I love sports, but I'm terrible at sports. But we were huge sports fans growing up.

MICHAEL KAY: So after high school, you go to Northwestern University. Were you a brainiac?

SETH MEYERS: I wasn't the best student, but I tested pretty well. I studied radio/television/film, but then I realized how patient you have to be to be a filmmaker. So much of it is technical, taking the time to get things perfect, and that was not how my brain was built. I realized I needed to do something else. And then at Northwestern I found my way into this improv comedy troupe called Mee-Ow, which is sort of famous, as famous as you can call a college improv troupe. Julia Louis-Dreyfus was a member, and other people who found their way into *SNL* in the early eighties were members. That sort of changed my whole outlook.

MICHAEL KAY: It seems like Chicago is such a hotbed for comedy and improv, and it's famous for Second City. Did you ever go to Second City?

SETH MEYERS: I never did Second City, but I auditioned for it and I desperately wanted to do it. Postcollege, that was my dream, to do Second City, mostly because of the litany of people who have done that, and you always thought, "That'll be the stepping-stone to whatever comes next." But I didn't make it that round. Instead I joined an [Amsterdam-based English-language improv troupe called Boom Chicago], and I moved overseas and lived there for two years. That was the greatest thing on earth. I would do two hundred shows a year, and I learned so much about comedy. But eventually I realized it was time to go, because you obviously hit a ceiling as an American actor in Holland. But it was a great time, I met great friends. Ike Barinholtz, who's an actor on *The Mindy Project,* was over there, and Jason Sudeikis and Jordan Peele from *Key and Peele.* So it was a really exciting time to be there.

MICHAEL KAY: Tell me how the *SNL* thing happened.

SETH MEYERS: So I come back from Amsterdam with this girl Jill Benjamin, who had sort of become my comedy partner over there. We come back to Chicago, we start doing this little two-person show called *Pick-Ups and Hiccups* in a seventy-seat theater in Chicago, a theater called the Live Bait. I remember in one of the first shows we did, there were eight people in the audience, and only one of them wasn't a blood relation. [*Laughter*] That was sort of the level we were at. But it became a small Chicago hit, it ran for a couple years. Then someone called me and said somebody from *SNL* had seen that show and wanted me to send in an audition tape.

MICHAEL KAY: When you got that call, did you freak out?

SETH MEYERS: I totally freaked out. So they wanted an audition tape, and I had to find a friend with a video camera, it wasn't like everybody had one. And it's just this terrible video. I remember watching it recently; I'm standing there doing weird impressions and characters. I sent the tape off, and I thought that was the end of it. Six months later *SNL* reached out again and said if I wanted to send another tape, they'd love to see it. I did, and then a whole 'nother six months passed and they called me in for the audition.

MICHAEL KAY: What's the funniest thing you said in the audition?

SETH MEYERS: One of my audition pieces was Russell Crowe as a talk show host, and he would just tell humorless monologue jokes, and then when no one laughed, he would scream [the line from *Gladiator*], "Are you not entertained?" and throw the mic into the crowd. [*Laughter*] Then I flew back to LA, and two days later I got a call that Lorne wanted to meet me. I flew back to New York and he hired me. It was the day I most wish I could go back and relive because I got to call everybody and say I got hired on *SNL*. A lot of times when people get jobs in show business, you don't know what it is. When Jennifer Aniston got *Friends*, nobody knew what *Friends* was then. But when you get *SNL*, you know your eleven-year-old nephew knows what it is, your grandmother knows what it is, everybody in your life knows what it is. It was just such a great day of calling people and letting them know that news.

MICHAEL KAY: So you get the *Saturday Night Live* job. You're a newbie. Anybody take you under their wing?

SETH MEYERS: I started with Amy Poehler, who I had known just from seeing her onstage in Chicago. Rachel Dratch, Horatio Sanz, were also Chicago people, they were very kind to me. Chris Kattan is someone who took me under his wing. There's this history of it being a very hard, backstabbing place, but my entire history with the show is the opposite. It was people looking out for one another.

MICHAEL KAY: You are so identified with "Weekend Update," but the first time you tried out for it, you didn't get it, right?

SETH MEYERS: I didn't get it. I auditioned for it, but it was one of those audition situations where you go in thinking, "Am I the right person for this job?" I was thinking Amy Poehler was the right person for the job. They went with Amy and Tina [Fey]. But then I lucked out because when Tina left, Poehler was a perfect person for me to do it with, and I finally believed I should do it.

MICHAEL KAY: So you become the "Weekend Update" host with Amy. Was it everything you wanted it to be? Was that the best time of your run?

SETH MEYERS: That was the best of times for me. Once I got to do "Weekend Update," and once I got to be co–head writer [with Tina Fey], it took me out of this time of self-doubt. Being a cast member on *SNL* was a dream come true, but I realized it wasn't really my skill set.

Before I was on *SNL*, I wasn't doing a lot of characters, I wasn't doing a lot of impressions, a lot of my comedy was coming from me as me. Which was what "Weekend Update" allowed me to do. You know, my first year on the show I thought I was okay, but there were a lot of people on this show who were better than me. I decided I had to find a place on the show where I was as good as they were at what they were doing. And ultimately I think "Weekend Update" became that for me.

MICHAEL KAY: So you were at *SNL* for a long time and then you leave to do *Late Night*. How emotional was that last show?

SETH MEYERS: It was very emotional, but you also have to do the show. I wanted my last "Update" to be a good one, so I didn't want to be so upset that I blew a joke my last night. Obviously I was gonna have a send-off of sorts on "Update," but I also wanted to do my work as a writer during my last week. Melissa McCarthy hosted my last show, and my last sketch, the last *SNL* sketch I ever wrote, I had written for Melissa and Bobby Moynihan. And Lorne and I were watching it during dress rehearsal, and it completely bombs. I wrote there for a long time, I wrote a lot of really good things, and I wrote a lot of really bad things. But I'm sitting there thinking, "It's my last sketch and it's the worst thing I ever wrote." So I'm watching it with Lorne, and it's just dead silence, and I looked at Lorne and said, "What are you gonna do without me?" [*Laughter*]

MICHAEL KAY: Now you're a very successful person. Do you ever walk past a mirror in your house and wink and go, "Yup"?

SETH MEYERS: [*Pauses*] Yeah, I think I have. And the really sad thing—the reason it took me long to answer—is because I think it's like second nature now, I don't even realize I'm doing it. [*Laughter*]

MICHAEL KAY: *Late Night* hearkens back to Dick Cavett and Johnny Carson, it's not all yucks, there are times when you really want to talk seriously. You're bringing in political guests.

SETH MEYERS: Our [taped] show airs at twelve thirty-five at night. We always want the first twenty minutes to be a lot of comedy, jokes, silliness, and then as it gets later in the night, we want to try to have our show have a different kind of people—politicians, authors, people who are experts in fields I don't know anything about. I think that if people are gonna stay up, they want to see something interesting like that.

MICHAEL KAY: At twelve thirty, do you sit up in bed and watch your show?

SETH MEYERS: First of all, I want to give a shout-out to everybody who watches my show, for keeping us on the air. Since I've started doing the show, I don't know if I've been awake once when it's come on TV. I'm home at eight. And my wife has regular hours and we get up at six forty in the morning to spend some time together, so to be up at twelve thirty to watch my show would be tough. With that said, I can't stand watching myself, either. [*Laughter*]

MICHAEL KAY: Do you find interviewing hard or easy?

SETH MEYERS: I really like the interviewing, especially when we have guests that I find very interesting. The biggest limitation is how short the interview segments have to be—seven, eight, nine minutes. Sometimes that can fly by if I'm talking to a really interesting person. And very rarely, it can feel like an hour when I'm with someone who is not interesting—but that doesn't happen that much.

MICHAEL KAY: With network talk shows there are big-time pre-interviews. So is the interview scripted, or are you allowed to just go off?

SETH MEYERS: I'm allowed to go off. But sometimes the pre-interview is really helpful. For example, last week we had Amy Schumer on the show and Paul Rudd on the show, they were doing huge press pushes for their movies. They've been on ten talk shows already, so the pre-interview is just a way to not have them come on and tell the same stories that they've told on other shows, you know? So the segment producers will say, "Here's something that happened to you that we just read about. Is that something you'd want to talk about?" Really the pre-interview is just a blueprint, and then you can go away from that during the course of the interview.

MICHAEL KAY: In May 2011, you host the White House Correspondents' Dinner. I've always wondered how tough that is, 'cause the president's sitting there. You have to make jokes about the president, the most powerful guy in the world.

SETH MEYERS: It was very stressful. When I was preparing for the White House Correspondents' Dinner, I was so stressed-out I couldn't even have a conversation with my wife for three weeks. All I did was live, breathe, and eat the writing of the thing. Then I ran into Robert Smigel, the great *SNL* writer, great *Conan* writer, and he had some great advice. He said, "When you're up there, you'll realize the audience is not looking at you. They're looking at the president looking at you. Because that's more interesting." That was a good thing to know. President Obama has an incredible sense of humor. The meanest thing he does is that he goes first at the White House Correspondents' Dinner, he goes up and kills, he brings the room down, and then it's like, "Ladies and gentlemen, Seth Meyers." [*Laughter*]

MICHAEL KAY: Now, most people thought you killed, that you were hilarious and you couldn't wait for the positive press. But something happened.

SETH MEYERS: I thought I did a great job, I felt really excited, and it went to my head a little bit and I started thinking, "This is Saturday, and when the news comes on Monday, all they're gonna do is talk about how funny I was—as long as nothing happens on Sunday." And then what happened on Sunday was, President Obama went on TV and announced that SEAL Team Six had killed Osama bin Laden [in a raid at Abbottabad, Pakistan]. I'm ashamed of this, but I was the one person in New York City whose first reaction was "No! Tonight? Ten years they've been looking and they got him tonight?" Nothing good ever happens to me. [*Laughter*]

MICHAEL KAY: Did the president say anything to you after you finished at the dinner?

SETH MEYERS: I told my last joke, and the president came over and shook my hand, told me I did a good job, but, you know, on C-SPAN you couldn't hear what we were saying. I always wanted to dub him saying, "Good job," and me saying, "Check out Abbottabad. I think there's this house in Abbottabad . . ." [*Laughter*]

MICHAEL KAY: I am such a fan of *SNL*, but you hear these stories about the bacchanal that it was. Was it like that when you were there?

SETH MEYERS: It wasn't as crazy as it used to be, but, look, if you had a good show, you want to go celebrate; if you had a bad show, you want to go get over it. There were some really late nights in New York City.

MICHAEL KAY: If you had a mulligan in life, what would you do differently?

SETH MEYERS: Oh my goodness. What would I do differently? I feel so happy with where I am now, I don't know if I'd go back and change much.

MICHAEL KAY: It's been such a blast, thank you so much.

SETH MEYERS: Thank you for having me here, I really appreciate it.

Alan Alda

When we booked Alan Alda to do the show, we knew we'd be visiting with show business royalty. As Hawkeye Pierce on *M*A*S*H*, he'd created one of the most indelible characters in television history. As long as there are moving images on the screen, Alda's portrayal of Pierce on one of the most popular TV shows of all time will sit atop the medium's Mount Rushmore.

Although Alda's career will always be defined by *M*A*S*H*, the actor's work goes so much deeper, including sparkling film and stage work as well as other television shows. He's one of the greatest actors of his generation, and of all time.

You'd think that having lived a life of excellence, he'd carry himself with a star's bearing. But it was the opposite. He arrived at the studio with his wife, Arlene, and had no handlers or PR people around him. He was kind and warm and exactly what you'd want Hawkeye to be if you'd met him when he came back from Korea. He couldn't have been more gracious to the staff and didn't "big-time" a single person. I only bring that up because, as I've said previously in this book, people of lesser accomplishment often arrive at the *CenterStage* set putting on airs and exuding less warmth. It's not that they're rude; they're just much more transactional and don't make much of an effort to connect. That wasn't Alda.

He wasn't much different from the kid who was born in the Bronx, went to Fordham University, and was on the staff of the student-run radio station, WFUV. When he realized that we had that in common, our conversation flowed even more freely through the years, hitting all the stops on the way to six Emmys and six Golden Globes. It has been a life well lived, and this legendary actor took us all along on the journey.

The Interview

MICHAEL KAY: Today's guest was born in New York City and grew up in the wings and the back stages of Manhattan theaters watching his father perform as a burlesque singer and actor. His acting breakthrough came as the sarcastic but tenderhearted surgeon Hawkeye Pierce on the celebrated TV series *M*A*S*H*. It ran for over a decade and became one of the most popular programs in television history. He has been nominated for an Oscar and received six Golden Globes, plus five prime-time Emmys. You have seen him in Woody Allen films, on the hit TV series *The West Wing* and *The Blacklist*. He has also been on Broadway stages and the host of PBS's *Scientific American Frontiers*. This affable and hardworking actor, writer, and director also serves as a visiting professor at the State University of New York at Stony Brook School of Journalism. Please welcome one of America's favorite and most talented actors, Mr. Alan Alda. [*Applause*]

ALAN ALDA: That was nice, thank you.

MICHAEL KAY: Your birth name was Alphonso Joseph D'Abruzzo. How did that become Alan Alda?

ALAN ALDA: My father [Robert Alda] chose the name Alda before I was born, because in those days, you didn't use an ethnic name for show business. So he took the *A-L* from *Alphonso*, which was his first name, too, and the *D-A* from *D'Abruzzo* and made *Alda*.

MICHAEL KAY: You were born in New York City. What was your family like?

ALAN ALDA: My father was in burlesque, he was a singer and a straight man. And my mother was a homemaker. The first four years of my life were spent in the wings watching burlesque.

MICHAEL KAY: So you spent most of your formative years as a child around naked women? [*Laughter*]

ALAN ALDA: I thought that's what life was like, and I was kinda pissed off when I saw that women wore clothes. . . . [*Laughter*]

MICHAEL KAY: Was it a tough way to grow up? It was very transient, I guess. . . .

ALAN ALDA: No, I enjoyed it. The chorus girls mothered me, they were very sweet to me. The tough part was my mother was unfortunately schizophrenic and paranoid, and so my whole childhood was difficult because I never knew what was real and what was her reality. I didn't understand why she had these episodes that were so violent and suspicious. In those days, nobody talked about mental illness, my father and I didn't even talk about it, even though we both had to cope with it. So I was completely in the dark until I was an adult.

MICHAEL KAY: Did you play sports?

ALAN ALDA: I wasn't interested in them 'cause I had polio as a kid. It wasn't until the seventh grade that I played football for the first time. And I remember this so clearly: I caught the ball and ran toward the goal line, and I was very proud of myself. And my teammates said, "You went in the wrong direction." [*Laughter*] Because the goalposts look exactly alike. . . .

MICHAEL KAY: [*Laughs*] Your father's first film was the very successful *Rhapsody in Blue*, and that meant your family moved to Hollywood, and seven years later you moved back to New York [where your father played Sky Masterson in *Guys and Dolls* on Broadway]. Being around show business, did you say, "This is what I want to do for a living"?

ALAN ALDA: When I was eight years old, I wanted to be a writer and I started writing things, and later in life—when I was nine—I wanted to be an actor.

MICHAEL KAY: [*Laughs*] Now, you started college at Fordham University in 1952, near and dear to my heart, 'cause that's where I went, too. And you worked at WFUV, the student radio station?

ALAN ALDA: I went there because I thought they had a good theater department, but they closed it down the year I came. So I majored in English. For the station I wrote radio plays, directed them, and acted in them and had my own record show where I played show tunes. I'd say all these intelligent things about these shows that I got off the back of the album cover. And one time I was describing the great lyricist of this show I was playing, and I had the wrong album cover. And so people kept calling in saying, "Doesn't this guy know who wrote *South Pacific*?" [*Laughter*]

MICHAEL KAY: Is it true you never wanted to take acting lessons because you thought it would ruin the natural ability?

ALAN ALDA: First of all, I couldn't afford it. But I also felt that if I took lessons, it would destroy my natural genius. [*Laughs*] And then I learned about twenty years later that everything I thought was my natural genius was actually just annoying mannerisms. I finally got rid of them by trial and error. [*Laughter*]

MICHAEL KAY: So in 1957 you're in New York, your dad's in show business, so it's probably easy for you to break into the business, right?

ALAN ALDA: No, it took about nine years before I could make a living at it.

MICHAEL KAY: So while you were trying to make a living as an actor, what else were you doing in those nine years?

ALAN ALDA: I drove a cab, I was a doorman, I was a dancing clown at parts stores and gas station openings. I was dancing at a gas station once in the hot sun and a guy said, "What do you get for that?" I said, "Twenty-five dollars for six hours," and he says, "Boy, you got it made!" [*Laughter*]

MICHAEL KAY: As part of a Ford Foundation effort you won a fellowship to go to Cleveland as an actor in a regional theater. After Cleveland you move to an improvisational company, at the Yachtsman in Hyannis Port [Massachusetts], and you also worked with their sister group in Chicago, which eventually became Second City. Were you considering yourself as a comedy actor or a more serious actor?

ALAN ALDA: I just thought of myself as an actor. I can be funny when called for, and I love to make people laugh, but I love the theater at its heart, because of all it can do to move us, to make us look inside ourselves. Sometimes comedy alone does that, and the combination of comedy and a tough view of life is probably my favorite form.

MICHAEL KAY: Your career ascends to the point that in 1964 you get cast in the romantic comedy *The Owl and the Pussycat* [on Broadway]. And also something historic happens that you didn't even know was historic when it happened—an interracial kiss [with black actress Diana Sands]. That was the first time ever on Broadway.

ALAN ALDA: She and I had worked together in an improvisational company in Hyannis Port, and we knew each other very well, and it didn't seem to us that there was anything special about this interracial romance that we were playing onstage. But we got some hate mail.

MICHAEL KAY: You end up being in the movie *Paper Lion*, from the George Plimpton nonfiction book about [him] trying to play for the Detroit Lions. You played George Plimpton's part in the movie. How much did you actually play, and how much did you get hit?

ALAN ALDA: The Detroit Lions played themselves in the movie, and they had this idea that it was fun to tackle me. And at one point eleven guys tackled me, piled on top of me, and [Lions defensive tackle] Alex Karras kept kicking me in the ankle. [*Laughter*] My ankle was asleep for a half an hour. It was fun to them. They didn't really try to hurt me, but they wanted to scare me. But I worked on it. I could throw a football fifty yards and hit the guy with the ball—but I could only do it once a day and then I had to sleep with an ice bag.

MICHAEL KAY: *M*A*S*H* was a Robert Altman movie, with Elliott Gould and Donald Sutherland. Did you like the movie *M*A*S*H*?

ALAN ALDA: I didn't like it that much. I thought it was a little silly in places.

MICHAEL KAY: Then they decide to make it a television series. How did it come to you?

ALAN ALDA: When I got the script for the pilot episode, I was at the Utah State Prison filming a movie. . . .

MICHAEL KAY: Not serving time? [*Laughter*][*Laughs*]

ALAN ALDA: And it was the best script I had ever read the whole time I was in prison. [*Laughs*] I decided that I would really love to do this.

MICHAEL KAY: It's been thirty years since the final episode of *M*A*S*H*, and Hawkeye Pierce still resonates. Did you ever think it would last this long and be this popular?

ALAN ALDA: No. At first we thought, "This thing could run a year." Then it ran eleven years. [*Laughter*] But once we started doing it, we all knew how special it was. We were very glad to spend much of our lives doing this.

MICHAEL KAY: The first season the show did not do that well on the ratings.

ALAN ALDA: We were at number seventy. But the second year we were a real hit.

MICHAEL KAY: I thought at first it was pure comedy, and then it became almost dramedy. There was a lot of fluff on TV, but what you were doing was serious, you were trying to give a message. Did

CBS ever give you pushback? Did they ever say, "This is a little too heavy"?

ALAN ALDA: I think the first time somebody died on the operating table was in the middle of the first season. We all were interested in the tough part of the war as well as the comedy that we could do. And when the guy died on the operating table, the head of CBS said, "What is this, a situation tragedy?" They didn't want us to show blood in the operating room. They wanted us to stay out of the operating room. They thought that they had a standard military-service comedy, where even though there was a war on, we were just having fun. But that's not what appealed to the people. What appealed was this sense that even though sometimes it was crazy and silly, it had an awareness that people were getting hurt and other people were trying to do something about it. It was a reflection of the authentic lives that people lived when they were in Korea. And we interviewed about two hundred doctors and nurses who had lived through that experience.

MICHAEL KAY: Now, on every hit show there's a breakout character— it almost seemed like an ensemble at the beginning, but Hawkeye Pierce is a forever character. Did the other actors in the show get jealous because of the fame that—?

ALAN ALDA: No, except for an occasional knife fight. . . .[*Laughter*] No, wait, it was guns. [*Laughter*] No, we all loved each other and we learned to live with one another. Everybody had a quirk of one kind, including me. We sat around and did the equivalent of group therapy. Once a week we'd sit in our chairs and look at each other and say, "What's the problem?" We really worked it out.

MICHAEL KAY: You found fame in your midthirties. Was fame everything that you thought it was going to be?

ALAN ALDA: It was even worse. A lot of people think that their problems will be solved if they get famous, but you just get more problems. I don't recommend fame to anybody, but in some professions you can't avoid it. You have to be famous to be a politician, and you risk being famous if you're an actor. And they expect you to be famous, you know. You make a movie, the studio has it in your contract that you're supposed to go around and talk about it on television. So fame is woven into our culture in certain professions. It doesn't do anything positive for you except once in a while maybe you get a nice table at a restaurant. But then you also get people staring at you, watching what you eat, and then texting it around the world.

MICHAEL KAY: Do you have a fondness for Hawkeye Pierce? Are you part Hawkeye Pierce?

ALAN ALDA: I didn't think I'd be able to play that character 'cause he didn't seem anything like me. But what an actor has to do is find out who there is in him that's the same as the person he's playing and go for that. I just jumped into it and everything was okay. But I don't look back on any character I play.

MICHAEL KAY: Do you ever watch reruns of *M*A*S*H*?

ALAN ALDA: No. Sometimes going past a channel, I'll look at it for a few seconds. I used to be able to tell what the story was, then I couldn't remember unless I had directed it, then I couldn't remember unless I had written it. Now I don't know what anything is. But it seems like a very nice show. [*Laughter*]

MICHAEL KAY: There's a certain pressure with a beloved series ending. You wrote the final episode, and you directed it. How do you think you did?

ALAN ALDA: I wrote it with seven or eight other people, but I was the leader of the pack. I think it was too long, two hours, but I really wanted to give everybody a goodbye, even down to the extras, the people with no character names. We knew their faces over eleven years, and I wanted to give them a goodbye, too.

MICHAEL KAY: And a hundred and twenty-five million people watched it.

ALAN ALDA: That shocked me. I don't think anybody really knows how many people watched because they made their statistics as they usually do, which is, if a television set is hooked up to the system, they figure two or three people are watching it. But this was shown in some town halls where hundreds of people were watching. One way we realized how big it was, we were driving to a restaurant together that night and the streets were deserted—it actually had an effect on the traffic. Not only that, I found out the next day in the paper that in New York, so many people were watching the show at the same time that when the commercials came on and they all went to the bathroom at once, it affected the water system. I never had a salute like that. [*Laughter*] I think all of us felt that we were part of something that was bigger than all of us, and we did our part to make it as good as we could, but nobody can really take credit for what happened when that show connected with the consciousness of the country.

MICHAEL KAY: Why did it end? It was still doing well. Had you run out of stories to tell?

ALAN ALDA: I was one of the people who felt that we were either repeating ourselves or in danger of repeating ourselves, and we didn't want to run it into the ground. We probably could have gone on a few more years.

MICHAEL KAY: In 2004 you return to TV and join the cast of *The West Wing*. What drew you to that? The great writing?

ALAN ALDA: What I loved was that although the political point of view of most people who wrote the show was on the liberal or Democratic side, when they wrote the character who I played, a Republican, they wrote him with respect and they gave him arguments that were solid arguments. I think it elevated the conversation on television for a while. If you don't have a respectful dialogue between those two points of view, you don't get anywhere.

MICHAEL KAY: You're kind of on the cutting edge technologically. I read somewhere that you fix your grandchildren's computers.

ALAN ALDA: Yeah, and I fix all my friends' computers. In fact I have a little service called Celebrity Tech Support. And the slogan is "Why let a nobody touch your stuff?" [*Laughter*]

MICHAEL KAY: You wrote a book about the things you learned in life. . . .

ALAN ALDA: Yeah. *Never Have Your Dog Stuffed, and Other Things I Have Learned.*

MICHAEL KAY: You have to explain the stuffed dog.

ALAN ALDA: When I was a kid I had a dog, named Rhapsody, after the movie my father did, and when I was eight years old, the dog died, and I was heartbroken. My father must have read someplace that it's a good idea to get the child involved in the funeral of a pet, so we took shovels and dug a hole to bury the dog. And digging the hole for the dog just destroyed me, I was sobbing. So my father thinks maybe he made a mistake. He said, "Well, maybe we should have him stuffed. We'll take him to a taxidermist and he'll stuff him, and you'll always be able to keep him." So the taxidermist stuffed him, and when he came back, the stuffed dog had this horrible, snarling look on his face. We kept him in the living room by the fireplace, and people were afraid to come into the living room. And I couldn't even remember the real dog anymore, just this thing with the horrible look on his face. I didn't realize it then, but as I looked back on that part of my life, I realized that you can't hang on to things forever, you have to let some things go. Enjoy them while they're there. If you stuff them, if you try to memorialize them in some way, even with photographs, it's not the thing itself.

MICHAEL KAY: Thank you so much.

ALAN ALDA: Thank you, I really appreciate it.

Larry David

Larry David is the cocreator of *Seinfeld*, a show considered by many to be the best in television history. He is also the creator and star of HBO's *Curb Your Enthusiasm*. When we booked him for *CenterStage*, it was hard to curb *my* enthusiasm. I loved both those shows in which he was involved and was particularly obsessed with *Curb* because we finally got to see David in front of the camera. He'd never appeared on *Seinfeld* except for a few well-hidden cameos, so *Curb* was a window into that famous comedic mind.

I was anxious to find out how much of the Larry David on *Curb* was Larry David in real life, and this hour with him gave me a bit more insight. He tells the story of his unlikely climb from a limo driver to a respected-by-other-comedians stand-up who was far from being a star. Not even close. His struggle as a comedian and as a short-lived writer for *Saturday Night Live* was a source of frustration, but also a source of endless stories to mine for *Seinfeld* and *Curb*. His unlikely pairing with the polished-onstage Seinfeld ended up creating television brilliance in which they both became part of forever in the entertainment industry.

When people ask me which of the more than two hundred *CenterStage* interviews I've done was my favorite, this is the one I always choose. David is brilliant, and you have to keep up with him or he'll devour you along the way. He knows what you're looking for in content, but he's going to make you earn it. I relished the challenge of going one-on-one with one of the most facile entertainment minds of all time.

David ended up paying me the ultimate compliment when, about a year after this interview, he called me up and told me he'd promised to talk to the students at Emerson College in Boston because one of his daughters, Cazzie, attended the school. I told him that would be a great experience for the students, but he said, "I hate talking like that for an hour. What I'd want to do is a question-and-answer format with someone—like what we did with *CenterStage*." I told him that made sense, then he said, "Yeah, I want you to come to Boston and do that with me onstage." I was stunned but flattered, so I agreed, and we had the most enjoyable hour and a half mesmerizing Emerson's students with David's stories.

Incidentally, Larry David in real life *is* almost the same as Larry David on *Curb*, but a little less mean in what would hurt people. But, as this interview will show, he does go right up to the line and, tantalizingly, always seems poised to step over it.

The Interview

MICHAEL KAY: Thank you, everybody, and welcome to *CenterStage*. Today's guest was born in the Sheepshead Bay neighborhood of Brooklyn. He grew up rooting for the Yankees despite the Dodgers being in Brooklyn, and they were still a fixture in that borough for many more years. Unsure of a career, he first experienced stand-up comedy in New York. Often misunderstood by audiences, things began to turn around for him in LA as a writer and performer for a short-lived TV comedy series by the name of *Fridays*. After a brief, insignificant stint as a writer for *Saturday Night Live*, he was asked by Jerry Seinfeld to help him work on a pilot for NBC. And the rest, as they say, is history. For seven years he was the creative catalyst behind one of the most innovative and popular sitcoms in the history of television. In 2000 his own HBO comedy special was expanded into a series and put the Must See back into TV. Over the past five years, *Curb Your Enthusiasm* has been the show that everybody either wants to watch or be on. Please welcome the guy who makes TV shows about absolutely nothing, Larry David. [*Applause*]

LARRY DAVID: Thanks, guys, very nice. You tolerate me, you really, really tolerate me! [*Laughter*]

MICHAEL KAY: So, you grew up in Sheepshead Bay, Brooklyn. How did Sheepshead Bay shape your life, your comedy?

LARRY DAVID: I grew up in an apartment building. My aunt and uncle and my two cousins were next door, my uncle and my grandmother and another cousin were on the third floor, I had neighbors to the left and the right of me, all over. Just a lot of people on top of you, very cramped, crowded, screaming, a lot of screaming and yelling, a lot of aggravation. People on top of each other, Jews on top of each other like that, it's a recipe for comedy. [*Laughter*]

MICHAEL KAY: A lot of people think comedians don't have happy childhoods.

LARRY DAVID: I used to have a line in stand-up, "I had a wonderful childhood, which is tough, because it's hard to adjust to a miserable adulthood." [*Laughter*] But I did have a very normal, good childhood. I wasn't an unhappy kid.

MICHAEL KAY: Now, you're a Yankee fan, and this started when you grew up in Brooklyn. Did you do this to be a contrarian?

LARRY DAVID: No, no. I'd like to say I did it to be a contrarian. My brother did it to be a contrarian. My brother is four and a half years older, he was a Yankee fan, and I looked up to my brother, so I became a Yankee fan, too.

MICHAEL KAY: Did you get a lot of abuse?

LARRY DAVID: Oh my God.

MICHAEL KAY: Really?

LARRY DAVID: It was unbelievable, yeah. Because everybody was a Dodger fan.

MICHAEL KAY: So, you end up going to the University of Maryland.

LARRY DAVID: Yep. The reason I went there is because I liked the name Terrapins. I loved the school nickname, the Terps. I wanted to say I was a Terp. [*Laughter*] That was the main reason I went there. There was also something about the state of Maryland I always liked, I liked the way it's shaped on the map. [*Laughter*] It wasn't that far from Brooklyn, and it was a big university. I wanted to experience the whole college life, and you didn't get that if you went to Queens or Brooklyn College.

MICHAEL KAY: What did you major in?

LARRY DAVID: I majored in history. And when I was in college, people would say, "Well, what are you going to do?" And my standard answer was "Something will turn up." I really had zero idea what I was going to do. Zero.

MICHAEL KAY: When you graduated, what turned up?

LARRY DAVID: I went to an employment agency and they sent me out on an interview, and it turns out it was an interview to be a bra salesman. Of course that was an episode I did on *Seinfeld*. The first day there my boss gave me a big paper bag full of bras. He said, "Take these home and study them." So there I was on the subway that night carrying a big paper bag full of bras that were spilling out the top of the bag. True.

MICHAEL KAY: You also did the taxi-driver stuff. How'd that go?

LARRY DAVID: Nothing ever went well. [*Laughter*]

MICHAEL KAY: So how did you stumble into being a comic, then, after all of these failed careers?

LARRY DAVID: So I was out of college for four years, and I was really kind of floundering.

MICHAEL KAY: Were you miserable?

LARRY DAVID: Oh, yeah. I was miserable. My parents were miserable.

MICHAEL KAY: What did your parents want you to do?

LARRY DAVID: They wanted me to work in the post office! They wanted me to take a civil service test and work in the post office. My mother wouldn't let up on it: "Larry, just take a civil service test, you'll have benefits, you'll be a postman." So I was really, really depressed, didn't know what I wanted to do. I was a private chauffeur for a while, driving a limo for an old woman who was half-blind. I was driving the Jewish version of Miss Daisy, I was driving Miss Tushman. [*Laughter*] I would take her up to the Bronx or Manhattan to shop, and I'd sit in the car. One day I was parked in Manhattan, with the chauffeur cap on, smoking a cigarette—I used to smoke—and all of a sudden this guy I knew in college comes walking down the street and sees me with my uniform on, leaning against the car. He looked at me and just continued walking, he couldn't even say anything. And I go, "What am I going to do?" So I took an acting class.

MICHAEL KAY: Right.

LARRY DAVID: But I didn't really like the acting class very much. And then one day I was talking to a friend and his wife from New Jersey, and his wife said to me, "You're so funny, why don't you do comedy? Why aren't you a comedian? You're so funny." I go, "Nah," but then I went to the Improv, just to see the show one night. And I was watching the comedians and I was thinking, "Jesus, that doesn't look that hard." Then I talked to someone I knew from college who was doing stand-up, and he gave me the lowdown of what to do. He said, "You have to have some material," and I go, "Material?" And he says, "Material, yeah, you have to write funny things and then go up and say the funny things you've written." So I started telling everybody I'm going to do it, I'm going to start to do stand-up. I did it to the point where I couldn't back out of it. And the first place I went was this place in the Village, Gerde's Folk City.

MICHAEL KAY: How was it?

LARRY DAVID: I was terrible. I had the worst material. I did some impressions, believe it or not. It was awful. But I got up once, and if you get up once, you could do it again, and that's all it is, just doing it the first time. And the more I did it, the more I realized that I probably could [make a living at it].

MICHAEL KAY: Did you love stand-up, or did you just hate it?

LARRY DAVID: I loved it—and hated it. I loved it when it was going well, but, you know, it was tough. Every night, I didn't know what was going to happen. It was kind of scary. The audience, when they had their share of drinks, they'd yell out very rude, horrible things. So it was hard to deal with.

MICHAEL KAY: Now, after the New York comedy scene, you moved to LA and you get a job as a writer and a performer on *Fridays*.

LARRY DAVID: Right. I auditioned in New York for a show called *Fridays*; it was kind of like *Saturday Night Live*, only on Fridays. The title was a rip-off, and because it was sketch comedy, it was a rip-off, but there were some really, really talented people working on that show. It was on for two years, I made some great friends, started writing sketches—that was fun—and that led to a writing job on *Saturday Night Live*.

MICHAEL KAY: Was that a dream job for you, Larry?

LARRY DAVID: You know, I didn't really have many dream jobs. When you think you're so incapable of doing anything, you don't really dream, because then you'll get it, and they'll see that you're incapable. Sounds funny, but it's true. So, no, it wasn't a dream job, but once I started doing it, it, it was kind of a dream job. I'm living in New York, I'm walking to work at Rockefeller Center, on this show with all this great history. And the writing wasn't hard, [except that] they never used my material.

MICHAEL KAY: That's what's shocking to me. I read that you were there a couple years and you had only one sketch on the show.

LARRY DAVID: Right, right.

MICHAEL KAY: And you had kind of an ugly almost-ending there where you told [NBC executive] Dick Ebersol to stick the job?

LARRY DAVID: Yes, I did quit. I was outraged because my sketch got cut again, and I walked up to him five minutes before the show is about to air, and I went, "This show stinks! I quit! I hate this show! I'm done, done, it's over!" And I walked out. And as I'm walking home, I'm beginning to compute the amount of money I had just cost myself. I thought, "Well, that was stupid." I go tell my neighbor Kenny Kramer, the guy who the [Seinfeld] character was based on, and he said, "Well, just go in on Monday and pretend it never happened." I said, "I think you got something there." So Monday morning I walk into the office and sit down at the morning meeting, and nobody said a word. And Ebersol never brought it up. I guess he just thought, "This is what nutty writers do."

MICHAEL KAY: Now, shortly thereafter, in 1988, Jerry Seinfeld hooks up with you and says he's going to do a pilot for NBC. What was the genesis of that?

LARRY DAVID: Jerry and I always had a strong comedic rapport with each other. We always enjoyed each other's company, occasionally we would get together, and he would go over some of his premises, and I would tell him some of mine, and we would kind of write a little bit together. He came up to me one night at Catch a Rising Star and asked if I'd be interested in working on something with him for NBC. So we came up with pretty much the idea of what the Seinfeld show became, and they liked it. So that's how that started.

MICHAEL KAY: Did you say at the time that you didn't care if it was a success?

LARRY DAVID: I must have, yeah. First of all, I didn't think I could do it, okay? Then the show got picked up, and I was unhappy because I thought, "What the hell am I going to do now? How am I going to write this? This is impossible. I'm going to write thirteen episodes? This is crazy." You know, I almost started crying from it.

MICHAEL KAY: Where did the premise of a show about nothing start?

LARRY DAVID: Well, that very night that Jerry and I first talked about it, we went to a grocery store to buy some stuff, and we were just talking about some of the products, having the kind of funny discussion that we normally would have, and I said, "This is the show, this is what the show should be, this kind of dialogue." You know, the way we talk with each other. We wanted to be able to capture that kind of dialogue on TV.

MICHAEL KAY: There was, like, a motto of the show, "No hugging, no learning." What did that mean?

LARRY DAVID: That meant that we wouldn't have a little life lesson at the end of the show and wrap everything up neatly, and everybody would kiss and make up, and life would be wonderful. That happens on a lot of sitcoms, they have to have these happy endings where everything is reconciled, and people learn a lesson at the end of it. But you can't really be too funny learning lessons every week.

MICHAEL KAY: Let's talk about the Yankee connection to the show. Did you have to get permission from George Steinbrenner for every single script [his character was featured in]? And was it tough to get?

LARRY DAVID: We did have to get permission. It took a phone call from Jerry to get his permission to do it.

MICHAEL KAY: He [Steinbrenner] once told me that the reason he gave the permission was because it was a bigger deal to his grandchildren that he was on *Seinfeld* than owning the Yankees.

LARRY DAVID: There you go! [*Laughter*]

MICHAEL KAY: I'm actually still ticked at you and Jerry for ending the show. Everybody loves *Seinfeld*, they still want it on. Is there ever going to be something like *A Very Brady Christmas*? Do you think there's ever going to be a *Seinfeld* [reunion show]?

LARRY DAVID: No.

MICHAEL KAY: No way? What if they throw a billion dollars at you and Jerry?

LARRY DAVID: Well, maybe a billion. [*Laughter*]

MICHAEL KAY: I know you don't cry as an adult, but after the final show, did you get sad?

LARRY DAVID: You're trying to have a Barbara Walters moment with me here. It's not going to happen. I've got to have comedic credibility, you're not going to see me weeping.

MICHAEL KAY: But were you sad or were you happy that, you know, it's a great thing to have done in my life.

LARRY DAVID: I don't get too sentimental over these things. I don't really think that way.

MICHAEL KAY: *Curb* is coming back for a sixth season, but there had been rumors that it might not. Were you on the fence about it? And if so, what put you over the fence?

LARRY DAVID: I'm always on the fence because I hate to work. It helps me get through the year by thinking that it's my last one.

MICHAEL KAY: It seems like when people watch *Curb*, it's almost like driving past an accident: they get uncomfortable, but they can't look away. Do you sense that? Is that what you try to foster?

LARRY DAVID: I had no idea that that was going to happen. I swear to you. When we first started doing the show, people would say, "I had to leave the room." I go, "Really, you had to leave the room?" I had no idea that it was having that effect on people. Certainly nothing on *Seinfeld* had prepared me for that. Nobody ever had to leave the room on *Seinfeld*. I was talking to my friend the other day, and he said it's a "horror comedy."

MICHAEL KAY: Now, you know, you mentioned *Seinfeld*, and when *Seinfeld* was on, people were always wondering, "How close is that to Jerry?" But now on *Curb* people wonder, "How close is that to Larry?" The actual character, how close is that to you?

LARRY DAVID: It's the character that I would want to be, if I could. Because it's things that I'm thinking about and not really saying, and that's why it's so much fun to do.

MICHAEL KAY: It's pretty well-known you don't have scripts, you write an outline and then it's improv. Would the show be as good if you sat down and wrote everybody's lines?

LARRY DAVID: Oh, God, no way.

MICHAEL KAY: No way? But *Seinfeld* was good.

LARRY DAVID: Yes, I know, but this is a little different. First, *Seinfeld* was played in front of an audience. So it had to be precise. You couldn't go out in front of an audience and improvise and do seven, six or seven takes like we do. And when you're playing in front of an audience, there's lines that are designed to get laughs. So it's a little more theatrical than this is. In this show, it would never be as good if there were lines.

MICHAEL KAY: This was great. Thank you so much.

LARRY DAVID: Thank you.

Rob Reiner

Rob Reiner is no Meathead.

Though he's often associated with his iconic character Michael Stivic, the beleaguered son-in-law of Archie Bunker in *All in the Family*, Reiner is *so* not that. He's so much more.

Reiner has established himself as one of the country's greatest filmmakers, directing such iconic films as *This Is Spinal Tap*, *Stand by Me*, *When Harry Met Sally*, *A Few Good Men*, *Misery*, and *The Princess Bride*.

It's been a long, interesting journey from the Bronx, where Reiner grew up in the borough's Grand Concourse neighborhood. His father, Carl, was a television legend who created the iconic *Dick Van Dyke Show*, and Rob explained in our interview how much of his early life was spent trying to get his famous father's approval.

When Reiner came on *CenterStage*, he was promoting his film *And So It Goes*, a movie starring Michael Douglas and Diane Keaton. The film became a modest hit financially but was not a critical success.

But Reiner came ready to play, moving away from talking up his film to taking us on his fascinating show business odyssey, which started with his being the son of a famous man and resulted in his becoming *more* famous than that man in ways Rob could never have envisioned.

The Interview

MICHAEL KAY: Today's guest was the kid from the Bronx who moved to the suburbs before spending his teenaged years in Beverly Hills, California. He first came to prominence during the early 1970s playing the "meathead" son-in-law on the groundbreaking TV series *All* *in the Family.* A decade later he shifted to directing and compiled an eclectic list of successful and memorable films, which include the comedy cult classic *This Is Spinal Tap*, as well as *Stand By Me*, *The Princess Bride*, *When Harry Met Sally*, *A Few Good Men*, *The American President*, and *The Bucket List*. Politically and socially active, he continues to be a vocal advocate for early-childhood development and educational programs. Please welcome one of the film industry's most accomplished creative forces: writer, producer, director, and actor Rob Reiner. [*Applause*]

MICHAEL KAY: I have to start out with this. Have you been "Meatheaded" yet today? [*Laughter*]

ROB REINER: You're the first.

MICHAEL KAY: Is it always at least once a day your whole life?

ROB REINER: At least once a day.

MICHAEL KAY: And does it bother you?

ROB REINER: No, it doesn't bother me. It's a badge of honor at this point. I love that show, I love being associated with the show. I've often said, it doesn't matter what I do in my life, if I win the Nobel Prize, [the headlines] will say "Meathead Wins Nobel Prize." [*Laughter*]

MICHAEL KAY: Now there's a generation of younger fans that don't know Meathead, they know you as Leonardo DiCaprio's dad from *The Wolf of Wall Street*.

ROB REINER: Yes. Which is unusual, because when Martin Scorsese asked me to play that part, I thought, "What's more unbelievable? That Leonardo DiCaprio is a Jew, or that I'm his father?" [*Laughter*] And then I thought, "Well, maybe I'm handsomer than I think I am." [*Laughter*]

MICHAEL KAY: So you were born in the Bronx, and I'm sure we all know that your father, Carl Reiner, was an entertainment-industry legend. So was it always going to be show business for you? Or did you have another career path in mind?

ROB REINER: Well, I don't know. I looked up to him, I idolized him, and I wanted to be just like him. But I was intimidated. I mean, he's brilliant. He had done *The Dick Van Dyke Show*, he won twelve Emmys, the guy is a brilliant comedy genius. And I never thought I could be anything like him. I was this kind of brooding kid. I don't think my father thought I had any humor in me at all. [*Laughter*]

MICHAEL KAY: When was the first time your father realized you had talent and told you so?

ROB REINER: I was nineteen years old, and I had directed a production of *No Exit*, by Jean-Paul Sartre, that Richard Dreyfuss was in, and my father came backstage and he looked me straight in the eye and he said, "That was good." That's when, for the first time . . . [*Pauses, sighs*] It felt unbelievable.

MICHAEL KAY: All right, so you're in the Bronx, then you move to New Rochelle, then your family moves to Beverly Hills. Beverly Hills High, you're a kid from the Bronx, how'd that work out? Was it fun?

ROB REINER: It wasn't so much fun initially because every kid would come up to me and say, "Say *water*." And I'd say, "Wadda," and then they'd laugh. "Ha, ha, listen to the way he talks." But I was a baseball player, I could play a little bit, and if you could play ball, you could get in with the group, so . . .

MICHAEL KAY: You went to UCLA after Beverly Hills High, the film school. So you definitely had the bug.

ROB REINER: Oh, yeah. I was wanting to do that. When I was at UCLA, I started my own improvisational theater group. I had Richard Dreyfuss, and Larry Bishop, who was Joey Bishop's son, and I directed this show and acted in it. We had our own theater for a year, and then we played in clubs around the country, and that's how I got started. And I started getting acting jobs. I was, like, the resident Hollywood long-haired hippie. I was on *The Beverly Hillbillies*, *Gomer Pyle*—whenever they needed a hippie, they would call me. And then when I was twenty-one, I got a writing job with *The Smothers Brothers Comedy Hour* [TV show].

MICHAEL KAY: I don't know if people realize how big they were.

ROB REINER: Yeah, that was a cutting-edge show in the sixties. The Vietnam War was going on, there were all kinds of race riots, civil rights was bubbling up, and they took on those issues. We ran afoul of the censors all the time. It was a renegade group of writers there, we were all radicals from the sixties, and we were all pushing Tommy [Smothers] to go further, go further. Looking back, and knowing what he had to go through, I have tremendous respect for what he did.

MICHAEL KAY: There was a show in England called *Till Death Do Us*

Part, and Norman Lear wanted to do something like that in America. How did you get involved with what became *All in the Family*?

ROB REINER: Well, they did two *All in the Family* pilots at ABC, before it went on CBS, and I auditioned for that and didn't get the part. Then Sally Struthers and I did it for CBS, and we got the parts. But we all thought, "This'll only be on for a few weeks, it's too edgy, it's not gonna go anywhere." [*Laughter*] But eventually people caught up with it.

MICHAEL KAY: It was the number one show for five consecutive seasons. Did it change the face of television in your opinion?

ROB REINER: It did at the time. All of a sudden, much more hard-hitting things came on. But I don't know that you could do a network television show like *All in the Family* now. Probably it would have to be a cable thing, 'cause it's a little too un-PC. But here's something that's fascinating to me, and it shows how things have changed. When we did *All in the Family* we were a country of about two hundred million people, and there was no DVR. If you wanted to watch it, you had to watch it when it was on television. So every week forty million people would watch and have that shared experience. The power of that was incredible. We did an episode that was about homosexuality, and nobody had ever touched that subject on television. We did another episode about my character being stressed-out over exams, and not being able to perform, you know, being impotent. CBS initially refused to air it, but Norman stood his ground. So we were able to do a lot of things, and we became part of the national dialogue. But now we're in a country of over three hundred million people, and if you get ten to fifteen million people watching, you're a monster hit—and they're not all watching it at the same time. So it's different.

MICHAEL KAY: So you won two Emmys, the show ends in 1979. And your film directing debut was *This Is Spinal Tap*, the [1984] rock mockumentary. Talk about hittin' a home run in your first at bat. How did this come about?

ROB REINER: Well, if it was a home run, it's a ball that left the bat very slowly and took twenty years to get into the stands. Because it wasn't a hit right off the bat. We previewed it in Dallas, and people were dumbfounded. They didn't know what the heck to make of it. People came up to me and said, "Why would you make a movie about a band that nobody ever heard of? And one that's so bad?" [*Laughter*] I said, "No, this is satire," but they had no idea what it was. So it took many years before people started catching on to it. And now it's become this [cult classic] thing.

MICHAEL KAY: [*Laughs*] Now, your follow-up movie is *The Sure Thing*, a kind of a coming-of-age love story. And then *Stand by Me* [about four young boys growing up in the 1950s]. Was it tough directing four kids like that?

ROB REINER: It was tough, but at the same time it was a lot of fun. Because young actors don't have a lot of bad habits, and they've got great instincts. And if you cast the right kids in the right parts, they're going to do what they need to do. By the time we started shooting, they had become a real unit. They were like a well-oiled machine.

MICHAEL KAY: It was based on *The Body*, which is a Stephen King novella. And Stephen King has said that nobody's ever been able to take his work to the screen better than you. . . .

ROB REINER: Well, he said it was the best thing that's ever been done of his work. And then he added, "But that's not saying much." [*Laughter*] He put that little caveat in there. But, yeah, he liked it.

MICHAEL KAY: So after the success of *Stand by Me*, you start Castle Rock Entertainment, and you're the guy who figures out how to put *The Princess Bride* on film.

ROB REINER: Yeah. I'm an idiot. It was my favorite book. As a young guy growing up, I read everything that William Goldman had ever written. And I was a huge fan. And I thought, "You know, they make movies out of books, maybe I'll see if I can get *The Princess Bride*." And what I didn't realize was that Robert Redford had tried, and François Truffaut, and Norman Jewison. All these people had been trying for years to get it done. And they couldn't. And so I called William Goldman, and he had seen *Spinal Tap*, and he agreed to have a meeting with me. I explained that I was trying to protect his book, and he agreed to have me do it. It was the greatest moment for me, that this person that I idolized was happy to have me do it.

MICHAEL KAY: So after that, [in 1989,] *When Harry Met Sally . . .* Where does this come from? Nora Ephron wrote it, but was it out of your experience?

ROB REINER: Yeah. I was married for ten years [to actress/director Penny Marshall], and then I was single for ten years, and during that ten-year period I was making a complete and utter mess of my personal dating life. I starting thinking about the idea "Can a man be friends with a woman, and not have sex come into it? And if it does come into it, does that ruin the friendship?" I went to Nora Ephron and I said, "I have this idea about two people who kind of come in and out of each other's lives, and they don't know what to do, it's this dance that they do around each other before they're able to get together." And she wrote it, and Billy [Crystal's] character is kind of like an extension of me, and Meg [Ryan's] character is kind of an extension of Nora.

MICHAEL KAY: Now, there's an unforgettable scene in the movie. . . .

ROB REINER: Okay. I think I know which one you're talking about. . . .[*Laughter*] [Meg Ryan's character's fake orgasm in the deli.]

MICHAEL KAY: And it was your mother who had the great line "I'll have what she's having." [*Laughter*]

ROB REINER: That was Billy's line. He came up with that. And it was interesting, because I needed somebody who was an older Jewish woman at the deli, and I thought my mother would be perfect. But just in case, I said, "Look, Mom, if this line doesn't get the big laugh at the end, I may have to wind up cutting it." And she said, "Oh, that's fine, I don't care, I just like to spend the day with you!" [*Laughter*] And that line, it became one of the top five lines in American Film Institute history. You've got Clark Gable saying, "Frankly, my dear, I don't give a damn," and [Clint Eastwood saying] "Make my day," and Humphrey Bogart, "This could be a beautiful friendship." And then Estelle Reiner is in there with "I'll have what she's having." It just gives me a tremendous kick.

MICHAEL KAY: Speaking of great lines . . . Jack Nicholson, "You can't handle the truth!" From *A Few Good Men*, the 1992 Oscar-nominated film, based on a play by Aaron Sorkin. Why did you want to do that film?

ROB REINER: Well, I loved the play. The theme, inside the obvious political courtroom drama, is a young guy who's a lawyer, and he has a father who's a very famous lawyer, who was a great trial lawyer, and this young guy is not willing to test himself. He doesn't want to get in a courtroom. And ultimately it's about his coming to grips with the shadow of his father. I felt that this was something I could understand how to do.

MICHAEL KAY: You had Tom Cruise, Jack Nicholson, Demi Moore, Kevin Bacon, the late J. T. Walsh, Cuba Gooding Jr., Kiefer Sutherland. That's a lot of star power. Was that hard to wrangle?

ROB REINER: You know why it was not hard to wrangle? Because of Jack Nicholson. When we had the first reading of the script, of all of us sitting around the table—the great Jack Nicholson, one of the great screen actors of all time, and all these great young actors—and when we started reading it, he read it full out. He wasn't just reading—he was *acting*. I mean, he gave a full performance the first day. And that's rare, it's very rare. This is a guy who just loved to act; it didn't matter if he was on camera, off camera, he loved to do it. It sent a message to everybody else, and it made everybody else step up. It was like everybody's taking batting practice, you hit a couple of balls, get your seven licks in, and you get out. Then all of a sudden Babe Ruth steps in the cage, and he starts hitting 'em into the upper deck. And everybody gathers around and watches, and then you realize, if the best guy is doing this, we better get our game together.

MICHAEL KAY: It's just an amazing film. Now, you're a Hollywood legend.

ROB REINER: *Legend?* That's a nice word. It means either you've accomplished a lot, or you're old—or both. [*Laughter*]

MICHAEL KAY: But you've also raised a lot of money for causes, and you've had propositions passed in California.

ROB REINER: Yeah, we've done a lot of things. We overturned Proposition Eight in California, which means gays and lesbians are now allowed to get married. We've been involved in a lot of programs promoting early-childhood development.

MICHAEL KAY: Ever think of running for political office, maybe governor of California? I mean, actors have done it before.

ROB REINER: Yes, I have heard that. [*Laughter*] I was actually considering it at one point, seriously thinking about it. And then I sat down with my family—I have three kids, and they were much younger at the time—and we discussed it. And we took a vote, and I basically polled forty percent—in my own family! And so I thought, "Well, if I can't carry my own family, I'm probably in trouble." [*Laughter*]

MICHAEL KAY: You have accomplished so much. [In addition to the other films] there's *Misery, The American President, Ghosts of Mississippi, The Bucket List.* It just goes on and on. But if given a mulligan, a do-over, what would you do differently?

ROB REINER: What would I do differently? You know, there's probably a million things that you might say you'd do differently, but ultimately I don't want to do anything differently. Because you learn more from the things where you mess up than you learn from the things that you do well. So . . .

MICHAEL KAY: This has been so much fun. Thank you, Rob.

ROB REINER: Thank you, Michael.

PART FOUR

THEY PUSHED
THE BOUNDARIES

Quentin Tarantino

Quentin Tarantino has morphed from a video-store movie nerd into one of the most influential figures in the history of cinema. His films are memorable for their singular style, featuring crackling dialogue, vivid characters, and sometimes gory violence and nonlinear story lines. Often, after seeing a Tarantino film, one leaves the theater exhausted by the sheer intensity of what one has just witnessed. Most moviegoers think about his films long after they've seen them.

Tarantino's filmography features some of the finest and most memorable films of all time. *Reservoir Dogs* started his career, and *Pulp Fiction* brought him firmly into public consciousness. When he sat down on *CenterStage* in 2007, he was there to talk about his latest film, *Grindhouse: Death Proof*. Since that day, he has helmed *Inglorious Basterds*, *Django Unchained*, *The Hateful Eight*, and *Once Upon a Time in Hollywood*.

His work is magnificent, and the process he uses to get his ideas on film is fascinating. When he sat down, he explained the journey from movie geek to film genius. He's as agile verbally as he is with the written word, which turned this hour into a riveting study of cinema—an essential primer on moviemaking. The conversation also gave us a peek into what makes Tarantino tick.

The Interview

MICHAEL KAY: Today's guest is an actor, writer, producer, and director who first began watching films in Knoxville, Tennessee, before moving to Southern California as a young child. At the age of fourteen, he wrote his first script. Two years later, he dropped out of high school to pursue a full-time film career. He first gained notoriety within the industry by writing a lengthy screenplay that would eventually be made into two notable movies. In 1992, he directed his first film, *Reservoir Dogs*, and with the release of *Pulp Fiction*, he became one of the biggest names in Hollywood's independent film revolution. His use of nonlinear story lines, edgy tough-guy dialogue, and stylized violence bred new life into traditional American film archetypes. Please welcome one of Hollywood's most innovative and creative forces. Here he is, Quentin Tarantino. [*Applause*]

MICHAEL KAY: Thanks for coming. That's a lot of stuff.

QUENTIN TARANTINO: I know. I was actually pretty impressed myself. [*Laughs*]

MICHAEL KAY: Tell me what *Grindhouse* is.

QUENTIN TARANTINO: It's a double feature. Back in the sixties and seventies we lived in a different world as far as movies went. You used to have double features all the time. *Grindhouse* is like what you saw in the old dilapidated theaters in the urban area of cities, whether it be New York, Forty-Second Street, or downtown Los Angeles or Kansas City. There would be these old dilapidated theaters showing all these wild B movies with all these lurid subgenres, whether it be sexploitation movies, cheerleader movies, blaxploitation movies, kung fu, monster stuff. And so we decided, "Let's do an old-fashioned double feature, with two movies for the price of one, but really create it like a night at the theater, not like a drive-in in the seventies." [*Laughs*]

MICHAEL KAY: And this all began in Knoxville, Tennessee. You were named after a Burt Reynolds character?

QUENTIN TARANTINO: My mom was sixteen years old when she had me. And my mom was half Cherokee and half Irish, so I am a quarter Cherokee. And at the time my mom had a crush on Burt Reynolds, who had played a half-breed Indian on the TV show *Gunsmoke*, a guy named Quint Asper. She was either gonna name me Quentin or Burt.

MICHAEL KAY: Now, you spent your childhood going to movies. Kung fu movies, blaxploitation movies. Did you ever just go to a *Gone with the Wind* sort of movie?

QUENTIN TARANTINO: I literally saw everything that came out.

But there was something about those lurid, sensationalistic movies. There was something about that sensationalistic material that was like a moth to a flame to me.

MICHAEL KAY: In reading the research about you, even when you were a kid, your mom treated you like an adult. And she took you to adult-themed movies. . . .

QUENTIN TARANTINO: Yeah, I was always able to see movies that none of the other kids in school were allowed to see. I saw *Carnal Knowledge* when I was in the third grade. [*Laughter*] The thing is, they talk about sex in *Carnal Knowledge*, but they don't have sex all the time. And it went right over my head. At one point there's this whole running dialogue between Candice Bergen and Art Garfunkel, and he goes, "Come on, let's do it." And she goes, "No, I don't want to do it." Then it's "Come on, let's do it." "No, I don't want to do it." "Come on, let's do it." And then I said, very loudly in the theater, "Mom, what's he want to do?" [*Laughter*] And everybody in the theater is laughing.

MICHAEL KAY: Did you like sports as a kid?

QUENTIN TARANTINO: Actually, it's a misconception that I was unathletic. People are like, "Oh, he's a movie geek, so obviously he lived his whole life by the TV." Well, that's not one hundred percent true. I never played team sports, I was never in Little League or in the flag football team. And I didn't get a chance to do any sports in high school because I didn't go to high school, because I quit in ninth grade. But back in elementary school, when we would play football on the playground during recess, I was always a big guy, so I wasn't the last guy picked. I was, like, the fourth guy picked.

MICHAEL KAY: Now, you like martial arts. Did you ever take any lessons?

QUENTIN TARANTINO: Nah, that's a little too much commitment for me. But right around the time I did *Desperado*, I started taking boxing lessons. I always wanted to be a boxer when I was a kid, and I always thought I would be pretty good at it. And so then I started doing it, and lo and behold, I am pretty good at it.

MICHAEL KAY: Who wins in a fight, you or Stallone?

QUENTIN TARANTINO: Stallone, I would think. But he'll know he was in a fight. [*Laughter*]

MICHAEL KAY: Do you like the *Rocky* movies?

QUENTIN TARANTINO: I love the *Rocky* movies. And I love Rocky Balboa. Not only do I love the *Rocky* movies, but Stallone was a huge influence on me, as a writer wanting to break into movies and everything. And his whole story about writing *Rocky*, and all of the false starts he had in his career—that inspired me more than any other story in Hollywood.

MICHAEL KAY: So you come to California, and one of your first jobs is at a Manhattan Beach video store, kind of a well-known store, Video Archives. But it wasn't just a video store, it was an eclectic mix of people that would hang out there, right?

QUENTIN TARANTINO: I didn't go to college, but a big part of the college experience is being with a bunch of like-minded individuals your own age. And that was my experience at Video Archives. It's a misconception that I got hired there and then became this film expert. I got hired there because I *was* a film expert. But it actually stopped me from having to get a real job for five years.

MICHAEL KAY: Your first stab at filmmaking was with a friend?

QUENTIN TARANTINO: Yeah. For five thousand dollars he's trying to complete *My Best Friend's Birthday*. It started off as a short film, then I got delusions of grandeur and tried to turn it into a feature. And I work on it for about five years, just financing it through my minimum-wage job. I would save up two hundred dollars and then we would go and shoot for a weekend. I wasn't in film school, but I had friends who were in film school, so we would have access to a sixteen-millimeter camera, thank God; that's what gave us the ambition to do anything at all. And through my film school friends I could check out lighting equipment and stuff. So we would shoot for a weekend, because if you rent the equipment on a Friday, you got it all weekend for just the price of one day, and you had to bring it back on Monday morning. So we would never sleep, all weekend long we would just shoot, shoot, shoot, and then bring the equipment back. I do that for about four years, and then eventually I get enough of the film together, and I start trying to edit it. And I realized that I don't have what I thought I had. [*Laughs*] And it is kind of demoralizing, actually. [*Laughs*] For four years I'm telling everybody, "I'm gonna make this movie, and it's gonna be so good," and I've got nothing to show for it. But I didn't quit. Anybody else would have quit. You try to put something out there, and you fail, and you might think, "Well, I guess it's just not for me." But in looking at the footage that I had shot, the majority of the stuff that I did the first couple of years looks very amateurish, but over the course of four years, the last stuff was a lot better. And so I just said, "Well, that was my film school." So around the time that I realized that *My Best Friend's Birthday* wasn't gonna work, I go, "Well, let me sit down and write a real movie. And this one I'm gonna finish. This will be my first screenplay." And that was *True Romance*.

MICHAEL KAY: Now, you also split that [script] into *Natural Born Killers*, and you ended up selling *Natural Born Killers* to Oliver Stone. From everything I have read, you were not cool with the way it turned out.

QUENTIN TARANTINO: Not at all. I just hated what he did with it.

MICHAEL KAY: Do you ever run into Oliver Stone? Do you ever get in each other's grill over that? [*Laughter*]

QUENTIN TARANTINO: No, we've kind of made up on it. But the reason that I really took him on in the press was, I did not appreciate him rewriting me. And I wanted to let Hollywood know, "Don't mess with me that way." I know that screenwriters get rewritten all the time, that's the way it is, and they cry all the way to the bank. Not me.

MICHAEL KAY: Around this time, you meet a guy named Lawrence Bender at a Hollywood party. And he starts to get together with you for the financing of *Reservoir Dogs*. How do you get this movie out, which turns out to be a great movie?

QUENTIN TARANTINO: I had always hooked up with a partner who had never done anything, but Lawrence had actually produced a couple of movies. They were very low-budget movies, but he had had a track record. He had a guy who wanted to put two hundred thousand dollars [in a film], and I had this idea for *Reservoir Dogs*, so I sat down and wrote *Reservoir Dogs* in about two weeks and gave it to him. And then he read it and goes, "Okay, wait a minute. We can't do this for two hundred thousand dollars." [*Laughs*] "This is a real movie." Now, at the same time, I finally sold my script for *True Romance*, and I wasn't even in the Writers Guild, but I got paid Writers Guild minimum, which at the time is, like, thirty-three thousand dollars. I had made about ten thousand dollars in my entire adult life, so that was a lot of money. So I wasn't going to wait [for financing], I was gonna take this thirty-three thousand dollars and I was gonna make *Reservoir Dogs* with it. And Lawrence was like, "Quint, look, chill out. Give me three months. Let me see if I can get a deal to get it made for real money. If we can't, then we will make it for thirty-three thousand dollars." Lawrence's friend was the husband of one of Harvey Keitel's friends at the Actors Studio, so we gave it to Lawrence's friend, he read it, he liked it, he passed it on to his wife. She liked it so much she actually gave it to Harvey Keitel and said, "Look, I don't normally do this, but I think this is a good piece of material, and I think you should read it." All of a sudden I get a call, and it's Harvey Keitel. And he is like, "Not only do I like it, I want to help you get it made. I want to be one of the producers on it. Let's do it." And he changed my life.

MICHAEL KAY: The total budget for the movie was $1.5 million. Do you ever sit back and wonder, "What could I do if I had a budget of $250 million like they could do for *Spider-Man* or for *Titanic*?" Can you even picture having that much money to make a movie?

QUENTIN TARANTINO: I don't really want to spend that much money. One of the reasons that I am able to do what I do is that I keep the budgets reasonable. But I do want all my movies to make money for the people who invest in them, and I want to be able to keep making movies.

MICHAEL KAY: After the success of *Reservoir Dogs*, you get offers to do *Speed* and *Men in Black*, and you turned them down. And those are big-time movies. Why'd you turn 'em down?

QUENTIN TARANTINO: By that time I was already writing *Pulp Fiction*. On *Reservoir Dogs* I made, like, fifty-five thousand dollars, and that was a lot of money to me, man. I had never been anywhere, and I had always wanted to travel in Europe, so as soon as I was done with *Reservoir Dogs*—finished, done, no take-backs—I took some of that money and I went to Amsterdam and I got a little apartment. And that's where I started *Pulp Fiction*.

MICHAEL KAY: *Pulp Fiction*, the first time I saw that in a theater, I sat there and it was just riveting. Did you know when you were writing it that "Yeah, I nailed this"?

QUENTIN TARANTINO: I knew I nailed it. But I didn't know it was gonna be this phenomenal big thing.

MICHAEL KAY: How would you explain the concept behind *Pulp Fiction*?

QUENTIN TARANTINO: The idea was taking the most basic nuggets you have always seen before: the mob guy is gonna take the boss's wife out—but don't touch her. And the boxer is supposed to throw the fight and he doesn't, and now the mob is after him. Old chestnuts you have seen a zillion times before, and then I just have my way with them.

MICHAEL KAY: And you kind of reinvent John Travolta. Why did you think Travolta would be good for that role?

QUENTIN TARANTINO: I was always a huge, huge fan of John Travolta, I always thought he was a terrific actor, and I felt bad that his career fell on hard times. There was that time period where he was the biggest star in the world, and any part that came out that he could possibly play, it was offered to him first. Nobody really had that situation since Brando. One of my favorite writers is the critic Pauline Kael, and I remember they quoted her in an *LA Times* article about Travolta's career. They ask, "Do you think John Travolta can come back?" And her response was "He has to. Because movies need him."

MICHAEL KAY: You don't win the Best Picture Oscar for *Pulp Fiction* because you run into a little buzz saw called *Forrest Gump*. Did it bother you that you lost for Best Picture?

QUENTIN TARANTINO: No.

MICHAEL KAY: Do you think that in Hollywood they don't want you to do well, because you are totally not that phony type of film school guy, and you have gone your own way? Are there fans of yours in Hollywood?

QUENTIN TARANTINO: I think there are. I have a very lucky and enviable position, and I get a tremendous amount of respect. I have gone my own way, but not like the jerk who can only hear the sound of his own voice. I am an artist, that's the way it is. I am not a journeyman director, I'm not looking for a job. Don't send me your scripts so I can read them; I write my own stuff. And when I finish, it's always about starting from square one all over again, it's about me looking at a blank piece of paper and having to fill it. Starting all over again—every single time. That's one of the reasons that I don't make more movies than I do. If I was a director that said, "Hey, send me stuff that I might find interesting," then I could make a movie all the time. But I don't even want to make a movie every year.

MICHAEL KAY: You make *Jackie Brown*, and then you take six years off. I was thinking before the show, "Is Quentin gonna be upset when he is sixty-five and he doesn't have as many movies that he could have made?" You have a form of genius, obviously. Do you feel that you are wasting it by not going pedal to the metal?

QUENTIN TARANTINO: No, I don't actually. Maybe I could have got one more movie in those six years. But I don't think about it that way. [During that time] I bumped into Uma Thurman, and I hadn't seen her in a couple of years. And I had come up with the idea for what would become *Kill Bill* while we were doing *Pulp Fiction* together. And so she brought it up, and then I realized, "That is what I should do." And I ended up spending another year and a half writing that.

MICHAEL KAY: When all is said and done with the movie career, what do you want your legacy to be?

QUENTIN TARANTINO: Well, I don't know if I'm going to get there or not, but truthfully, I want to be considered one of the greatest artists of the twentieth century. I want to transcend movies like the way J. D. Salinger transcends literature, or the way Bob Dylan transcends being a singer/songwriter, and Helmut Lang transcends being a designer. I want my writing—and I'm not saying it will be—but I want my writing to be up there with Mark Twain and Charles Dickens, if that's possible.

MICHAEL KAY: Wow. This has been a blast. Thank you so much for coming here.

QUENTIN TARANTINO: Thank you so much.

Kareem Abdul-Jabbar

Kareem Abdul-Jabbar could be intimidating both on the court and off. He was one of the greatest players to ever play high school, college, and pro basketball—but he was also notoriously difficult with the media. He was so much *more* than a basketball player, his mind always wrestling with social issues and causes more important than whether his next skyhook would fall.

After his twenty-year Hall of Fame career, which landed him six MVPs, nineteen All-Star appearances, and six NBA titles, Abdul-Jabbar never got the chance to become a head coach in the NBA. He was an assistant with the Clippers and the SuperSonics, but never got the top job he thought might come his way. He suspected his difficult relationship with the media contributed to his never getting the opportunity.

But Abdul-Jabbar's inability to add *head coach* to his résumé didn't keep him from exploring what he was capable of. Instead, he appeared in movies and on TV, delivering an especially memorable performance as Roger Murdock, the copilot in the hit movie *Airplane!* Over the years, he's also become a prolific author, writing or cowriting sixteen books, many not about sports. When he visited *CenterStage* in May of 2004, he was promoting the book *Brothers in Arms: The Epic Story of the 761st Tank Battalion, World War II's Forgotten Heroes*, but we spoke about everything. Abdul-Jabbar was riveting, so much so that this was the only show we ever produced that ran an hour and a half on air. We usually tape a bit more than an hour, then edit the show to sixty minutes with commercials. But Abdul-Jabbar was so open and fascinating that the standard edit became impossible, and we allocated a full ninety minutes to the airing.

There's nothing that Abdul-Jabbar didn't address, and he was especially interesting discussing his beginnings in New York City at Power

Memorial Academy and his subsequent dominance at UCLA. His time with the Bruins accelerated an awakening that was both academic and spiritual and led to his changing his name from Lew Alcindor to Kareem Abdul-Jabbar.

Abdul-Jabbar's determination to shape his NBA destiny by demanding a trade from the Milwaukee Bucks foreshadowed the paths blazed by future NBA stars. Unfortunately for Knicks fans, the New York franchise dropped the ball on a possible homecoming deal, and the big man took his prodigious talents to the LA Lakers. The rest, as they say, is history.

This interview is essential reading for any NBA fan, but also for anyone interested in riding shotgun on an amazing American journey.

The Interview

MICHAEL KAY: You run out of superlatives when describing Kareem Abdul-Jabbar and his contributions to the game of basketball. Known for his indefensible skyhook and his unsurpassed skills on the court, he redefined the game. Always a winner, he led UCLA to three national titles in his three seasons playing. He helped take an emerging Milwaukee Bucks team to the NBA championship in only his second year, then had a stellar career with the LA Lakers, winning five more titles. When he retired in 1989 after twenty seasons, no other NBA player had scored more points or racked up more MVP awards, snaring six. [He has appeared in numerous films and TV shows, from *Airplane!* to *The Fresh Prince of Bel-Air* and many others.] He's also an author, a historian, and has written five books, including *Brothers in Arms: The Epic Story of the 761st Tank Battalion, World War II's Forgotten Heroes*. Please welcome to *CenterStage* a New York native, Hall of Famer, and one of the greatest basketball players ever, Kareem Abdul-Jabbar. [*Applause*]

KAREEM ABDUL-JABBAR: Thank you. . . .

MICHAEL KAY: You grew up in New York, and your dad was a transit cop. Was he an authoritarian figure as a dad?

KAREEM ABDUL-JABBAR: Well, he had to work around the clock, on different shifts, so I only got to see him when I'd be awake when he was awake. So a lot of the time he was just a guy sleeping in my mom's bedroom. [*Laughter*]

MICHAEL KAY: All right now, your role models. Tell me about them.

KAREEM ABDUL-JABBAR: Jackie Robinson, most definitely, the Reverend Adam Clayton Powell, Dr. Martin Luther King, Malcolm X. They inspired me to be courageous and stand up for something. They were very influential on me when I was growing up. And in sports I would have to say [Boston Celtics center] Bill Russell. Starting when I was in the eighth grade, I got a chance to go down to Madison Square Garden and see them play all the time. And I was very impressed with him as an athlete and as a human being. He had dignity and intelligence, and he wasn't a buffoon. There was still too much of the minstrel era that had survived, and it was really a source of shame for black people. Bill Russell never gave in to that. It was a demeanor that I tried to adopt to show people that I was serious.

MICHAEL KAY: Is that why you went to basketball? Or did your height [six feet eight at age fourteen, eventually seven feet two] just dictate it?

KAREEM ABDUL-JABBAR: I think my height dictated it. That and the fact that in playing baseball I couldn't get my fastball over the plate all the time. I could pitch a little, but control was still a very serious issue by the time I got to high school. So I decided to give that up and stick with basketball.

MICHAEL KAY: Did you really love baseball?

KAREEM ABDUL-JABBAR: I really loved baseball. I had dreams of replacing Gil Hodges at first base for the Brooklyn Dodgers. That's what I wanted to do.

MICHAEL KAY: Let me ask you about why you picked Power Memorial Academy [an all-boys Catholic high school in New York City]. I guess you could have gone anywhere.

KAREEM ABDUL-JABBAR: Well, I had gone to Catholic school my whole life, and Power was a very good school academically, and they had a good basketball team. The coach, Jack Donohue, was a really funny Irishman and an excellent basketball coach. And it was pretty close to my home. So it made a lot of sense for me to go there.

MICHAEL KAY: [Your high school team had a 79-2 overall record when you were there, and you set scoring records.] At that time, people didn't go right from high school to the pros like LeBron James, but do you think you could have done that?

KAREEM ABDUL-JABBAR: It would have been a struggle for me, because my body hadn't matured and I really needed time to fill out physically and learn a little bit more about the game. But I probably would have considered it, especially at the salaries that they're paying today. I mean, you got to be crazy to pass that up. [*Chuckles*]

MICHAEL KAY: What was it like to have almost every college in this country want you? Everybody wanted [the young player then named] Lew Alcindor. How does a kid deal with that?

KAREEM ABDUL-JABBAR: I was really lucky in that the people around me didn't let it get to my head. They kept me grounded a little bit. I was getting letters on a regular basis from all the colleges, and my coach said, "Don't even deal with these letters. If a school has a basketball program, they want you, okay? So you just decide where you want to go and you'll get a scholarship."

MICHAEL KAY: You end up choosing UCLA. You weren't freaked out about going three thousand miles away?

KAREEM ABDUL-JABBAR: No, I *wanted* to go three thousand miles away. I wanted to get away from parental supervision. [*Laughter*]

MICHAEL KAY: I guess [UCLA coach] John Wooden was kind of a parent figure to you. What did he mean to your life?

KAREEM ABDUL-JABBAR: John Wooden was a great example and just a totally grounded and fundamental guy. He felt that his whole mission in life was to have a good effect on the guys that played for him, to make sure that they got out of school and learned the things they needed to learn about life—things that had nothing to do with basketball.

MICHAEL KAY: At that time, as a freshman you weren't allowed to play varsity. Is it true that your freshman team was actually better than the varsity team at UCLA?

KAREEM ABDUL-JABBAR: Well, in my freshman year the UCLA Bruins were the defending NCAA champs, so they were number one in the country. Then we played them in a freshman-varsity game and we beat them. So that made them number one in the country and number two on campus. [*Laughter*]

MICHAEL KAY: How was it playing at UCLA and almost never being beaten? I mean, you got beaten a couple of times, but every time you went out on the court, you expected to win, right?

KAREEM ABDUL-JABBAR: It was great being considered that good, but it also took away some of our sense of discovery. If we won the games, we were just doing what everyone thought we would do. And if we lost, they would say we couldn't live up to our promises. We achieved what we needed to achieve, but it really took away a lot of enjoyment for my last two years in college.

MICHAEL KAY: So you finally graduate [in 1969] and the NBA wants you. So there's a coin flip between the [Phoenix] Suns and the [Milwaukee] Bucks, and the Bucks end up winning. You're an erudite kid from New York, college at UCLA, what's it like in Milwaukee? Is it kind of a letdown?

KAREEM ABDUL-JABBAR: Milwaukee was a *frozen* letdown. [*Laughter*] Oh my goodness, I get out there and I said, "I'm from New York, I know all about winter." But I didn't know anything about winter. It was a different kind of winter. But there were great fans and great management, and they treated me very well. They paid me well, and they looked after me.

MICHAEL KAY: Was it hard for you to adapt to the NBA lifestyle, 'cause that's pretty wild? I don't know if it was as wild then as it is now, but it's still different than being a kid.

KAREEM ABDUL-JABBAR: It wasn't real wild. Because of all the minutes I played, I had to sleep all the time, on planes, on my days off. I rarely got to do much other than practice, play, and sleep.

MICHAEL KAY: Now, at that time, Kareem, and even throughout your career later on, people looked at you as kind of aloof. I don't know if it was shyness or what, but you weren't friendly with the media. Is that an accurate assessment?

KAREEM ABDUL-JABBAR: That's accurate. I was shy and I didn't trust the media. I knew that when dealing with them, you could step on a land mine.

MICHAEL KAY: What was the genesis of the distrust? Had they ever done anything to you?

KAREEM ABDUL-JABBAR: No, they really hadn't done anything to me. But I didn't like what they did to Muhammad Ali. I figured they would do that to me, too, after I announced to the world that I was

Muslim. So I was just wary. Maybe I was a little too wary, and people took my wariness and shyness for hostility. At that point I didn't have the people skills to know how to deal with that.

MICHAEL KAY: Tell me about the conversion to become a Muslim, and changing your name. Was that a difficult thing for you?

KAREEM ABDUL-JABBAR: By the time I changed my name, I had been Muslim for four years. I had become Muslim after reading *The Autobiography of Malcolm X*. That really affected me, and it caused me to go and investigate Islam. And in Islam I found a monotheism that I felt was the right thing to practice, and I have tried to hold on to it since. I'm not a gung ho type of person, I am pragmatic and probably very secular. But I still believe in my faith, and it's been a great moral anchor for me.

MICHAEL KAY: Did you encounter racism from fans around the league because of the decision?

KAREEM ABDUL-JABBAR: No, I didn't. Some people would make fun of my name, but they would make fun of my Christian name anyway. They were rooting for the Kings or the Hawks, and I was with the bad guys, so . . . That's just what fans do, and I could accept that. People who knew me well realized that I was sincere about my religious conversion and I wasn't doing this to say that, you know, I hate America—because I've never hated America. And people in Milwaukee were pretty open-minded about it. When they saw that I wasn't out to make waves politically, they more or less let it slide by.

MICHAEL KAY: Now, in '75 you were with the Bucks and you demand to be traded to either the Knicks or the Lakers. Had you just become tired of Milwaukee?

KAREEM ABDUL-JABBAR: In Milwaukee we had reached a point where we couldn't get the players we needed to win the world championship. And I wanted to get out of there, and they accommodated me. They were able to make the deal with Jack Kent Cooke of the Los Angeles Lakers.

MICHAEL KAY: Was LA everything you expected it to be?

KAREEM ABDUL-JABBAR: It was. I knew what Southern California was all about, and returning there was really nice.

MICHAEL KAY: Now, it eventually becomes the "Showtime" [era for

the Lakers, with a lot of flashy "run-and-gun" play]. You were a great player, but you were never a showy type of player. Was that awkward for you?

KAREEM ABDUL-JABBAR: No. It was funny, Earvin [Magic Johnson] could do the Showtime thing, he had all the pizzazz and the zest for the game, and I just did my job. And it fit, we were two pieces that fit together, and then you add people like Norm Nixon and James Worthy and Jamaal Wilkes and Bob McAdoo, and we ended up doing very well.

MICHAEL KAY: Now, Magic Johnson was a star, and he got all of the adoration. You were okay to sit in the background and just score your points, right?

KAREEM ABDUL-JABBAR: Yeah, it, that was okay with me.

MICHAEL KAY: April fifth, 1984, against the Jazz, [you shoot a] skyhook and you break Wilt Chamberlain's NBA all-time scoring record [with 31,420 career points]. What did that mean to you?

KAREEM ABDUL-JABBAR: That was great because I never thought I would beat Wilt's record. He was always superhuman to me.

MICHAEL KAY: In '89, after twenty years in the league, you decide to retire. How tough was that for you? You had been playing your whole life, and all of a sudden you say, "That's it."

KAREEM ABDUL-JABBAR: It wasn't tough. I probably had another year or two in me, but I was really burned-out. I worked very hard every summer to get ready for the next year, and then all of a sudden the incentive started to wane. At that point I knew that maybe I should be doing something else.

MICHAEL KAY: You left a lot of money on the table, though. You could have played another couple of years for maybe three or four million dollars a year, right?

KAREEM ABDUL-JABBAR: Yeah, probably. Looking back on it, when I see some nice toys that I want to buy, sometimes I think, "Jeez, I should have played that last year. . . ." [Laughter] But you know, that's life.

MICHAEL KAY: When you retired, did you have an interest in coaching?

KAREEM ABDUL-JABBAR: No, I didn't. I needed to get away from the game. I wanted to get away and see what life was like as a normal citizen. I started writing at that point, and that became a special thing for me.

MICHAEL KAY: All right, it's a perfect day, you have nothing to do, you can just chill. What do you do?

KAREEM ABDUL-JABBAR: I listen to jazz, I read. I like the beach and the ocean—I spend a lot of time in Hawaii—and I like to swim.

MICHAEL KAY: You jump in the water, your feet are still on the bottom, right? [*Laughter*]

QUESTION FROM AUDIENCE: You made the skyhook shot famous, but we rarely see hook shots anymore. Why not?

KAREEM ABDUL-JABBAR: You don't see hook shots anymore because it's not that sexy, you know? The young players today, they want to dunk the ball like Michael Jordan or Dr. J or shoot a three-pointer. [Shooting] six or eight feet from the basket just doesn't seem sexy to them. It's not going to get them a date. [*Laughter*] So it's a dying art. The style of the game really has changed.

MICHAEL KAY: Now, you can be modest or you can be immodest, but who is the greatest NBA center in history?

KAREEM ABDUL-JABBAR: Jeez, that's a tough one. You'd have to consider Bill Russell for the success that his team had, and you'd have to consider Wilt Chamberlain for just his singular dominance as an individual. I think you could consider me because of my personal success and my team's success. But you know, that's an argument people are going to have forever. Whatever your opinion is, I'll accept it.

QUESTION FROM AUDIENCE: How would you compare the athleticism of today's players with the players of your time?

KAREEM ABDUL-JABBAR: Well, the athletic ability that the players have today is based on what they learned from the players in my generation. I think they've just taken it another step, and I salute them for that. But I don't know if they're more athletic. They should learn the game fundamentally, which is something I don't think they always stick to. They go with their own abilities, the things that they work on by themselves. But it's the team game that gets you championships, and that's something they don't seem to understand.

MICHAEL KAY: You've had team honors, individual honors, you've done it all in your sport. You've written books, you've appeared in numerous films and TV shows. As you sit back now, what are you most proud of in your life?

KAREEM ABDUL-JABBAR: I'm most proud of the fact that all five of my children have graduated from college and they're all doing well. I'm really proud of that, and I'm happy for them. It justifies my life.

MICHAEL KAY: Before we let you go, as we said, at the beginning of your NBA career people seemed to think you were aloof, and in turmoil. You seem so centered and happy now. Is that accurate?

KAREEM ABDUL-JABBAR: I think so. I've learned a little bit about life, and I have had my ups and downs. But I feel good and I'm looking forward to the second half of my life. The second half is supposed to be the best half, so I'm going to enjoy it.

MICHAEL KAY: Thank you so much.

KAREEM ABDUL-JABBAR: Thank you.

Serena Williams

Time is money, and studio time is a *lot* of money, so when we produce *CenterStage*, we try to be lean and mean. The longer we keep the crew and stay in the studio, the more money each show costs. When we tell a guest we'll start taping at 10:00 a.m., we mean 10:00 a.m. sharp. We don't keep the guest longer than initially forecast, and we expect the guest to be there on time.

That didn't happen with Serena Williams. Serena was supposed to be at the studio for the cameras to roll at noon. She wasn't there. Executives started to sweat, phone calls were made to her people. Our first concern was that she was okay. We'd sent a car to pick her up at her hotel and take her to the studio. We got hold of the car service, which told us the driver who'd picked up Serena had been instructed by her to take her to Barneys to shop.

Now we were in a bit of a jam. How exactly do you hurry up one of the greatest athletes of all time without getting on her bad side and possibly killing the interview? One of the YES Network executives at the time, Janice Platt, was having none of this and took a cab to Barneys on Madison Avenue in New York City and found Serena serenely shopping for clothes. Platt told her that an entire crew was waiting to interview her and she had to come with Janice right this moment. Serena was a bit taken aback when Janice took the clothes Serena was clutching and asked the salesperson to hold them for later, then told Serena to get in the cab with her. Williams went with Platt and wasn't in the best mood when she arrived at the studio. The behind-the-scenes people told me this wasn't going to be easy because Williams was red-hot after being forced to leave Barneys. Before each show I always pop into the guest's dressing room to just say hello so the first time the guest sees me isn't onstage. I don't like to have a drawn-out conversation because I don't want to start the interview before the show begins, so I walked into Serena's dressing room with some trepidation, but she couldn't have been nicer. She was smiling, friendly, and said she was looking forward to the interview. The crew was amazed. They said it was like seeing two different people.

When the lights came on, Williams was more than ready—as she always has been in her career. We conducted this interview in 2004, and since then she has continued to win majors, capturing twenty-three Grand Slam singles titles and being acknowledged as the best female tennis player ever. Our talk in 2004 illuminated the path she and her sister Venus followed to greatness out of the rough streets of Compton, California. It's a fascinating journey, much more than might have been predicted by the journey from Barneys to the studio.

The Interview

MICHAEL KAY: Ladies and gentlemen, we're so proud to have with us today one of the most dominant female sports figures in the world today, and an unbelievable tennis player as well—Serena Williams. When Serena Williams and her older sister Venus burst onto the women's tennis scene, they brought new energy, vitality, and an interest to the sport. The sisters have come a long way from the public courts in Compton, California, where, urged on by their father, and with the help of a tennis manual, they learned to play with old racquets and found tennis balls. In 1999 at the age of seventeen, Serena captured her first US Open championship. She was the number-one-ranked player in the world in 2002, and when she won the Australian Open at the beginning of 2003, she achieved what has come to be known as the Serena Slam—winning all four Grand Slam tournaments—the French Open, Wimbledon, the US Open, and the Australian—in a row. She's also proven a success off the court, expanding her interest into fashion design, acting, and writing. Her athletic talent, temperament, and power game make her one of the most dominant players on the women's circuit today. Please welcome the smart, multitalented, and vivacious Serena Williams to *CenterStage*. Welcome to the show. [*Applause*]

SERENA WILLIAMS: Thank you so much.

MICHAEL KAY: When was the first time you picked up a tennis racquet?

SERENA WILLIAMS: I cannot answer that. I really don't remember the actual first time that I picked up a tennis racquet. I just remember always playing tennis and just being out on the court and having fun with my parents and my sisters.

MICHAEL KAY: Now, your dad, though, had it in his mind, he was gonna make you a champion, right?

SERENA WILLIAMS: He did. He had a vision. And I think it's important in life to have a vision. Set goals for yourself or—or goals for your family, and you know, he set these unbelievable goals and he achieved them. I set my goals to the sky, and I might not get to the sky, but at least I set my goals really high. And it's just amazing how he set his goals so high.

MICHAEL KAY: I've heard the story that he went to your mom after seeing a tennis match on TV and somebody got a thirty-thousand-dollar check. He said, "We gotta have kids and make them tennis players." Is that true?

SERENA WILLIAMS: That's one version I heard. [*Laughter*] But I've heard so many different versions. It becomes urban legend after a while, right? But, no, my sister and I believe we were already born and then he started us in tennis. Like I said, tennis was a part of our family, and I always remember just being on the court. I saw a picture of myself when I was really young. I was in the stroller. And I was on the tennis court. I wasn't hitting, obviously, but my mom and my dad were practicing.

MICHAEL KAY: Let's talk about your dad a little bit more because he obviously has meant so much to both of your careers. He's outspoken. He's been criticized. You think any of it's fair?

SERENA WILLIAMS: I think my dad is a great guy, and he's the sweetest person in the world. He's so nice. He's incredibly talented, in every aspect. I think a lot of things are taken a little out of hand with him. He's the greatest guy in the world. I really don't listen to what everyone is saying.

MICHAEL KAY: Do you ever remember not liking tennis or did you love it right away?

SERENA WILLIAMS: I never remember not liking it. I remember

sometimes having to go on the court and I wanted to do something else. But I think sometimes you have to make a little sacrifice if you want to be the best in what you want to do.

MICHAEL KAY: Now, the court that you and your sister played on, in Compton, California, that's not exactly Beverly Hills. I mean, it was dangerous, right? I heard that there were stray gunshots and stuff like that.

SERENA WILLIAMS: On one occasion, yes, there was.

MICHAEL KAY: When you were young, your family didn't have money. So it was used tennis racquets and used balls, right?

SERENA WILLIAMS: It wasn't used everything. We weren't the richest, we weren't living in Brentwood, but we weren't dirt-poor by any means. My mom had a very solid job. She worked as a nurse. And my dad had his own security company. So that's kind of the evolved urban Super Cinderella story of it. We had new racquets sometimes, but we accepted older racquets if we wanted to. And we always used the used balls, and I think it was for the best that we never had the new balls. Because when we got to play in the tournaments with new balls, it was like we were superfast—we were used to the old balls not bouncing so well.

MICHAEL KAY: How did you balance playing all the tennis and getting as great as you've gotten and going to school and earning A's?

SERENA WILLIAMS: Well, we weren't allowed to practice if we didn't get A's. We weren't allowed to bring home B's, actually. We had to study harder and stuff, but, you know, it always came easy for me, the education part. I love school to this day. I love school.

MICHAEL KAY: Now, obviously this is not the normal childhood because you guys were being raised to be great. Did you feel you were robbed of anything, Serena?

SERENA WILLIAMS: I feel I experienced a full childhood life. I know some players, they go pro at, like, fifteen years old, and then they don't get to finish high school. They don't get to have fun with just extracurricular activities and getting to know themselves as a person. And then it's like they get burned-out really easy. But my parents made sure that we finished high school. I actually went to college for two and a half years.

MICHAEL KAY: Now, in regular families there are sibling rivalries, and your sister Venus is also a great tennis player. How do you avoid that? Because everything I read is that you guys adore each other.

SERENA WILLIAMS: Yeah, we do. We were raised as Jehovah's Witnesses, so our religion teaches us to be loving towards one another, to love your brother and your sister and your neighbor and to just treat each other with so much love. I like to look at it this way: I'm not gonna be playing professional tennis twenty years from now, but my sister will be there twenty years from now. And I don't want to ever make up any strife or anything to put us in a really bad situation and have a bad relationship.

MICHAEL KAY: Now, about your first match. Thirty minutes, straight sets, you're out. At any point did you say, "This isn't what I want to do, this isn't working out."

SERENA WILLIAMS: I can't think of any point where I've ever said that.

MICHAEL KAY: Did they accept you right away, the other players? Did people ignore you, did they treat you poorly? Because you were new and different?

SERENA WILLIAMS: Well, my sister was first, so she kind of went through everything. They obviously weren't really accepting because it's something new, you see faces that aren't your usual faces that you see in tennis. I mean tennis is predominately a white person's sport. And so to see two African Americans come into it and not only just come into it, but do so well and get to the top, wasn't the easiest thing.

MICHAEL KAY: Did you feel you were paving the way for other African Americans to get into the sport?

SERENA WILLIAMS: I try to feel as if I'm paving the way for anyone who wants to become a great tennis player, and that's how I like to look at it.

MICHAEL KAY: Now, the way it was planned, Venus was gonna win the first championship, and you kind of threw a wrench into that and you won the '99 US Open. What was that like?

SERENA WILLIAMS: I don't think it was ever actually planned for her to win the first championship. I just knew I was gonna win that year. I just told myself I was gonna win the US Open.

MICHAEL KAY: Who does the family root for?

SERENA WILLIAMS: My mom told me once that if I'm down, she

roots for me, or if Venus is down, she roots for her. It just depends who's down at that moment in the match, but it must be hard. I couldn't do it.

MICHAEL KAY: In 2001 you played Venus in the US Open final. Now, that must be strange. Tell me what that's like.

SERENA WILLIAMS: That was good. I know I wanted to do well in that tournament. I was having a slump. We both got to the final, and I was really happy for Venus, I was really proud of her. I think she won the Wimbledon, US Open, and the Olympics, and she just was winning everything, so I was just really all pro-Venus. She beat the daylights out of me in that match. There was nothing I could do.

MICHAEL KAY: It ended up being a tough year for you to learn how to beat her. What finally got you over the hump?

SERENA WILLIAMS: I think I was playing at the French Open, in the final, and it was, like, five all in the first set, and she missed a shot and I won the set and I won the match. When I'm playing Venus, I'm not playing Venus Williams my sister, I'm playing Venus Williams my opponent. Because when we play each other in the final of a Grand Slam, there's history on the line. So I'm not playing my sister.

MICHAEL KAY: Now, you and your sister have been accused—and it's just an accusation, that's why I'm asking you—

SERENA WILLIAMS: I'm accused of a lot of stuff. [*Laughter*]

MICHAEL KAY: —that you feign injuries when you're supposed to play each other. Any truth to that at all?

SERENA WILLIAMS: I've never heard this one actually.

MICHAEL KAY: Would you guys rather not play each other?

SERENA WILLIAMS: Like I said, it's an opponent out there. We both have jobs—and my job is to play her sometimes and do the best that I can do.

MICHAEL KAY: *Hmm-mm.* Let's talk about some of the opponents that aren't related to you. Who's the toughest one to play?

SERENA WILLIAMS: Um, Venus?

MICHAEL KAY: Okay, after Venus.

SERENA WILLIAMS: I don't know. I can't say that anyone is. Mentally I can't tell myself that they're tough to play.

MICHAEL KAY: Your family has obviously gotten you through a lot. I mean, this is not an easy thing that you and your sister have done.

SERENA WILLIAMS: No.

MICHAEL KAY: And then you suffered an internal family tragedy, you lost your sister, one of your sisters. [Her sister was shot and killed in Compton in 2003.] How do you deal with that?

SERENA WILLIAMS: We're dealing.

MICHAEL KAY: Let's talk about the Olympics situation. You and your sister won gold in 2000 in Sydney, and you guys were, like, you loved it. I mean, you've done so many other things, why were the Olympics so important?

SERENA WILLIAMS: The Olympics are amazing. I'm still disappointed that I couldn't go this year, but the Olympics are like no other. I can play the US Open every year. I can play Wimbledon every year. I can play all these tournaments every year, but with the Olympics it's every four years. And all my career I've always thought, "Okay, I want to win the US Open, I want to win Wimbledon, I want to win the Australian Open," but I never thought about winning a gold medal. So I played in the Olympics and I got a gold, and when I got home weeks later, I was just reflecting on my gold medal and I thought, "You have people who work their whole lives for that one moment to have what I have. That's definitely the best win in my career."

MICHAEL KAY: People don't only come to watch Serena play tennis but also to see what she wears to play tennis. Let me ask you about the obsessions that people have with what you're wearing. Do you like that or does it freak you out?

SERENA WILLIAMS: It definitely does not freak me out. I'm really a fashion guru. I love fashion. I love setting trends and starting trends and being a part of everything that I'm gonna wear. So it doesn't bother me at all.

MICHAEL KAY: Now, two years ago at the US Open you wore the famous catsuit. Did you think it was gonna get that much play?

SERENA WILLIAMS: I really didn't. I was just really nervous to go out and play in it. Because it was skintight and I'm thinking to myself, "Wow, this is weird playing in this outfit." [*Laughter*] And it really had never been done before. So, yeah, I was really nervous. But once I got over that, it was fine. It was so comfortable. I was like, "Oh, this is the best thing in the world."

MICHAEL KAY: Now you have your own fashion label, too.

SERENA WILLIAMS: I do. It's called Aneres—*Serena* spelled backwards. I don't do tennis clothes actually because I'm not really into the tennis wear. At Aneres we just wear fun stuff, things that you'd wear every day. I do all the designing, all the sketches, I do everything but sew.

MICHAEL KAY: Does it bother you that not only are you a tennis star but you're kind of turning into a sex symbol?

SERENA WILLIAMS: Not really. I'm okay with it. Because I'm not gonna shy away. I'm just gonna be me.

MICHAEL KAY: You and your sister have really redefined the female athlete, the way people look at female athletes.

SERENA WILLIAMS: I think I definitely have. I think we have a major impact in that. Because a lot of female athletes, they get to be these wonderful athletes, but then they think that they have to be strong and really unfeminine-like. But myself and my sister, we're extremely feminine. We're really into fashion. We're really into things like that.

MICHAEL KAY: I think that as minorities you've also helped tennis a lot, too.

SERENA WILLIAMS: Absolutely. Every day someone will come up to me and say "Oh, I never watched tennis until you and your sister played" or "I never watch tennis unless you and your sister play." It's an unbelievable feeling in my heart when people tell that to me.

MICHAEL KAY: I would think it's unbelievable. Because tennis was almost exclusively white.

SERENA WILLIAMS: Yeah, it was. And it still is a pretty dominant white sport, tennis. But I'm seeing more and more black people in the locker room, so it's pretty encouraging.

QUESTION FROM AUDIENCE: Hi, I'd like to know, how does the crowd affect your play?

SERENA WILLIAMS: Well, the crowd is usually not for me. Because I guess they always like to see the champion lose, because they just want the challenger to win sometimes. So when I go places and the crowd is actually for me, I get really nervous. I feel like something bad is gonna happen. It's been really weird. I always feel better when they're against me, which is about ninety percent of the time.

MICHAEL KAY: Do you feel at any point racism from the crowd because it's a white sport?

SERENA WILLIAMS: I did at one point in my career, at this one tournament I played in Indian Wells. I was, like, eighteen or nineteen, really young. And I was playing Kim Clijsters, and she's a great girl. And at the moment I walked out, it was just boos, ridiculous boos. And everyone in Palm Springs is predominately—about ninety percent of the population is—are white, and everyone is about seventy and above. So it was kind of weird to have seventy-years-olds and above booing a nineteen-year-old black girl.

MICHAEL KAY: Weird. Has it been like that since?

SERENA WILLIAMS: No, it hasn't.

QUESTION FROM AUDIENCE: What accomplishment outside of your sport would you say you're most proud of?

SERENA WILLIAMS: What am I most proud of? My relationship with my family, how tight we are and how close we are and how I haven't let fame or anything come between us at all. And a lot of people do. They get famous and they lose their relationship with God and with their family.

MICHAEL KAY: Where do you think you're gonna be in ten years? And where do you think you're gonna be in twenty? Because in ten years you might still be playing tennis.

SERENA WILLIAMS: Yeah, in ten years I still envision myself playing tennis and hopefully have a lot of titles. I'll probably be ready to wind it down at that point. In twenty years I guess I hope to have a family by then, and hopefully I'll be living a little bit vicariously through them, through my kids.

MICHAEL KAY: Do you want them to be tennis players?

SERENA WILLIAMS: No, I wouldn't put them in tennis. It's too grueling on the body. Traveling eleven months out of the year, and staying so focused. And you don't want your kid to be under Serena Williams and Venus Williams. I would never want my child to feel any type of pressure to be that, the next Williams generation.

MICHAEL KAY: Serena, this has been fun. Thank you so much.

SERENA WILLIAMS: Thank you very much.

Lawrence Taylor

Lawrence Taylor is an enigma. He's one of the best players in NFL history, and he's charming when you meet him. But there are demons. So many demons. And he has fought those demons throughout his life. He has also been enabled like few before or since, his prodigious talent encouraging authority figures to turn away and ignore rather than confront and deal. His ability to create havoc on the football field has given him a sometimes puzzling "get out of jail free" card.

Most people's immediate reaction to those who let Taylor run wild off the field in order to run wild *on* the field is disgust, but when you sit down and talk with him, you realize there's something more there. There's trouble, but you wonder if it's willful or something he can't control.

When Taylor answered my questions in 2009, he took the *Center-Stage* audience into the huddle of his life, detailing his amazing exploits as well as his missteps and conspicuous drug use. He sat down with us on June 15, and sadly, about a year later, he was arrested for having sex with a sixteen-year-old girl in Montebello, New York. Lawrence always maintained that he thought the girl was nineteen; nevertheless, he pled guilty to two misdemeanors, sexual misconduct and patronizing a prostitute.

You can see from this interview that Taylor is most comfortable in the daily routine and protective cocoon of being on a team. Left to his own devices, he has little structure and less reason to stay straight. It's a cautionary tale of fame and fortune with particular relevance to the modern athlete. The only hope is that Taylor finds his way before more serious trouble finds him. Again.

The Interview

MICHAEL KAY: Thank you, everybody, and welcome to *CenterStage*. Today's guest was born and raised in Williamsburg, Virginia, where he didn't begin playing high school football until his junior year. He made a name for himself in the University of North Carolina and was selected as the second pick of the 1981 NFL draft by the New York Giants. A linebacker with explosive speed and power, he was in reality more like a feared force of nature in the NFL. He led the Big Blue Wrecking Crew to the first of two Super Bowl championships in 1986 and was so dominating that season that he became only the second defensive player in NFL history to be named the MVP. Quite simply, he changed the way the game of football was played. He is a member of the NFL's Seventy-Fifth Anniversary All-Time Team, and in 1999 he was inducted into the Pro Football Hall of Fame. Please welcome, unquestionably one of the greatest football players ever, Lawrence Taylor.

MICHAEL KAY: Now, Lawrence, I have always heard that there is an *LT*, and there is a *Lawrence*. What's the difference?

LAWRENCE TAYLOR: Well, one is the badass. [*Laughter*] That's LT. He's gonna play hard on Sunday, he's gonna play hard on Monday, Tuesday, Wednesday . . . But that's when I was young. I like the person I've turned out to be. It hasn't always been that way, but I like him now.

MICHAEL KAY: So I am talking to Lawrence? And Lawrence is kind of mellow and LT was wild. The Giant players are always quoted as saying that they loved LT on Sundays. Did they like that wild guy during the week? Did you hang out with Giant players during the week, or were you a lone wolf?

LAWRENCE TAYLOR: There were some guys that I would hang out with, and some of the older guys, like Harry Carson and Brian Kelley and Brad Van Pelt. We used to have a ball. Those guys taught me everything about NFL football.

MICHAEL KAY: We had Harry Carson on our show a while back, and here is what he had to say about LT. [*Starts film clip*]

HARRY CARSON: I know what he could have been, and I think *he*

knows what he could have been. I think once he left football, I think he lost it. I think his Maker has really given him a second chance, because he is clean. He has resurrected himself. I think that he has been at the bottom, and he has worked his way back up, and I think he is a better person now. I used to say, "The best thing that Lawrence Taylor could do for himself is to get LT to commit suicide and just become Lawrence Taylor." I didn't necessarily like LT, because LT could be very rough, very abrasive, and LT was the one who was going out and getting in trouble, not Lawrence Taylor. [*End film clip*]

MICHAEL KAY: He said he wished that LT would commit suicide. How do you lose a part of your personality like that, Lawrence?

LAWRENCE TAYLOR: It's just growing up. It always was the question, would you rather be feared or respected? I wanted to be feared 'cause I felt if you are feared, that's a sign of respect, and they are probably not gonna mess with you. And I was with that LT mentality so long that even after football was over, I kept that same mentality, and it got me in a lot of trouble. It wasn't until '98 when I got out of my last rehab, and I changed my environment. And I tell you what, I am a much better man for it. I enjoy every day. I wake up in the morning, and I look at the guy in the mirror, and I say, "Hey, you know what? You all right." And I like myself, I really do.

MICHAEL KAY: It's interesting, Lawrence, you helped the Giants win two Super Bowls, but you went through all these problems, and you know at times you weren't a great guy. But New York fans adore you. Why do you think people love you so much? Do you sense it?

LAWRENCE TAYLOR: I like people in general, I believe in people, I believe in the goodness of man, so to speak. I believe everybody has something good in them. And I think people can sense that.

MICHAEL KAY: So it started in Williamsburg, Virginia, which people know as Colonial Williamsburg. And you are one of three kids, and Clarence and Iris are your parents. And what did they do for a living?

LAWRENCE TAYLOR: My mother was a schoolteacher. And my daddy was a supervisor at a shipyard.

MICHAEL KAY: And he was an ex-boxer, too?

LAWRENCE TAYLOR: Yeah, and he did a lot of different things. He boxed, he played a little baseball, and he was a pretty good first base-man. So he was a pretty good athlete.

MICHAEL KAY: You didn't start playing football till you were a junior in high school. So before that did you play sports? And what were you good at?

LAWRENCE TAYLOR: I played baseball. I have always been a base-ball player. But after I started playing football, my baseball coach told me to quit football because, he said, "You'll never make it in football." [*Laughter*] So I decided to try to prove him wrong, and I decided, "Forget baseball, I'll play football." I went out there for the football team, and they beat my butt every day in practice. Every day I just got beat up, beat up, beat up every day, but I stayed with it. I didn't start my junior year, but then about the fifth game of the season, our first-string guy went down and they put me in. I had a helluva game, won the game for the team. Never had a bad game in high school. Every game I just got better and better and better. Fif-teen games later, I am All-American.

MICHAEL KAY: It just came to you, then?

LAWRENCE TAYLOR: Yes, some things you know how to do. Beat up and hit people, I knew how to do that. . . . [*Laughter*]

MICHAEL KAY: As a senior in high school you are six-one, two hun-dred pounds. And obviously, you are good. How many colleges recruited you, and why did you end up in North Carolina?

LAWRENCE TAYLOR: Well, I got recruited, but not by a whole bunch of colleges. In the neighborhood I lived in, I didn't know anyone who actually went to college. In my neighborhood, the "college" we went to was usually the penitentiary. But this one guy I played base-ball with, he went to the University of North Carolina, so they asked me to come down for an official visit, and he was there. He said, "Okay, why don't you come to school here?" I am really pleased with that decision I made because I had a ball. Carolina was a fabulous school. And plus, you can learn something there, too.

MICHAEL KAY: That's a plus. What happened the first year at North Carolina? Were you great right away?

LAWRENCE TAYLOR: The first year I was playing behind Kenny Sheets and T. K. McDaniels. I was a rookie, and they don't really let rookies play. But I played on the special teams. It wasn't until my junior year that I settled down at one position, outside backer. And just like in high school, playing NC State, I had a very good game. I caused a fumble, sacked the quarterback a couple of times. And I remember all the publicity and all the snapshots and all of the reporters wanting to interview me. And how the next day, they talked about me in the paper, and I said, "Wow." And from that game on until I left school, I never had a bad game. I got better and better and better *every game*, until I was All-American again, I was Player of the Year, and I got all of the types of accolades and stuff. I learned that it's not how many plays you make, you just gotta make the big play. You make the big plays, you are a hero.

MICHAEL KAY: How important was the Gator Bowl after your junior year—and you beat Michigan seventeen to fifteen—to put your name on the map? Now, that's a pretty big program to beat, and you played well in that game.

LAWRENCE TAYLOR: Wangler, the quarterback, he was killing us the first quarter. He had two hundred and twenty-five yards passing already. The coach come up to me and says, "You gotta do something about him." And the next play, I accidentally broke his leg. [*Audience moans*] And we won that game. And I'll tell you what, it really propelled our program. We got all the way to number six in the nation. That's the first time Carolina had ever been that high.

MICHAEL KAY: Now, after your senior year, in the NFL draft, the Saints don't pick you, they pick George Rogers. Was that disappointing to you? Did you want to be the number one? And did you mind going to the Giants? 'Cause the Giants weren't the Giants back then, Lawrence. You made them the Giants again.

LAWRENCE TAYLOR: It didn't bother me. I am sitting there, on draft day, and they say, "The Saints pick . . . George Rogers." And I said, "Now I gotta wait and see where I'm going." But about ten seconds later: "And the Giants pick Lawrence Taylor." And I was happy.

MICHAEL KAY: Okay, so the Giants take you. Are you embraced by your teammates right away, or did they go, "Who is this brash guy?"

LAWRENCE TAYLOR: Well, I am supposedly making all this money, which is funny, because they weren't paying me shit, and they are a little upset with that because I'm a rookie, I haven't done anything. I haven't proved myself. But it only took 'em about an afternoon to say, "Well, maybe he's gonna be all right, and maybe we shouldn't talk about his money." After the first practice I knew—and I am quite sure they knew—that I could play in this league, that I could play with these guys. So we had no problems after that.

MICHAEL KAY: Now, the year before you got drafted, the Giants were four and twelve. And you come, and they are nine and seven and they make the playoffs. You are the NFL Rookie of the Year. The Defensive Player of the Year. How satisfied were you with all that? Did you think, "Hey, I've made it"?

LAWRENCE TAYLOR: My rookie year, a lotta people would say to me, "You're gonna be All-Pro," and I didn't believe it.

MICHAEL KAY: Now, the next year you guys were four and five in a strike season. Then Bill Parcells gets the job. And you go three, twelve, and one. They were gonna fire him. How much did you have to do with him keeping his job?

LAWRENCE TAYLOR: Well, they had brought in a guy from Miami [Howard Schnellenberger] and they were gonna hire him, and I told 'em I won't play anymore. They could've called my bluff, 'cause I still had three years left on my contract. Bill was my drinking buddy, I wasn't gonna let him go!

MICHAEL KAY: At what point did you realize this is a really good team?

LAWRENCE TAYLOR: I thought the '85 team could make it to the Super Bowl. And in '86 we were by far the best team in the league. There was no team that could touch us, we was killing people, we weren't just beating 'em, we was killing 'em, we were destroying people. I'd put that team against any football team that's ever played.

MICHAEL KAY: Now, I wonder how much of this stuff is made up, but you read stories that you actually showed up at a [team] meeting once in handcuffs? A young lady couldn't find the keys. . . .

LAWRENCE TAYLOR: Well, that's another story. I was in the wrong place at the wrong time. [Laughter]

MICHAEL KAY: Now, during this time you win the Super Bowl, you've got it all, you got the big money, and although you're great, you're starting to drink and all that. . . .

LAWRENCE TAYLOR: Starting? [Laughter]

MICHAEL KAY: Starting to get really heavy. Did that set off alarms in the Giants? Did people come up to you and try to stop you, did they try to help you?

LAWRENCE TAYLOR: They can't stop me.

MICHAEL KAY: Didn't you know it wasn't good for you? Did anybody try to say, "Hey, Lawrence, you're gonna kill yourself"?

LAWRENCE TAYLOR: The Giants took out an [insurance] policy on me. They didn't think I was gonna live to be thirty anyway. So they took out an insurance policy so they were covered.

MICHAEL KAY: Did you think that you were spiraling outta control, did you ever get scared? Or were you just having fun?

LAWRENCE TAYLOR: I really didn't think of it that way. I drove cars at one hundred and forty miles an hour, and that's the way I lived. Anything for a good time. You really don't think of things like that until you get a little bit older. Now the good thing is the NFL's changed a little. You're stopped from doing that long before you get outta control. Now that it's got so many rules in place about your conduct, and you can't even drink. I mean you get a DUI, you're suspended.

MICHAEL KAY: Now, you won the Super Bowl, you beat Denver, it was thirty-nine to twenty. Is it true the Giants put a chaperone on you the week of the Super Bowl?

LAWRENCE TAYLOR: They called it a chaperone, I called it a detective. [*Laughter*]

MICHAEL KAY: Now, in the 1987 season you fail your first drug test.

LAWRENCE TAYLOR: That's the first one you *knew* about. [*Laughter*]

MICHAEL KAY: How did you elude the drug testers for so long?

LAWRENCE TAYLOR: In '87, I failed the drug test, it wasn't the first one, but that's the one that counted. And so I had to go to rehab. And I still have problems with that one, because actually, it wasn't my urine.

MICHAEL KAY: So you took somebody else's urine?

LAWRENCE TAYLOR: Yeah, and I failed the drug test and he was still on the team. I couldn't understand it. But to this day I still wonder how the hell it happened. But it was a great thing for me. I get suspended. Now I have to get tested three times a week and monitored. So it was good for me.

MICHAEL KAY: You loved football so much that that stopped you?

LAWRENCE TAYLOR: Absolutely. It was like, "Do I wanna play? Or do I wanna go this route?"

MICHAEL KAY: You went five years without testing positive. Were you clean?

LAWRENCE TAYLOR: Who knows? During the season we're getting tested three times a week, but who knows what's happening off-season? I don't remember. But it turned out well.

MICHAEL KAY: Now, going back to '85, in that season, there's probably the most memorable television moment in sports, with you and Joe Theismann. [Theismann's leg was broken in two places in a Lawrence Taylor sack.]

LAWRENCE TAYLOR: Oh, you mean when I kissed him? [*Laughter*]

MICHAEL KAY: Yes. How tough was that for you? Obviously you don't want to hurt somebody like that.

LAWRENCE TAYLOR: No, but he was in the wrong place at the wrong time. [*Laughter*] But seriously, I heard it just crack, and I knew when he was in the bottom of that pile, with all those bodies on him, with his leg going nine different directions, and I just couldn't imagine what he was going through.

MICHAEL KAY: Is it true that you've never seen a replay of it?

LAWRENCE TAYLOR: Never. I called him the next day, though, and he starts bitching and moaning, he's like "Oh, man, you broke both bones." And I say, "Joe, you know I don't do shit halfway." [*Laughter*] But we've been friends ever since.

MICHAEL KAY: Now, let's fast-forward. You end up retiring after a great career. And you go back to using drugs. Was that a tough call for you?

LAWRENCE TAYLOR: Not for me. The night before I retired, I got this thought in my head that I wanted to go back to recreational drugs. And once I got it in my head, I couldn't get it outta my head. I just wanted to retire because I wanted a chance to do recreational drugs—

MICHAEL KAY: Really? You retired 'cause you wanted to do drugs again? Was it worth it?

LAWRENCE TAYLOR: Overall, or that night?

MICHAEL KAY: Overall.

LAWRENCE TAYLOR: No, it's not worth it, but I don't even look at it like that anymore. It's a part of my life, what I've done. I'm very fortunate because my kids have seen what their daddy went through, and they don't mess with drugs. To me that's a fair trade-off. If I have to go through it so they don't have to go through it, it's a fair trade-off for me.

MICHAEL KAY: Was there a particular breakthrough moment for you where there was clarity and you said, "Okay, I'm done with this"?

LAWRENCE TAYLOR: Yeah, when the Feds put the handcuffs on me. When the Feds come for you, it's real clear.

MICHAEL KAY: [That was for back taxes and stuff.] So those are different handcuffs than the ones in the [team] meeting?

LAWRENCE TAYLOR: Yeah, those weren't recreational handcuffs. [*Laughter*]

MICHAEL KAY: What's the best piece of advice anyone ever gave you?

LAWRENCE TAYLOR: Just say no.

MICHAEL KAY: What's the most important thing that you've learned from your life?

LAWRENCE TAYLOR: I know that there's no shortcuts. What you do in life, you're gonna pay for it at some point. Maybe not today, but at some point everything comes back to haunt you.

MICHAEL KAY: Do you have any regrets?

LAWRENCE TAYLOR: None. I don't regret anything. There's some bad times and some good times, but I don't look where I've been, I look where I'm at right now. I'm happy with it.

MICHAEL KAY: Thanks so much, man—

LAWRENCE TAYLOR: Thanks, thank you.

John McEnroe

John McEnroe is a force of nature. The intensity he brought to the tennis court as one of the game's greatest stars has reappeared in the broadcast booth. The difference is, while during his playing days Johnny Mac sometimes seemed unable to control his demons, these days, as a tennis broadcaster, he is calm, cool, and extraordinarily analytical. Unexpectedly, he has become perhaps the best analyst of all time. In any sport. He's that good.

McEnroe in the broadcast booth can appear as if he's just combed his hair with a shoe and is wearing rumpled clothes pulled out of a satchel. But what he *says* is sharp and stylish as he deconstructs the genius occurring on the court with quick bursts of words that make it easy for the layman to understand.

Knowing of McEnroe's excellence in two fields and of his somewhat fiery temper when nudged the wrong way, anybody interviewing him has to be sure to be ready to play verbal three-dimensional chess.

Making my 2010 *CenterStage* interview with him more fun was the specter that hung in the air of "what might have been." When ESPN Radio in New York started in September of 2001, there'd been talk of pairing me with Johnny Mac to host a show. The executives set up a secret meeting in the basement of a restaurant near Madison Square Garden and directed the two of us to enter at different times and through different entrances. Once together, we were encouraged to "talk sports"—to see if there was any chemistry. There was. McEnroe has strong opinions on every sport and thoroughly follows them all. That was important since what was contemplated was the two of us teaming up to host a general sports talk show, not a tennis show.

After a couple of hours of watching McEnroe and I swap observations on sports, the suits decided they wanted to start the *Mac and Kay*

Show, but it never happened. McEnroe's tennis broadcasting schedule was so full that it would have been impossible for him to be in the studio with me much. Still, negotiations went on for months before ESPN New York decided to just put me on the air alone and later hooked me up with Don La Greca.

I'd heard rumors that McEnroe was mad at me because I'd taken the job and didn't wait for him to work things out. Although I wasn't happy that he thought I was at fault, I never second-guessed my decision because the radio execs had assured me the logistics of bringing McEnroe on board were just too difficult to resolve.

Because of what I'd heard, though, I was somewhat apprehensive about how McEnroe would be with me. I needn't have worried. He was a great interview, offering strong opinions and telling us how he'd accomplished all that he had.

The minute we booked McEnroe for the show, I should have expected excellence. Seven Grand Slam singles titles, nine Grand Slam doubles titles, and a combined 155 singles and doubles titles in his career suggest that this enigmatic superstar would thrive in any arena. Centre Court at Wimbledon couldn't unravel him, so *CenterStage* in New York was no match for him, either.

The Interview

MICHAEL KAY: Thank you, everybody, and welcome to *CenterStage*. Today's guest was raised in New York City and, as a kid in Queens, began playing tennis at the age of eight. As an eighteen-year-old amateur he won the mixed doubles title at the French Open and made it to the men's singles semifinal match at Wimbledon. The next year he turned pro and won the US Open, the first of his seven Grand Slam singles titles. He was ranked as the number one player in the world for four consecutive years and acclaimed for his shot-making and volleying skills. Both a winner and a whiner, he commanded tennis fans' attention like no one before him or since. This fiery competitor's on-court tirades, comments, and antics are legend. In recent years, he's gained a reputation as the most knowledgeable, insightful, and candid tennis commentator on television.

You're probably thinking to yourself, "You cannot be serious." Well, we are. Please welcome a true New Yorker, and one of the greatest tennis players ever, John McEnroe.

JOHN McENROE: Thank you. But I'm too old to be a whiner now. [*Laughter*]

MICHAEL KAY: I've always wondered about the on-court antics that we talked about. You were one of the greatest tennis players ever, but people always talk about the behavior. Do you think that people didn't notice the genius, because of the other stuff?

JOHN McENROE: If you don't perform, ultimately I don't think they really give a damn. Maybe people realized that I was so good, and they thought that I was rubbing it in their faces, so they didn't take to that too kindly. But—can I just say something to get this outta the way quickly? You know this from baseball. If you go up to an umpire and say, "Blank you," what are the odds of you getting the next call?

MICHAEL KAY: Not very good.

JOHN McENROE: So I spent many years telling guys, "You're the worst, you're the pits of the world, you suck, you're terrible," among other things. I felt I was just being honest, telling them what I actually thought. Because Lord knows in the beginning when I was on the tour, the quality of umpires was pretty dicey.

MICHAEL KAY: But you're a bright guy, and you knew that it wasn't getting you calls. Couldn't you stop yourself from doing it? Because you might've won easier.

JOHN McENROE: My father always said to me, "John, you don't need to do this, you're better than these guys, just go out there and play." But I grew up in Queens, so I thought what I was doing was sorta normal. I was a product of my environment. [*Laughter*] I'm not saying that everything I did was perfect, but I tried to stand up for myself.

MICHAEL KAY: What's the best piece of advice anyone ever gave you?

JOHN McENROE: "It doesn't matter whether you win or lose . . . until you lose." [*Laughter*]

MICHAEL KAY: When's the first time you picked up a racquet, and did you know right away, "Yeah, this is it"?

JOHN McENROE: I don't remember not knowing how to play tennis, to be honest. I remember I was about eight and a half, and I already knew what to do with a tennis ball. I went to tennis academy a year or two later. I played every other sport, but clearly this was the best one.

MICHAEL KAY: Okay, so in 1976 you enter your first ATP [Association of Tennis Professionals] tournament as a wild card, and you end up being the top junior player in the world at that time. Where's your head at this point, because you could either go pro or go to college. How tough a decision was it?

JOHN McENROE: Well, most people were encouraging me to turn pro. You know: "Why in the world are you going to college?" But I was eighteen, and I did want to experience college. I was trying to find a school that combined some academics with the best tennis program, so it was sort of narrowed down pretty quickly to the West Coast—USC, UCLA, Stanford. Stanford was the best school academically, along with a program more to my liking in terms of the way they approached training and letting me do my thing. And I was [ranked] twenty-one in the world, and I thought, "It's going to be good with the girls—"

MICHAEL KAY: They must have been all over you, right?

JOHN McENROE: They didn't give a damn. [*Laughter*] And that's forgetting the part that nine-tenths of the girls in California are good-looking, and the other tenth go to Stanford.

MICHAEL KAY: Oh, you'll get letters!

JOHN McENROE: I'll get a letter or two, but I'll make a donation [to the university], it'll be okay. [*Laughter*]

MICHAEL KAY: Now, in the beginning your main competitor, your main rival, was Jimmy Connors. What was your relationship like with Jimmy?

JOHN McENROE: We had respect for each other, but we didn't get along real well. For example, the first time we played in Wimbledon, in '77, he didn't acknowledge me or speak to me whatsoever. It made it all the more difficult to deal with the situation I was about to deal with. I had never been on the Centre Court of Wimbledon. [Connors's behavior] made me even more nervous, so I was pretty much shaken by the time I went out there.

MICHAEL KAY: Did you guys ever get better, you and Connors?

JOHN McENROE: We would go through a period of time where we wouldn't speak for six months to a year, and then suddenly he'd be like, "Hey, John, you want to practice tomorrow morning?" And stupidly I would say yeah, because he was great practice. I remember particularly, before Wimbledon in '82, he did that, he said, "Let's practice together." We were on opposite halves of the draw, so I said, "Okay, that's good, because the odds are Jimmy and I are not going to play against each other." Unlikely, but not impossible. [So we practice together], and then sure enough, we play in the final, and he's picking my serve every time I hit it, and I end up losing to him in five sets.

MICHAEL KAY: And you think the practice let him become more familiar with your play?

JOHN McENROE: I think so. Bonehead move on my part. [*Laughs*]

MICHAEL KAY: All right, so you went to Stanford for one year, you won the singles title, and then in January of 1979 you beat Jimmy Connors for the first time at the Masters tournament, and then Arthur Ashe in the final of the event. Is it kind of neat to beat those kinds of names?

JOHN McENROE: Well, especially since it was at Madison Square Garden. I mean, that's a place I went to since I was eight years old. I was a big Knicks and Rangers fan, so there's a lot of history there for me as a New Yorker. Jimmy didn't give me the full satisfaction, though; he defaulted at seven–five, three–love.

MICHAEL KAY: Did you want to kill him?

JOHN McENROE: I sort of wanted to kill him, but I wasn't going to let him spoil it. And I saved a few match points against Arthur Ashe, who had had a great sort of comeback to his career. We actually always got along, Arthur and I, off the court, we had great conversations.

MICHAEL KAY: Was he as classy a guy as everybody says?

JOHN McENROE: He was the greatest ambassador our sport ever had. Without a doubt.

MICHAEL KAY: Now, that same year, after you beat Arthur in the Masters, you end up winning the US Open. What did that mean to you?

JOHN McENROE: Well, it was an incredible feeling. The only bad part was that Vitas Gerulaitis, who I played in the finals, and I were both from Queens. He was from Howard Beach, I was from Douglaston, and we had become reasonably close. I was four years younger than him, and he was nice enough to take me a little bit under his wing. He would be the one who would get me into Studio 54.

MICHAEL KAY: Was it as Sodom-and-Gomorrah-like as they made it out to be?

JOHN McENROE: I didn't see that part as much as I would have liked. [*Laughter*] You had to be on the really A-list to do that. I remember times where I wasn't with Vitas, and there would be hundreds and hundreds of people outside, and I'd be like, "Please let me in, I'm number five in the world!" And they're like, "We don't care. . . ." [*Laughter*]

MICHAEL KAY: Now, in 1980 at Wimbledon, you lose to Björn Borg in that epic match. Although you lost, do you still remember it fondly, because it's considered one of the greatest tennis matches ever played?

JOHN McENROE: I remember it well. It was one of the only matches I ever played where I felt like I was part of history while I was playing it. That's unusual. And that match, there was an energy, and a feeling, and the way the match ebbed and flowed and went back and forth, that it really felt that something magical was happening.

MICHAEL KAY: Borg was the one player that you didn't ever really snap at, on the court. What was it about him that calmed you down, or was it a sign of respect to him?

JOHN McENROE: Both. When anything was going on, he'd just sort of sit there passively, you wouldn't even see him change his expression. So that meant that if I went up and started yelling, it would sound like it was three times louder. Also, he sort of took me under his wing.

MICHAEL KAY: So he was a nice guy.

JOHN McENROE: He was a great guy, one of the greatest guys you'll meet. We played a match early on, probably the third or fourth match we played, and I was going sorta crazy; this is in New Orleans back in 1979. And he motions me to the net, and I'm like, "Oh my God, he's gonna tell me I'm the biggest ass that ever lived." [*Laughter*] And I went up there expecting him to berate me, which I deserved, and instead he put his arm around me and he just said, "Look, it's okay, this is good." It just changed my perspective instantly.

MICHAEL KAY: When you burst upon the scene at Wimbledon, you weren't that well received. The British press called you Superbrat and all that stuff. Did that hurt you?

JOHN McENROE: Actually, I quite enjoyed it the first year. I thought they just didn't get me. If I got upset, and people started booing and stuff, I was thinking, "Why are they booing? I'm just upset at myself, it's got nothing to do with you, relax." When it first happened, I thought it was funny. But when I came back, and people in the States were saying to me, "Hey, you're the brat guy, you're the guy that got in trouble"—it seemed like they knew me for the wrong reason, and that sort of bothered me.

MICHAEL KAY: Now, you meet your first wife, Tatum O'Neal, in October of '84, you marry in '86, and you take a six-month break from tennis. In retrospect was that a good move?

JOHN McENROE: Well, it was mainly because we were gonna have a kid, and I was a bit burnt-out, I guess. I had gone extremely hard for seven or eight years on the tour. I needed to regroup a little bit, because I wasn't enjoying it the way I wanted to enjoy it. The plan was to get better, after I came back, not to get worse. Unfortunately, I didn't get better.

MICHAEL KAY: Did you like the Hollywood lifestyle, being married to Hollywood royalty, Oscar winner Tatum O'Neal? Was it tough for you?

JOHN McENROE: I wouldn't say that *tough* would be the right word. [*Laughter*] I thought Tatum was someone who could understand me because she had a lot of success at a very young age, and I needed someone who could relate to that. I didn't know that all of a sudden this would create this crazy interest because, quite honestly, Tatum hadn't worked for four or five years. But it took the relationship into a whole new league and level that I was unaware of. I never was in the *National Enquirer* till 1985. Certainly I was around Hollywood-type parties, and it's pretty hard not to think, "This is pretty good for a guy from Douglaston, Queens." The key is to be able to handle it, and I didn't do a particularly good job handling it. And at the same time, there was this huge change that took place in the sport, where all of a sudden people are using graphite racquets, and they're bigger guys and they're doing different types of training. It was a perfect storm in a way, and suddenly I go from being one or two in the world to being eight or ten in the world, and struggling to find my way back to the top five. That was frustrating.

MICHAEL KAY: We talked about you being on the air as a tennis commentator, and you're very frank, very honest. And I wonder, do you sometimes rankle some players? Do they get in your grill after the match and go, "What was that about?"

JOHN McENROE: Sometimes. But I think people respect honesty, particularly players, and for the most part the only thing I really get down on players about is when they don't make that hundred percent effort. I try to make myself always available for that very thing if they feel the need to blow off some steam. I still try to play on a seniors tour so that I don't lose sight of how tough it is to do what they're doing, when you're out there by yourself and trying to perform in front of a lot of people. Of course, I'm sure there are times where they want to strangle me.

MICHAEL KAY: Now, you've talked, John, about how the ATP [Association of Tennis Professionals] needs a commissioner. If that commissioner happened to be you, what would you do?

JOHN McENROE: Well, there's a lotta things. Cut the schedule, do more tournaments with men and women together. That would be something I would do. I would like to go back to wood racquets, but it's too late, I think the cat's outta the bag there. But we have to try more things, you know, I think that's the problem with our sport. Very little has changed.

MICHAEL KAY: You've said that when you were a young player, there were a lot of incorrect calls, but now there are challenges and there's unbelievable replay. Do you think you'd be less angry if you were playing at that top level now?

JOHN McENROE: I think so. I would spare a lot of that energy and I think I would've won some more bigger events.

MICHAEL KAY: Now, you've never really retired. There's a lot of people who think that if you played on the men's tour right now, you'd be very competitive and you could still win a lot of matches.

JOHN McENROE: I don't believe that for a second.

MICHAEL KAY: Could you win on the women's tour? [*Laughter*]

JOHN McENROE: I would do better on the women's tour. [*Laughter*]

MICHAEL KAY: John, thanks so much, this was so much fun.

JOHN McENROE: I appreciate it, thank you.

Snoop Dogg

The rapper known as Snoop Dogg appeared on *CenterStage* in April of 2008, and he came as advertised. Snoop was laid-back and had a big smile on his face as he discussed his iconic career, with special emphasis on the potential pitfalls of fame and fortune.

Snoop Dogg has crossed into the mainstream, and his honesty about who he is and how he got there can be endearing. He offers no apologies and makes no excuses. He has an unabashed love affair with marijuana, and he makes no bones—the pun is most definitely intended—about it.

Where Snoop has been in his career and what he has done are fascinating. Born Calvin Broadus Jr. in Long Beach, California, Snoop has had as many name changes as career milestones. He has gone by Snoop Doggy Dogg, Snoop Lion, and Snoopzilla, just to name a few.

He raps, acts, writes songs, produces, is a businessman, and is also a football coach in youth leagues. He's legitimately a big-time sports fan.

He has worked with hip-hop royalty and stands in that pantheon as well. He collaborated early in his career with Dr. Dre, worked with Master P, and has made music with pop stars as accomplished as Katy Perry and Justin Timberlake.

Snoop's reach is extraordinary, pulling in fans from the inner city to the suburbs. The Snoop buffet always seems to have something that someone will find tasty. His influence seems endless.

Doing an interview with Snoop Dogg on a show that is produced by a family-oriented network was a bit of a challenge because his work isn't for the easily offended. The words and images are raw, and the misogyny that sometimes emerges in his work is hard to ignore and, at times, stomach.

But again, Snoop made no excuses. He is what he is, and his refusal to apologize for that seems to make him more accepted, even mainstream. Throughout the show he told great stories and spoke with the same ease he displays in laying down his rhymes. Both in his work and how he interacts in an interview, he's laid-back and extraordinarily smooth.

At the end of our conversation the audience came away seeing why Snoop is so likable, even to those who don't like and approve of certain things about him.

I was fascinated with his story, but didn't know how Snoop felt the interview had gone. He was certainly cordial and friendly to the audience and to each and every member of the staff. But someone in the public eye should always display that persona. It's good for business. I couldn't help wonder, was he *really* pleased with how our conversation had played out?

Three years after we taped the show, I was at an ESPN Super Bowl party and Snoop Dogg was walking through the room with several friends. We hadn't seen or spoken to each other since the taping, and I'd never met him before he sat down on *CenterStage*, so I was stunned when he stopped, shook my hand, asked how I was doing, and then turned to his buddies and said, "This dude right here did the best interview with me ever. No shizzle. It was the best. We really talked." His friends nodded; Snoop smiled and then walked away onto the list of best interviews on *CenterStage*.

The Interview

MICHAEL KAY: Thank you, everybody, and welcome to the YES Network's hundredth *CenterStage* program. We've had quite an eclectic collection of prominent celebrities and sports stars. Today another icon joins us, from the world of today's hip-hop/rap culture. He was born Calvin Broadus Jr. and raised in Long Beach, California. As a child he learned to play piano, performed in the church choir and school plays. He was a gifted athlete in football and basketball, but his off-field life in a gang and dealing drugs landed him in jail. He refocused himself, and his homemade tapes would eventually catch the ear of a rap music producer, which led to a hugely successful debut album in 1993. It was something of a watershed moment in music, as it included the violent themes of West Coast urban culture and pushed it further into the public eye. Over the past fifteen years he's made the transition from gangsta rap to a lovable brand. His 2007 reality show, *Snoop Dogg's Father Hood*, revealed him to be a committed family man. Please welcome the man who puts the izzle in the sizzle, fo' shizzle [*laughter*], Snoop Dogg. [*Applause*]

MICHAEL KAY: Did I get that right?

SNOOP DOGG: You did, that was sharp.

MICHAEL KAY: Over the last couple of years, you've become very mainstream. Is that something that you consciously tried to do, or has it just happened?

SNOOP DOGG: I just feel like mainstream has finally opened their ears and their eyes to me. I'm not changing anything. I've done the same thing since day one.

MICHAEL KAY: Your new album is *Ego Trippin'* and it's got a little bit of a different style. It seems like the CD has a Marvin Gaye–Curtis Mayfield feel to it. Is that what you were going for?

SNOOP DOGG: Well, that was my musical influences, I'm influenced heavily by Marvin Gaye and Curtis Mayfield because they made such great music, and they came from a time when it wasn't about computers, it was about making music from their hearts and their souls. I just felt like that was a great time for making music, so I wanted to reflect back on that.

MICHAEL KAY: "My Medicine" on the CD, it's kind of a country song and it seems like it's influenced by Johnny Cash.

SNOOP DOGG: It definitely has a bluegrass-country feel, and it is definitely inspired by Johnny Cash. I love his songs, I love the fact that he went to Folsom penitentiary and did a show for the inmates in the penitentiary when nobody really cared about the guys locked up. Everybody in there ain't guilty.

MICHAEL KAY: You appeared on the CMT and CMA country music awards. Were you embraced by the people there?

SNOOP DOGG: Yeah, I went and got me some cowboy boots, some jeans, a cowboy hat. I was accepted well, it was a great day, a great time.

MICHAEL KAY: I heard your mother gave you the nickname Snoop. How'd that come about?

SNOOP DOGG: The *Charlie Brown* TV show was on in the seventies, and I used to watch it so much that she said I was starting to look like the dog, Snoopy. So she was like, "You watch this show so much, your name is Snoopy." [*Laughter*] And everybody just started calling me Snoopy.

MICHAEL KAY: Now, sports were a big part of your life. How did it start with you and what were your favorite sports growing up?

SNOOP DOGG: Sports started with me in 1979. I was watching a USC game, Charles White was the running back, and he was so sweet. I went to school the next couple days and I told my homeboys I wanted to play football. And I went and tried out for this team, and I started playing football, and from that I went to basketball and track. But my best sport was playing the girls. [*Laughter*] That was the sport that I ended up playing. That's why I didn't end up doing no professional sports or nothing.

MICHAEL KAY: Now, you were recruited for basketball by some small colleges, right?

SNOOP DOGG: Yeah.

MICHAEL KAY: What'd you play in basketball?

SNOOP DOGG: I played guard and small forward. But it wasn't my passion, I didn't really push, you understand what I'm saying? I didn't have the passion to wanna work out, to wanna practice, to wanna really put my mind on doing that. My mind was on selling drugs, getting money, rapping a little bit, hanging with the gang. But once I found out that that wasn't the right path, then I locked into making music and figured out that this is what I really need to do.

MICHAEL KAY: Now, when you graduated from high school, did you have a plan at that point?

SNOOP DOGG: Nah. When I graduated from high school, I'm lost, because a job is hard to come by, I don't really wanna go to college, I don't really wanna press myself and use my mind. I'd rather take the easy route. I could sell drugs real good, even though I knew at the end of the day if I got caught, it's a lotta jail time waiting on me. So I'm on the corner selling drugs until I get caught. And when I get caught, I go to jail and do a little bit of time, and that gives me time to settle down and see what I really need to be doing, it helps me refocus. When I'm rapping in there [in jail], the fellas are telling me,

"You too good to be in here, dog, you could do better than half the guys that's on the radio." They got to the point where they was like, "Man, we don't even wanna see you in here no more, you come back in here, we gonna do something to you." [*Laughter*] And that really stuck with me because I seen that these guys cared enough to tell me that. And I ain't been back to jail since.

MICHAEL KAY: Were you afraid when you were in jail? Of getting hurt or—?

SNOOP DOGG: Never. That's the first thing you don't do, is to show fear.

MICHAEL KAY: Tell me how you got into the Crips.

SNOOP DOGG: It started off as a hustling thing, it wasn't about violence, it was just about money. We was always chasing money. And then it became "Well, we gotta protect our street." And if we see other gangs that we wasn't used to seeing, we'd throw our set and they'd throw up their set, and then it escalated to some next-level thing that didn't need to happen. And it just grew and it grew, to the point to where for me it was like, "Is this what I wanna do for the rest of my life?" Because when you in it, you're all the way in it, there ain't no time-out. It's full speed, whenever, however, forever. And I had to make a decision to myself, when I got into the music industry, to get out of it. I'm still connected to it, 'cause this is where I'm born and raised, I still got family that's from the hood. But now I denounce gangbanging, and I'm actually a peace advocate, I'm the one who pushes peace. I move with Bloods, Crips, Mexicans, gangs from other nationalities, I'm the one who brings peace to the situation, 'cause they respect my voice, and they know I walked that walk with them. It's a little different than someone who's never walked that walk trying to tell them to stop gangbangin'.

MICHAEL KAY: Now let's go to how the music started. How did you get involved with rap music, and who was your early influence in that?

SNOOP DOGG: One was a rapper named Jimmy Spicer, he had a song called "Super Rhyme." And there was a group called Whodini, and there was Run-DMC. We heard these records and they were a different style of music, and it just made us wanna imitate them. So I would take the raps of a rapper, for instance, if it was "the hip-hop, the hippy to the hippy-de-hip-hop, the hoppa you don't stop the rocka," I would take that and put my own words in there. I'd make it, "To the bang-bang boogie, say up jump the boogie, Snoop Dogg, and the place to be." So I was just free-styling to the beat, saying whatever came out my mind, and I was great at that and people was like, "Wow, he's good." I was like, "I don't need to write anything down," but I got rhymes from '84 I still remember.

MICHAEL KAY: Give us an early rhyme that you can remember.

SNOOP DOGG: [*Pause*] Uh, "I went to this place, where people was rapping, stomping they feet, and even clapping. I went inside and got me a table, and right beside me was a girl named Mabel." [*Laughter, applause*]

MICHAEL KAY: So you were hooked on music?

SNOOP DOGG: I didn't get hooked on it until Dr. Dre told me I was good. Because he was the standard. He was already the greatest producer to ever do it in rap.

MICHAEL KAY: How did he hear you?

SNOOP DOGG: Me and his brother, Warren G, and [my cousin] Nate Dogg, we was a group called 213. Warren G always used to make me make tapes, but I didn't like putting my voice on tape, 'cause I didn't think I was ready. I was iffy about myself, like I wasn't sure. But Warren G would play the tapes for people, and he took one of the tapes to Dr. Dre's bachelor party, and when the music cut off, he popped in my tape. And the party got back crackin'. And they were like, "Who is that?" And he was like, "That's my homeboy, Snoop." And then Dre called me the next day and said he'd like to see me. And I was like, "Who is this, this ain't no Dre." So I said, "If this is Dr. Dre, let me hear you rap." [*Laughter*] So I put him through all that, you know what I'm saying, and I finally figured out that it was really him. He brought me down and we recorded that song that I did. He brought in The D.O.C., and we started writing and writing and writing, and that's when I wrote " 'G' Thang" and I wrote "Deep Cover" and I wrote "Dre Day," and I just start writing all of these songs that became number one hit records for Dr. Dre.

MICHAEL KAY: Now, you end up signing with Death Row Records.

SNOOP DOGG: That was Dr. Dre's record label, why wouldn't I sign? You know what I'm saying? That's the greatest producer in the world and he wants to sign me? And he's starting off his own label, Death Row Records, and I can become one of the first acts on his label, and I can help write his album? I'd sign that contract for nothing.

MICHAEL KAY: But wasn't that still part of the gangsta world that you were still trying to get away from?

SNOOP DOGG: Nah. It was actually getting away from the gangsta world, and having the job to create something for myself.

MICHAEL KAY: And your first album was *Doggystyle*, and it sold eight hundred thousand copies the first week. I mean, are you just blown away at this point?

SNOOP DOGG: I didn't get none of that money so I don't know.... [*Laughter*] Nah, I was, as you say, "blown away." [*Laughter*] I was so happy, man, I was so thankful and so happy for people to really respect me and appreciate me for who I am and what I do.

MICHAEL KAY: Right around that time, there's talk of censorship because [in some] rap albums there's vilification of women, drugs, stuff like that. What are your thoughts on censorship and putting [warning] labels on CDs?

SNOOP DOGG: I don't know all the amendments, but I do know the first one says "freedom of speech." And that means you should be able to say what you wanna say, whenever you wanna say it.

MICHAEL KAY: Let me ask you this, though. You have kids. Do you want to monitor what they listen to?

SNOOP DOGG: Man, my kids listen to my records. There's no cut, I don't play radio versions for the kids, and when they hear me talk, I talk "rated R." No earmuffs in my house. [*Laughter*] I mean, you have to be real with your kids. You know, if they're hearing it from me, they don't have to go hear it from nobody else.

MICHAEL KAY: Now, we were talking before about how your life changed after the first record. You moved out of the neighborhood and you even had a bodyguard. Did you say, "Wow, I didn't think that this was all part of the deal of becoming a success"?

SNOOP DOGG: It was all given to me. You know, you need a body-guard, you need this, you need that. In the hood you're not trained to become a superstar celebrity. And that's what's wrong with half of us when we become famous, we have not been taught, and that goes for athletes, entertainers, for anybody from the inner city.

When we get money, we wanna go back and share our money with our homeys, our hood, our community. And sometimes that's a bad thing because everybody hasn't grown to the stage that you've grown to. We can't bring everybody from the hood with us when we make it. But we don't know that. And we think we're doing something wrong if we don't.

MICHAEL KAY: At this time there's a guy that's stalking you, and he tries to ambush you, and your bodyguard shoots him dead. Was this traumatic for you?

SNOOP DOGG: You know, everybody always says if there's one thing in life you could take back . . . For me it'd be that whole day. Because somebody lost his life. I just feel for his mother, you know what I'm saying? I don't feel responsible for it, he was in pursuit of me, trying to do something to me, and he ended up losing his life. But I wish it could've been a conversation, a fight, anything to where he could've kept living, that it didn't have to end like that. But I can't change it.

MICHAEL KAY: Now, you became friends with Tupac, and he gets murdered, Biggie Smalls gets murdered, in successive years, and there's a lotta violence in rap. Are you going to yourself, "Whoa, what's going on here?"

SNOOP DOGG: Well, after, after Biggie got murdered, I made a few phone calls, and with Russell Simmons and Minister Farrakhan we put together a day of peace where we brought all of the rappers together from all parts of the world.

MICHAEL KAY: What were they all angry about, though? Was it East Coast–West Coast—?

SNOOP DOGG: They weren't angry about nothing, the media hyped that up. We all had love for each other. But when the media started playing it that way, you gotta choose sides now.

MICHAEL KAY: Now, you were drawn into movies. How did that happen?

SNOOP DOGG: I always wanted to do movies. Then [rapper and record producer] Master P created my own movie, he created *Da Game of Life* for me. It wasn't the greatest movie in the world, but it showed me that I could really do it, and it opened Hollywood's eyes enough to say that "Well, he ain't good, but he can *become* good." [*Laughter*] Then I just started taking roles. You know, when I heard they were making the *Starsky and Hutch* movie [which featured a pimp-type character called Huggy Bear], I went to meet with the director, and I came in there with my pimp outfit on, I had my nails done, and I'm like, "I *am* Huggy Bear!" And they were like, "Okay, you're Huggy Bear." [*Laughter*]

MICHAEL KAY: Isn't it weird that there are other singers in the entertainment industry, [and often] they don't translate into being good actors? But rap stars seem to be good—why is that?

SNOOP DOGG: Because the rap life isn't like the actor's life. Because we have to create this character who you love, we have to create everything about him, his persona, his swag, his talk, his dos, his don'ts. And we have to live that, even when we don't want to. An actor can turn his characters on and off. But the rapper, his persona stays on.

MICHAEL KAY: Now, so many kids, black, white, Hispanic, they grow up in the inner cities and they're growing up with the thought of "Live rich or die trying." Do you agree with that?

SNOOP DOGG: I don't disagree with it. [*Laughter*] But it's not just about getting rich, it's about getting the finer things in life, whatever it is, if it's just peace, if it's just being happy and being healthy. It's not about having the biggest car or the biggest house. I know people who have big houses, big cars, but they don't have no families, and they feel so empty. But I see people who have families, and a small house, and they're just loving the life. Sometimes it's not about that material thing, it's about that real love.

MICHAEL KAY: Been a pleasure, thank you.

SNOOP DOGG: All right, man, thank y'all.

Jay-Z

Booking Jay-Z to do the show was a huge get for *CenterStage*. He was hip-hop royalty, and when we taped in 2006, he was one of the world's hottest musical acts. All these years later, he still wears the crown and sits atop the throne. We got him mainly because he was a part owner of the Nets, which was a minority owner of the YES Network and also the main winter programming on the network.

Jay-Z didn't disappoint. It wasn't difficult to draw an audience since people were aching to get close to this music icon. His story is amazing, from the poverty and crime of the Marcy Projects in Brooklyn to the rarefied heights of artistic and business megasuccess. His life could have gone bad in a hurry, but his brilliance with words and beats propelled him to a level of accomplishment that probably exceeded any of his dreams.

When you sit down and talk with Jay, you get an idea of how it all worked. He's razor-sharp, funny, analytical, and is able to communicate to all people. He charmed the jam-packed audience with stories of his unlikely journey.

All these years later, one answer he gave me still resonates. I was amazed at his ability to remember all the words to his densely packed raps and asked if he had to use a teleprompter during concerts. His laughter and the audience participation reminded me how popular and accomplished he is, and how his words are the soundtrack for an entire generation.

The Interview

MICHAEL KAY: The life of today's guest has been a journey from the poverty of the urban ghetto to the power of the corporate boardroom. In ten short years he went from selling records out of his car to being one of the most popular rap artists of all time, and a powerful music executive as well. As a businessman, he is the president and CEO of Def Jam Records and one of the co-owners of the Nets NBA basketball team. As a performer, he's won numerous awards, sold millions of records, and won the hearts of rap and hip-hop fans everywhere. Please welcome the undisputed heavyweight champion of hip-hop, Shawn "Jay-Z" Carter. [*Applause*]

MICHAEL KAY: Tell me why you got into the NBA, why'd you buy into the Nets.

JAY-Z: A better question is why they let me in. [*Laughter*] It's a long story, but to make it simple, it was really all about timing, luck, good fortune, and great calm.

MICHAEL KAY: And how about the fact that the Nets are moving to Brooklyn—the arena isn't built yet, it's in the planning stages—did that mean something to you?

JAY-Z: Brooklyn pride. It's hard to even put it into words. There's, like, a patriotism about Brooklyn. If you know anything about Brooklyn, you know Brooklynites are gonna embrace the Nets. And we haven't had a sports team since the Dodgers.

MICHAEL KAY: I've seen you at the Nets games sitting courtside.

JAY-Z: Yeah, I can get good seats. [*Laughter*]

MICHAEL KAY: What's cooler, running a record company or owning [a part of] the team?

JAY-Z: I'm in music, so that's second nature for me. The Nets thing is still surreal to me.

MICHAEL KAY: There's not a lot of minority representation in *any* sports at the ownership level. And most [team] owners are stodgy older guys, guys in their fifties and sixties who can't relate to the players—

JAY-Z: Mark Cuban is pretty hip.

MICHAEL KAY: Okay, he's hip. [*Laughter*] But there are other guys who are in their fifties and sixties. Do you have a hard time being an owner and a boss, or are you friends with any of the players?

JAY-Z: I pretty much just try to leave 'em alone for the most part. I have a piece of the Nets, I'm not principal owner. So it's not a situation where I can say, "If you don't play well, you're outta here." [*Laughter*]

MICHAEL KAY: You grew up in an area of Brooklyn called the Marcy Houses. That's a tough area.

JAY-Z: It's like any urban neighborhood. There's violence, but there's also an integrity and a sense of belonging that you have in the projects. If you carry yourself a certain way, if you're not a liar, if you don't cheat people, and if you're just a good person, for the most part you'll be okay. You have obstacles and things that you have to overcome. But if you're a strong person, you'll rise up outta there—and when you do, you won't forget where you come from.

MICHAEL KAY: Were you a tough guy growing up?

JAY-Z: No. Just cool. [*Laughter*]

MICHAEL KAY: No fights at all?

JAY-Z: We had fights, but nothing too bad, nothing outrageous.

MICHAEL KAY: You grew up in a family with music in the house. What kind of music did your parents listen to?

JAY-Z: Funk and soul, Parliament and Prince and Stevie Wonder and Michael Jackson—just everything.

MICHAEL KAY: I read that you'd listen to their music, but you'd write your own lyrics to it.

JAY-Z: That's what all rappers do, they find a break in a song that their mom and pops really liked, a break in there with no one singing, and they go crazy on that part. When I was about twelve, I started writing [lyrics], and it just felt natural.

MICHAEL KAY: You were one of four kids, and when you were eleven, your dad left the house.

JAY-Z: That was extremely tough, 'cause as a kid you look up to your pops like Superman. That's your first superhero, and not having him around is traumatic. So you can do two things: you can either fold or become strong. I chose to become strong.

MICHAEL KAY: Your mom is Gloria, and you're real close with her, right?

JAY-Z: We call her Lulu. She's my homegirl.

MICHAEL KAY: How great was it for you to reach your level of success and be able to take care of her?

JAY-Z: It was great, but she fought it. She's been working her whole life, and she's not used to anyone taking care of her. So she fought it the whole way.

MICHAEL KAY: Did you win?

JAY-Z: Eventually. [*Laughter*]

MICHAEL KAY: Now, you were kind of a street hustler, you sold drugs and things like that.

JAY-Z: Yeah, I did. I can say that now 'cause the statute of limitations is done. [*Laughter*] I was young, and it was almost normal, commonplace, what was going on. You gotta realize we grew up in an area that was infested with drugs and liquor stores on every corner, it was pretty heavy. But later you realize that what you were doing was keeping your own community down, keeping your own people down.

MICHAEL KAY: I've heard that you dealt drugs but never used them. How come?

JAY-Z: The movie *Scarface* had a line, "Don't get high on your own supply." That was my blueprint.

MICHAEL KAY: Was there ever a temptation?

JAY-Z: No, no, no.

MICHAEL KAY: What made you say, "I'm done with that life"?

JAY-Z: Because that lifestyle leads to two things—prison or dying. There's no escaping it, it's gonna happen, absolutely one hundred percent. Some people don't have anything to fall back on, but I had a talent.

MICHAEL KAY: You went to George Westinghouse Technical High School, and you had a couple of friends there—Chris Wallace, who turned out to be the rap star Notorious B.I.G., and Trevor Smith, known as Busta Rhymes. You were a pretty good student, but you decide to pursue music, and you quit high school to do it. Was that a tough decision, and did your mom dig it?

JAY-Z: My mom didn't dig it, but it was a great decision for me. [*Laughter*] It wasn't tough for me. I had my eyes on something and I was gonna get it done. I don't recommend that course for anybody else because there are very few successful rappers. There are tons of lawyers and accountants and managers and all these other people, and they have long careers. But rappers have short careers—for the most part, two or three years, and if you don't hit right out of the gate, you're in trouble.

MICHAEL KAY: How did Shawn Carter become Jay-Z?

JAY-Z: [*Laughs*] When I was young, my demeanor was really cool, they used to say, "That's a jazzy little kid. He's real jazzy." So I just took the *J* and the *Z* from *Jazzy* and became Jay-Z.

MICHAEL KAY: How did you learn about the rap business?

JAY-Z: I wasn't really thinking about the business when I first came in. I really just thought about a way to tell my story. I was really just trying to impress my friends, talking about stuff that we went through. I put it in rhyme and they thought that was really amazing.

MICHAEL KAY: You released your first solo single in '96, called "In My Lifetime." Is it true that you sold that song out of the back of your car?

JAY-Z: They had this record store down on Fulton Street. I would take records there and just hang out, you know, playing my music loud. And people would listen, and I had the CDs in my trunk and they'd buy them.

MICHAEL KAY: So you were a promoter, producer, distributor, the whole deal. Did you make money doing that?

JAY-Z: Yeah. Like, three hundred dollars. [*Laughter*]

MICHAEL KAY: You started Roc-A-Fella Records with Damon "Dame" Dash and Kareem "Biggs" Burks. What made you guys do that?

JAY-Z: We weren't geniuses, it was more out of necessity. We shopped our demo everywhere, and we couldn't get a deal. We were doing shows and I would perform places and we knew people liked the music. The record companies were the bridge to get us to a wider audience, but they weren't giving us the bridge. So we had to build it ourselves.

MICHAEL KAY: In '96 you released your first album, *Reasonable Doubt*. And that was with Primary Records and that was well received. Did it sell okay?

JAY-Z: Over time it went platinum, but when it first came out, it didn't sell well. It's considered a classic in hip-hop circles now—I guess in all circles, 'cause hip-hop music is world music.

MICHAEL KAY: That same year, Tupac Shakur was killed, and then your friend from high school Notorious B.I.G. was killed as well. Why was rap so violent? What was the East Coast–West Coast thing, can you explain it?

JAY-Z: East Coast–West Coast is a media-made name. We come from violent neighborhoods, so when you become a rap star, it's not like,

"I made it, you can't touch me now, I'm a rapper, I got a deal." You don't just cut off like that. The problems you had in the neighborhood can follow you into your career as a superstar. You still have your friends, you have your loyalty to your friends. Sometimes your friends have problems, you could be riding around with your friend and he had a beef last night, and then stuff happens.

MICHAEL KAY: You can't go back to the Marcy Projects now, can you?

JAY-Z: Of course I can.

MICHAEL KAY: Aren't you afraid?

JAY-Z: I'm not afraid of my own people. That's just crazy to me.

MICHAEL KAY: But there might be people who are jealous of Jay-Z's success. . . .

JAY-Z: I'm more afraid of the people in the corporate world who are afraid of my success. [*Laughter*]

MICHAEL KAY: In '98 you released your third album, *Hard Knock Life*, and it sold five million copies and made you an international star. You had a fifty-two-city tour that was sold out everywhere. Why do you think your music resonates with so many people?

JAY-Z: It's like watching any good movie, or any great story about things that you have to overcome. That message inside the music, it's always there. And the hook is pretty catchy and the tracks I picked were pretty good.

MICHAEL KAY: *Hard Knock Life* won the Grammy for Best Rap Album, and you were nominated for two other ones, but you boycotted the awards.

JAY-Z: The Grammys, they're getting better, but we still have a way to go. They wouldn't televise the rap awards. It was almost like a slap in the face, like people invite you over to their house for dinner, and then tell you, "You gotta eat in the basement." [*Laughter*] I just didn't see that we were being treated with respect.

MICHAEL KAY: You get your songs played on the radio a lot. And obviously you can't get 'em played on the radio with explicit lyrics. Do you sometimes try to not be explicit so they can be played on the radio?

JAY-Z: I don't believe in that. I believe in freedom of speech and I believe in your natural emotions. But I know there are formats such as radio where you can't send that out over the airwaves, so I'm cool with censoring the record and having clean versions.

MICHAEL KAY: Some people feel some aspects of rap music, particularly gangsta rap, are negative for the community.

JAY-Z: To broad-stroke the whole thing would be like me saying that the film industry is horrible. There are bad movies, movies that glorify violence. To put everybody in one box, I don't think that's fair.

MICHAEL KAY: Ten years, twelve albums, thirty-three million CDs, then in 2003 you decide to retire. *The Black Album* was gonna be your last. Was it like Jordan going out at the top of his game?

JAY-Z: I just felt that there was something else that I could contribute to music and the genre in general. Most artists, after they're done, they become *E! True Hollywood* specials, they don't become president-CEO of Def Jam Records.

MICHAEL KAY: I hear your music in the Yankee clubhouse every now and then. Alex Rodriguez comes to the plate [singing] "Numb/ Encore," Derek Jeter is "Bring Em Out"—

JAY-Z: That costs a lot of money to get those guys to do that. [*Laughter*] I'm just jokin'.

MICHAEL KAY: Why do athletes relate so well to your music?

JAY-Z: I think athletes and performers are pretty much cut from the same cloth. We're from the same type neighborhoods, we have the same upbringing. It's just that they get to go away to these basketball camps and baseball camps while we're stuck in the hood to do bad stuff. [*Laughter*] We're like the bad cousins.

QUESTION FROM AUDIENCE: What advice would you give a young artist trying to make it in the music business?

JAY-Z: The thing that worked for us is belief in ourselves. We could've stopped when everyone said that demo was horrible, or when people were offering us horrible deals. But we held out, and every time that we had that belief, it worked out for us.

MICHAEL KAY: You're pretty tight with LeBron [James], and he's gonna be a free agent soon. Is he coming to the Nets?

JAY-Z: [*Laughter*] We would have to write a really big check. [*Laughter*] He's my friend first, and I would never take advantage of that. But if we're committed to winning and building a championship team around him and have enough money for him, then . . . come on over.

MICHAEL KAY: You've never been a paid professional in sports, but I can sense in the way you do your business that you're competitive. You think you were just born with that?

JAY-Z: Brooklyn, and New York in general, breeds the competitive spirit. There's a different swagger to a New Yorker, bigger than anywhere else in the world. We're highly competitive.

MICHAEL KAY: How did you branch out into the clothing line?

JAY-Z: I had to. I was wearing this clothing line called Iceberg, like, early '96, '97, and I would do the shows and see that everyone had on Iceberg. So we went to Iceberg and said, "You should cut us a deal 'cause we got everybody wearing your stuff, you wanna be in business with us? We just need to use your private plane. . . ." [*Laughter*] And they threw us out.

MICHAEL KAY: Not a smart move.

JAY-Z: Yeah, not so smart. They shoulda given us the plane [*laughter*] 'cause then we started Rocawear [which soon had annual sales of $700 million].

MICHAEL KAY: The kicks you're wearing are your own. Pretty cool to wear your own sneakers, with your name on 'em. You were the first nonathlete to get your own sneaker. What's better, that or a gold record?

JAY-Z: Music is my first love, but it's great to have a Fortune 500 company [such as Reebok] investing in you. Because they didn't know how the sneakers were gonna sell. They thought we'd sell maybe ten thousand over a few months, and we sold ten thousand the first day.

MICHAEL KAY: Do you ever wear sneakers with a scuff mark on them? 'Cause when I was in the Bronx, if you got a new pair of sneakers, somebody would always come over to you and step on them. That doesn't work with you, right?

JAY-Z: Nah. [*Laughter*] In my neighborhood the guys that got their sneakers stepped on didn't do too well.

MICHAEL KAY: Yeah, they end up being the host. [*Laughter*] You eventually become the president and CEO of Def Jam. Do you like being called President Carter?

JAY-Z: [*Laughter*] I was with President Clinton the other day, and I was like, "Okay, you're President Clinton, I'm President Carter." [*Laughter*]

MICHAEL KAY: As the president and CEO of Def Jam Records, what is the biggest challenge you have? 'Cause some people say the music business is in a little bit of trouble.

JAY-Z: The music business is down, but the business of music is gonna last forever. It's like the soundtrack for people's lives. Once you open that digital world, it's hard to control, people are downloading stuff for free. So you just have to find the right way to get it out there and make sure the artists get compensated for their hard work.

MICHAEL KAY: When you're lying in bed, do you ever go, "Is all this really happening to me?"

JAY-Z: Every day. I'm not jaded, I'm still amazed by everything that's happened to me.

MICHAEL KAY: A lot of people who were poor and become rich, they always have a fear of becoming poor again. Does that happen to you?

JAY-Z: I have more fear of going back. I like to advance every year, to advance myself, spiritually, mentally, everything. I have more fear of going back than losing money. I've been broke, I've been rich, but money is just a by-product if you're doing something that you love to do. You wanna be paid, but you'll pretty much do it for free. [*Laughter*]

MICHAEL KAY: Do you love being rich?

JAY-Z: Well, I love freedom. The freedom of having money is you can do what you want.

MICHAEL KAY: Mick Jagger is sixty-five years old, and he's still doing his thing onstage. You're in your midthirties now, but can you see yourself performing at sixty-five?

JAY-Z: No, I'd sprain my hamstring or something. [*Laughter*] Can't do that.

MICHAEL KAY: So you've enjoyed your life so far, right?

JAY-Z: Yeah, it doesn't suck. [*Laughter*] Can you say *suck* on *Center-Stage*?

MICHAEL KAY: Well, we'll see. But this didn't suck, it was great. Thanks a lot.

JAY-Z: My man. Thank you.

Acknowledgments

With so many people to acknowledge for their help in creating the *CenterStage* show and now this book, let's give it a whirl and hope we don't miss anyone.

John Filippelli gets first call, since he created the show and tapped me to host it—and for that I'll be forever grateful. I'd also like to thank the president of YES, Jon Litner, for his understanding and guidance in putting the book together, and Randy Levine, the president of the Yankees and the chairman of the YES Network, for allowing us to use the transcriptions of these interviews. Lonn Trost, the Yankee COO, has also always been so supportive through the years.

CenterStage has had four producers, and each was a gently guiding hand in creating the scripts and helping to map out the flow of each show. Sue Podbielski, Vicky Pomerance Neer, Mike Kostel, and Mitch Kozuchowski were brilliant in making the show what it is.

I want to thank the directors who, over the years, called the camera shots and made the show look as great as it did. Jeff Kaye, Jeff Winn, Jeff Mitchell, John Purcell, and Mike Cooney have expertly directed the show over almost two decades.

Our associate producers, Liz Cavanaugh Kalisky, Shari Lampert, Jane Hirt, Christa Robinson, Jacqueline McCardle, Blayke Scheer, and Brielle Saracini made the trains run on time each and every show.

And thanks to our production managers, Carolynne Harris, Heather Smith, and Dana Rowinski, as well as our incredible editors, Allan Greene, Frank Murphy, Gary Fall, Joseph Calo, and Brian Weber.

And the management at YES has always been incredibly supportive of a show that is certainly not inexpensive to produce; they've made sure we had the best cameras, lighting, and set design. Big thanks go to VP of Programming Woody Freiman, VP of Programming Mark Rosenweig, Coordinating Producer Janice Platt, Creative Director Larry Kamm, VPs of Operations Ed Delaney and Mike Webb, and the head of Tupelo-Honey Productions, Cary Glotzer.

Our production team of Associate Director Carol Lehti; Stage Managers Jennifer Aiello, Ann Marie Kuehling, and Thom Gatewood; and Audience Coordinators Jacqueline Gonzalez and Tina Cirigliano always kept the show humming.

And thanks to Ashley Fugazy, who makes the YES Network work each and every day.

Before each taping we have a comedian who warms up the audience. I want to thank Pete Dominick for making sure that everyone laughed before we went to work.

Also, special thanks to our talent producer, Steve Bernie, who doesn't know how to take no for an answer. His relentless pursuit of big-name guests has been a big part of *CenterStage*'s success.

And a huge shout-out goes to Trish Taylor, the digital assets manager at YES, who made sure all of the show's transcriptions got to the right people for this book to be made.

I wish my late agent—and friend—Steve Lefkowitz were here to read this book. Years ago, he assured me I could handle both hosting the show *and* broadcasting Yankee games on YES. He always believed.

And thanks go to my literary agent, David Vigliano, who at the start of this project sought me out, believed in the idea, and arranged for a happy marriage with Scribner.

My editor at Scribner, Rick Horgan, has been a champ throughout this whole process, handling a first-time author with a calm but forceful hand—one that smoothed out some of the bumps the project suffered alone the way. Also, thanks go to Rick's assistant, Beckett Rueda, who put out many fires and made sure things happened when they were supposed to happen.

I also want to thank my colleagues at 98.7 ESPN Radio in New York since they always had my back if I was five minutes late after two *CenterStage* tapings or if I had to leave *The Michael Kay Show* a bit early for a later taping. My cohosts on the show, Don La Greca and Peter Rosenberg; my producers, Andrew Gundling and RJ Santillo; ESPN

NY general manager Tim McCarthy; and Program Director Ryan Hurley were always supportive throughout this project.

And mostly, I'd like to thank our incredible guests. The stories they told about their journeys are the heart, soul, and inspiration of this book.

Index

Parental Guidance (film), 190, 196
Parish, Robert, 40
Parry Sound, Ontario, 117–18
Parry Sound Shamrocks, 118
Parseghian, Ara, 109
Patterson, Floyd, 59
Pay It Forward (film), 134
Peele, Jordan, 232
People magazine, 9
Purdue Boilermakers, 110
Perry, Katy, 315
Pesky, Johnny, 169
Petrucci, Jeff, 109
Philadelphia Phillies, 17
Philadelphia 76ers, 103, 104, 220, 222, 223–24
Philadelphia Soul, 133, 134, 138
Philadelphia Warriors, 103
Phoenix Suns, 224–25, 226, 281
Piazza, Mike, 9
Piniella, Lou, 7
Pittsburgh Steelers, 14
Platt, Janice, 287
Playing for Keeps (Halberstam), 169
Plimpton, George, 243
Plunkett, Sherman, 35–36
Poehler, Amy, 229, 233
Powell, Adam Clayton, 279
Power Memorial Academy, N.Y.C., 277–78, 279–80
Powers That Be, The (Halberstam), 169
Presley, Elvis, 126, 130–31
Princess Bride, The (film), 195, 259, 260, 263
Professional Basketball Writers Association, 40
Pro Football Hall of Fame, 14, 31, 114, 143, 144, 298
Pryor, Richard, 231
Pulp Fiction (film), 269, 270, 274–75

Quaid, Dennis, xix, xx
Queens, N.Y., 124, 308, 309, 311, 313
Quinn, Pat, 121

Radner, Gilda, 179, 183, 185
Rambo (film), 24, 29

Ramos, Pedro, 191
Ramsey, Frank, 41
Ravenite Social Club, N.Y.C., 95
Reasonable Doubt (Jay-Z, album), 329
Red and Me: My Coach, My Lifelong Friend (Russell), 99
Redford, Robert, 263
Reiner, Carl, 259, 260–61
Reiner, Estelle, 264
Reiner, Rob, 195, 259–66
  All in the Family and, 259–60, 262
  And So It Goes and, 259
  background and family, 259–61
  Castle Rock Entertainment, 263
  as comedy writer, 261
  early TV roles, 261
  early years in Beverly Hills, 261
  A Few Good Men and, 264–65
  as film director, 259, 260, 262–65
  politics and, 265–66
  The Princess Bride and, 259, 260, 263
  Stand by Me and, 259, 260, 263
  The Sure Thing and, 263
  This Is Spinal Tap and, 259, 260, 262–63
  at UCLA, improv group formed, 261
  When Harry Met Sally and, 259, 260, 263–64
  The Wolf of Wall Street and, 260
Reservoir Dogs (film), 269, 270, 273–74
Reynolds, Allie, 174
Reynolds, Burt, 270
Rhinestone (film), 28
Rice, Jerry, 111–12, 149
Riggs, Bobby, 69
Ripken, Cal, Jr., 6, 10
Rivers, Joan, 182
Rizzuto, Phil, 211
Robinson, Jackie, 174, 279
Robinson, Sugar Ray, 82
Rock, Chris, 186, 204
Rock and Roll Hall of Fame, 124
Rocky (film), 23, 24, 28–29
Rocky Balboa (film), 24
Rocky III (film), 26